MW00790834

JESUS, INTERPRETED

JESUS, INTERPRETED

Benedict XVI,
Bart Ehrman, and
the Historical Truth
of the Gospels

Matthew J. Ramage

The Catholic University of America Press
Washington, D.C.

Copyright © 2017

The Catholic University of America Press

All rights reserved

The paper used in this publication meets the minimum
requirements of American National Standards for Information
Science–Permanence of Paper for Printed Library Materials,
ANSI z39.48-1984.

∞

Library of Congress Cataloging-in-Publication Data

Names: Ramage, Matthew J.

Title: Jesus, interpreted : Benedict XVI, Bart Ehrman, and the
historical truth of the Gospels / Matthew J. Ramage.

Description: Washington, D.C. : The Catholic University of
America Press, 2017. | Includes bibliographical references and index.

Identifiers: LCCN 2016036444 | ISBN 9780813229089 (pbk. : alk.
paper)

Subjects: LCSH: Jesus Christ--Person and offices. | Bible.
Gospels—Criticism, interpretation, etc. | Bible. Gospels—
Hermeneutics. | Benedict XVI, Pope, 1927– | Ehrman, Bart D.

Classification: LCC BT203 .R35 2017 | DDC 232/.8—dc23

LC record available at https://lccn.loc.gov/2016036444

For my father
Michael Joseph Ramage
1945–2016

[W]hoever obeys and teaches these commandments
will be called greatest in the Kingdom of heaven.

Matthew 5:17

The flower of earthly splendor in time must surely die,
Its fragile bloom surrender to you, the Lord most high;
But hidden from all nature the eternal seed is sown
Though small in mortal stature, to heaven's garden grown:
For Christ the man from heaven from death has set us free,
And we through him are given the final victory.

Hymn "O God Beyond All Praising"

CONTENTS

PREFACE

The subject of this book has played an important part in my own autobiography for many years now. *Jesus, Interpreted* is for my own life a lot like what the *Jesus of Nazareth* series was for Benedict XVI: an expression of my personal search for the face of Jesus Christ. The book is my own attempt at a response to Jesus' question, "But who do you say that I am?" (Mt 16:15). It reflects my appropriation of the question Peter asked Jesus, "Lord, to whom shall we go?" (Jn 6:68). In the particular enquiry at hand, the issue concerns whose interpretation of Jesus best captures his true face: the mainstream agnostic approach exemplified in the work of Bart Ehrman or, instead, the appropriation of critical scholarship within the context of Christian faith as practiced and taught by Pope Emeritus Benedict XVI.

Many individuals deserve my gratitude for their contributions to this book. As in the case of my prior volume, *Dark Passages of the Bible*, here I first have to thank our emeritus pontiff, who now humbly goes by "Fr. Benedict." I have been studying Benedict/Ratzinger intensely for more than a decade, and, though I have never met him in person, the emeritus pontiff has consistently been the model who shows me how, as a committed Christian, to engage, critique, and learn from the most serious challenges posed by modern biblical criticism.

As for those who have played a more direct role in the crafting of this manuscript, my colleagues at Benedictine College hold pride of place. In particular I thank James Madden and Andrew Jaeger in

Philosophy for thoughtful conversations which helped to refine the philosophical foundations of this work. My apologies to them for any philosophical infelicities in the text and for misapprehending what I garnered from them. And in my own department of Theology I especially thank Andrew Swafford and Andrew Salzmann for our frequent conversations over the years that continually refine my thinking and inspire me to be a more faithful disciple of Jesus Christ.

Some sections of this book originated elsewhere in different formats. Chapter 2 originated as an article in the international theological journal *Nova et Vetera*. I wish to express my heartfelt thanks to their editorial staff, especially Matthew Levering, who has been an inspiring model and source of encouragement to this young theologian over the past ten years. A version of chapter 6 first appeared in the *Josephinum Journal of Theology* and had its first antecedents in a series of short articles on my own theology blog, www.truthincharity. com. In addition, my thanks go out to Brandon Vogt for reviewing my previous book and for asking me to contribute articles to *Strange Notions*, his site that fosters dialogue between Catholics and atheists. The thought I put into those articles on Benedict XVI, Bart Ehrman, and the question of miracles was seminal for the eventual formation of this book. I am grateful also to Fr. David Meconi, editor of *Homiletic and Pastoral Review*, for publishing several of my articles which are cited in various places throughout the work.

I also would like to thank the staff of CUA Press, in particular John Martino and Brian Roach with whom it has been a pleasure to collaborate on two projects now. My copyeditor, Susan Needham, saved this manuscript from a multitude of errors.

Finally, I never would have been able to undertake this project without the total, continued support of my parents, wife, and children. Above all, I wish to thank my father, Michael Joseph Ramage, for everything he did in life and everything he taught me, especially the love of Christ and his Church. It was from my dad that I learned by example how to ask the hardest theological questions in a spirit of thankfulness and trust in Holy Mother Church. Though he did not possess the theological formation to explore the topic of this book in as much depth as I am able, it is precisely because of my dad's dedication to his children, and his desire for us to have the education he never could, that I am able to publish this volume. I hope that the practice of faith seeking understanding in this book gives him fitting honor, and I pray it will help many readers to see better the face of the Lord Jesus revealed in his sacred word.

JESUS, INTERPRETED

I

"WHO DO YOU SAY THAT I AM?" BART EHRMAN, BENEDICT XVI, AND THE PLAN OF THIS BOOK

Modern Biblical Scholarship and Ancient Christian Faith

I must confess that I really enjoy reading Bart Ehrman. A former Christian who now describes himself as an agnostic, Ehrman has written several bestselling books popularizing modern biblical exegesis and challenging believers to consider more thoughtfully the origins of the Bible and Christianity. Part of what attracts me to Ehrman's work is his accessible style matched with a personal touch and an intellectual humility that is often lacking in believers and nonbelievers alike. It might at first strike one as odd that a book concerned with upholding the truth of Scripture should begin by speaking so enthusiastically about a self-professed agnostic, but ironically the following lines from Ehrman concisely capture the conviction that undergirds the present volume: "My personal view is that a historical-critical approach to the Bible does not necessarily lead to agnosticism or atheism. It can in fact lead to a more intelligent and thoughtful faith—certainly more intelligent and thoughtful than an approach to the Bible that overlooks all of the problems that historical critics have discovered over the years."[1]

---

1. Bart Ehrman, *Jesus, Interrupted: Revealing the Hidden Contradictions in the Bible (And Why We Don't Know about Them)* (New York: HarperOne, 2009), 272.

In his various works, Ehrman goes to great lengths to make clear his conviction that modern biblical exegesis is not exclusively the domain of the agnostic or atheist. Yet far from everyone agrees that modern biblical criticism and the Church's ancient faith are compatible, especially when it comes to those within the Christian fold. Unfortunately, in my years of working with a mostly Catholic audience I have witnessed plenty to confirm Ehrman's observation that Christian writers, speakers, and teachers sometimes write off modern scholarship *tout court* as if it were an unholy and irredeemable endeavor. Placed in scare quotes, modern biblical authorities are frequently labeled "scholars," as if their lack (or perceived lack) of faith invalidated all their controversial positions. I suspect that Ehrman is right in remarking that his own books are sometimes dismissed because people—whether consciously or unconsciously—perceive his arguments as threatening to their faith.

Ehrman does well to take issue with those who dismiss modern scholarship out of hand as if it were practiced only by the godless. He remarks, "These scholars are not just a group of odd, elderly, basically irrelevant academics holed up in a few libraries around the world."[2] In a very important sense we owe our modern, translated Bibles to these very people—some of whom are indeed nonbelievers. Irrespective of their faith or lack thereof, these academicians have dedicated their careers to producing Bible editions that present us, as closely as possible, with the original texts of Scripture.

Many people fail to appreciate the importance of modern scholarship because they have little sense of just how complicated was the origin of the texts we now take for granted as "the Bible." For one thing, Ehrman constantly emphasizes for his popular audience something that all biblical scholars know: we do not possess the original biblical books fresh from their authors' pens. Moreover, he insists that the many—and much later—copies of texts we do possess contain important variants and points of seemingly blatant contradiction among

---

2. Bart Ehrman, *Misquoting Jesus: The Story behind Who Changed the Bible and Why* (New York: HarperOne, 2007), 208. For a helpful Christian critique of this same reactionary attitude, see Kenton Sparks, *God's Word in Human Words* (Grand Rapids, Mich.: Baker Academic, 2008), 303–8.

themselves. So which manuscripts ought to be considered authoritative or inspired? Even if this were able to be settled, then we still have to consider the question of how to interpret the authoritative texts that have survived from antiquity. On this score Ehrman writes, "If texts could speak for themselves, then everyone honestly and openly reading a text would agree on what the text says."[3]

Thesis and Goal of This Volume

Universal agreement in matters biblical is clearly not the reality today, and it probably never will be. Yet this is not to say that no headway can be made and that sincere dialogue on biblical questions will yield no fruit. On the contrary, an immense amount of work remains to be done in the field of biblical studies today. The Church is in need of faithful who are formed in the tradition, invested in dialogue with modernity, and zealous to help other believers face the myriad challenges thrown their way, whether by colleagues, teachers, professors, books, TV, social media, or even their children. It was this conviction, informed by Benedict XVI's call for scholars to help the faithful tackle the Bible's most difficult passages, that inspired my prior work, *Dark Passages of the Bible*. As its full title indicates, that volume articulated the exegetical programme of Benedict XVI and Thomas Aquinas with an eye to addressing the presence of problematic passages in the Bible, and within the Old Testament in particular.

This sequel volume likewise insists upon the exegetical vision of Joseph Ratzinger/Benedict XVI as a privileged avenue by which to address the thorniest issues in contemporary biblical exegesis.[4] However, the present text has a different concern, in that it does not address the

3. Ehrman, *Misquoting Jesus*, 216. For a scholarly but relatively accessible introduction to the complex history of New Testament manuscript traditions, see Bruce Metzger and Bart Ehrman, *The Text of the New Testament: Its Transmission, Corruption, and Restoration*, 4th ed. (Oxford: Oxford University Press, 2005). For the Old Testament, see Ernst Würthwein, *The Text of the Old Testament: An Introduction to the Biblia Hebraica* (Grand Rapids, Mich.: Eerdmans, 2014).

4. In this volume we shall ordinarily refer to this man with many names ("Fr. Ratzinger," "Cardinal Razinger," "Pope Benedict XVI," "Fr. Benedict," etc.) as "Benedict," although we may occasionally call him by his pre-papal names where that seems appropriate.

problematic Old Testament themes considered previously but rather tackles issues bearing directly on the heart of the Christian faith such as they emerge in contemporary New Testament studies. The thesis of this present volume is that Benedict's engagement with modern biblical scholarship is unique in its ability to navigate the most difficult challenges posed by New Testament exegesis while affirming the foundations of the Christian faith itself that have been cast into doubt by much modern scholarship. I aim to show that Benedict's hermeneutic of faith offers a plausible and attractive alternative to the mainstream agnostic approach to the Gospels that is exemplified in the work of Bart Ehrman, an alternative that is every bit as scholarly and no more reliant on unprovable assumptions. I believe that this enterprise is of paramount importance, for while scholars have touched upon topics within Benedict's biblical scholarship here and there in recent years, little has been done to address the interface of Benedict's exegetical project with the opposing method to which he is so concerned with providing an alternative.

In the present book, I could not possibly deal with every contemporary portrait of the life of Christ that stands as a rival to Benedict's approach. Engaging modern scholarship can simply be overwhelming, so one might ask, "Whose exegesis? Which interpretation?" While I certainly will interact here and there with other modern authors, I have chosen Ehrman for my principal representative of the modern academy because he tends to base his arguments on consensus views among scholars, because he is immensely popular, and because he is a fair-minded interpreter who is not so overcome by his own agenda as to think that every rational person ought to see things his way.[5]

I am passionate about this volume because its subject has played an important part in my own autobiography. Over the years I have been dissatisfied with the way some Catholic apologists simplistically

---

5. Over the course of this volume, other well-known challengers to Benedict's approach also will be engaged, especially John Dominic Crossan. Moreover, Benedict's arguments will be supplemented by the work of other recent scholars who have written on the subjects at hand. For the purpose of letting Benedict and Ehrman speak for themselves and to promote flow of the argument, the majority of these supplemental arguments will be placed in the footnotes.

dismiss modern biblical scholarship without first deeply understanding it.[6] For me, however, Benedict XVI has always proven himself the eminent exception to this rule. One can tell from reading his exegetical works that the questions he asks are not merely academic but also existential in nature. The emeritus pontiff's *Jesus* trilogy in particular represents the fruit of his personal quest for the face of Christ, a quest to answer Jesus' question to his disciples: "But who do you say that I am?" (Mt 16:15). In this endeavor, Benedict is always asking how, as a committed Christian, to engage, critique, and learn from the most serious challenges posed by modern biblical criticism.

The Problem of Engaging Modern Exegesis as a Christian: A Case Study in the Bible and the Question of Miracles

Of course, the worries of Christians concerning modern biblical exegesis are not entirely unfounded. Ehrman, after all, is not a believer and does not pretend that his conclusions are consonant with orthodox Christian doctrine. In this initial pass at Ehrman's thought, here I will only very briefly summarize his position concerning Christ's divinity and resurrection. Ehrman's arguments will be explored in greater detail later, but here the goal is to make plain what the Christian is up against in seeking to defend belief in the Bible generally and in Christ particularly. Then I will critique what I consider to be an inadequate but very common Christian response to skeptics of the Bible. I think that this effort will bring into relief the precise nature of

6. Though approaching the historical Jesus question as a Catholic rather than a Protestant, I can relate to the musings of Dale Allison, who writes of his own book *The Historical Christ and the Theological Jesus* (Grand Rapids, Mich.: Eerdmans, 2009), "It is my personal testimony to doubt seeking understanding.... Whatever one makes of the following pages, they are the stammerings neither of an apologist nor of a skeptic but instead of an oft-confused Protestant who has come to his conclusions, modest as they are, quite gradually, and who may alter his uncertain mind about much tomorrow." Allison, 5. Allison's book is a powerful testimony to the truth that "informed changes of mind should be welcomed, not feared." Ibid. In a similar vein, the following comments of N. T. Wright also reflect my vision in writing this book: "I cannot compel my readers to follow me in this particular pilgrimage, but I can and do hold out an invitation to see Jesus, the Gospels, ourselves, the world, and, above all, God in what may well be a new and perhaps disturbing light." Wright, *The Challenge of Jesus: Rediscovering Who Jesus Was and Is* (Downers Grove, Ill.: IVP Books, 2015), 18.

our task by identifying the sort of approach upon which the following chapters hope to improve.

Ehrman on Jesus' Divinity and the Failure of the "Trilemma" Argument

Ehrman's position concerning the divinity of Christ can be quickly grasped from his evaluation of C. S. Lewis's famous "trilemma" argument. According to Lewis, Jesus' lordship can be shown by reducing to the absurd the possibility that he was either a liar or a lunatic. But in *Jesus Interrupted*, Ehrman reveals a problem with Lewis's logic:

> I had come to see that the very premise of Lewis's argument was flawed. The argument based on Jesus as liar, lunatic, or Lord was predicated on the assumption that Jesus had called himself God.... I had come to realize that none of our earliest traditions indicates that Jesus said any such thing about himself ... not three options but four: liar, lunatic, Lord, or legend.[7]

At the risk of oversimplifying Ehrman's more lengthy narrative, his position is that Jesus' disciples began to profess his divinity only after they experienced him as risen from the dead. According to Ehrman's analysis of the data in *How Jesus Became God*, the earliest Christian sources (Paul and Mark) do not portray Jesus as divine but rather as an exalted human or an angel. While Jesus certainly existed as a historical person, for Ehrman he is nevertheless a "legend" in that he was not divine as Christians subsequently came to believe.

Ehrman on Jesus' Resurrection

One of the interesting features of Ehrman's work is his affirmation that at least some direct followers of Jesus sincerely believed their master had been raised from the dead. He suggests that "three or four people—though possibly more—had visions of Jesus sometime after he died." But he also states that the question of whether these putative experiences were veridical (i.e. whether Jesus was really there or whether they were hallucinatory bereavement visions) is beside his point. Rather, the claim he puts forth is the following:

---

7. Ehrman, *Jesus, Interrupted*, 141.

[A]nyone who was an apocalyptic Jew like Jesus's closest follower Peter, or Jesus's own brother James, or his later apostle Paul, who thought that Jesus had come back to life, would naturally interpret it in light of his particular apocalyptic worldview—a worldview that informed everything that he thought about God, humans, the world, the future, and the afterlife. In that view, a person who was alive after having died would have been bodily raised from the dead, by God himself, so as to enter into the coming kingdom.[8]

In Ehrman's view, it was the disciples' own apocalyptic worldview (informed by Jesus' teachings when he was alive) that led them to think of their visions of the crucified Jesus in terms of resurrection. This is certainly a far cry from the orthodox Christian view; indeed, denying the divinity and resurrection of Jesus could hardly be more opposed to it.

An Insufficient Christian Response

In the chapters that follow, we will be considering how one might respond to Ehrman's claims briefly introduced above. For the moment, I wish simply to comment on how we ought *not* to address the challenges posed by modern biblical criticism. For a case study of a typical approach, I refer the reader to Peter Kreeft's and Ronald Tacelli's *Handbook of Christian Apologetics*. In particular, I find inadequate the authors' response to the "quadrilemma" (Jesus is either a liar, lunatic, lord, or legend). With due respect to these thinkers, whom I admire, and recognizing that this represents just one wrinkle within a much larger book, I think their response to the "legend" issue unfortunately evinces a rather common, simplistic understanding of the biblical evidence. The authors state that our extant biblical manuscripts contain "very few discrepancies and *no* really important ones," but I think Ehrman's books *Misquoting Jesus, How Jesus Became God*, and *Jesus, Interrupted* sufficiently disabuse one of the notion that the Gospels differ only in accidentals such as order and number.[9] And Ehrman is by no means the only author who writes about this sort of thing; he is popularizing information that biblical scholars already know.

Moreover, the authors argue, "If a mythic 'layer' had been added

8. Bart Ehrman, *How Jesus Became God: The Exaltation of a Jewish Preacher from Galilee* (New York: HarperOne, 2014), 203.

9. Peter Kreeft and Ronald Tacelli, *Handbook of Christian Apologetics: Hundreds of Answers to Crucial Questions* (Downers Grove, Ill.: InterVarsity Press, 1994), 162.

later to an originally merely human Jesus, we should find *some* evidence, at least indirectly and secondhand, of this earlier layer." Here I think Kreeft and Tacelli have an unduly narrow view of "myth," and moreover I think they fail to anticipate the obvious response of a Bible scholar like Ehrman.[10] What might he say? The evidence for this earlier, nonmythical layer is right there in front of us: it is the Gospel of Mark, which most scholars (including Benedict XVI) recognize to be the earliest Gospel.

Finally, the authors of the *Handbook* ask who possibly could have invented such a myth about Jesus. I think they are on to something in remarking, "No one invents an elaborate practical joke in order to be crucified, stoned, or beheaded."[11] Ehrman agrees with this to some extent, insofar as he does not seem to think that the disciples maliciously invented the myth of a divine Jesus. (Remember, in Ehrman's view, at least some of the disciples really thought they saw Jesus alive after his death, and it is this that eventually led them to conclude he was divine.) The authors fail to envision reasonable counter-arguments when they claim, "Whether it was his first disciples or some later generation, no possible motive can account for this invention."[12] It is indeed difficult for a Christian to imagine someone inventing the notion that Jesus was divine, but is it fair to say that "no possible motive" could account for this? Could not the disciples themselves have been delusional, as Ehrman seems to suggest? Or could not they have been using the "risen" Jesus as a power play for their own (ultimately unsuccessful) personal ambitions? Now as a believer I am certainly not of the opin-

---

10. For a rich understanding of myth's presence within Scripture, see C. S. Lewis, *Miracles: A Preliminary Study* (New York: Macmillan, 1978), especially the chapters "Horrid Red Things," "Christianity and 'Religion,'" and "Miracles of the Old Creation." Equally valuable is Lewis's *The Weight of Glory, and Other Addresses* (New York: Macmillan, 1980), in particular the chapters "Transposition" and "Is Theology Poetry?" On the capacity of myth to convey truth by means of the human imagination, see also G. K. Chesterton's chapter "Man and Mythologies" in *The Everlasting Man*, which can be found, among other places, in *The Collected Works of G. K. Chesterton* (San Francisco: Ignatius Press, 1986). Finally, I recommend J. R. R. Tolkien's *Tree and Leaf: Including the Poem Mythopoeia* (Boston: Houghton Mifflin, 1965), with its chapters "Mythopoeia" and "On Fairy Stories."

11. Kreeft and Tacelli, *Handbook of Christian Apologetics*, 164.

12. Ibid.

ion that this is what actually happened, but one cannot properly call it an *impossible* scenario.

The same principle applies when it comes to another key matter to be discussed in this book: is it really impossible that St. Paul mistakenly believed that Christ would return within the first Christian generation? Frequently the possibility of such a conclusion is immediately denied by believers who are afraid that accepting it will crumble the foundations of the Christian faith. In this volume I hope to provide a way out of these problems not by avoiding but by going right through them, addressing them head-on. Indeed, Benedict has given us our marching orders for this task in pinpointing that a "criticism of the criticism" must come "from the inside" by those who engage in modern methods while remaining firmly grounded in the tradition.[13]

Benedict, Lewis, and Ehrman: A Critical Point of Convergence

I wish to complete this initial setup of the problem at hand by drawing attention to a common thread in Benedict, Lewis, and Ehrman which ought always to be kept in mind by anyone who desires a sincere marriage of faith and reason in matters biblical. Although they ultimately come to quite different conclusions about the Christian faith, all three of these thinkers—a Catholic, an Anglican, and an Evangelical turned agnostic—acknowledge that the problem of how to engage modern exegesis has a much deeper foundation than one might expect. As then-Cardinal Joseph Ratzinger famously avowed in his Erasmus Lecture, "The debate about modern exegesis is not at its core a debate among historians, but among philosophers."[14] Elsewhere Ratzinger expounds upon the Kantian premises that undergird the exegesis of contemporary figures such as John Hick and Paul Knitter:

Because of the structure of our cognition, what the Christian faith maintains cannot be, according to Kant. Therefore, miracles, mysteries or sacraments are superstitions, as Kant clarifies for us in his work *Religion Within the Lim-*

---

13. Joseph Ratzinger, "Biblical Interpretation in Conflict: On the Foundations and the Itinerary for Exegesis Today," in *Opening Up the Scriptures: Joseph Ratzinger and the Foundations of Biblical Interpretation*, ed. José Granados, Carlos Granados, and Luis Sánchez-Navarro (Grand Rapids, Mich.: Wm. B. Eerdmans Publishing Co., 2008), 8.

14. Ratzinger, "Biblical Interpretation in Conflict," 19.

its of Reason Alone. It seems to me that the questions from exegesis and the limits and possibilities of our reason, i.e. the philosophical premises of the faith, indicate in fact the crucial point of the crisis of contemporary theology whereby the faith—and more and more the faith of simple persons as well—is heading toward crisis.[15]

As Lewis puts it with regard to the question of miracles, "The difficulties of the unbeliever do not begin with questions about this or that particular miracle; they begin much further back."[16] At the end of the day, one's answer to the question of whether the Bible's portrait of Jesus is true depends first upon whether or not one believes that God exists and is of such a nature that he would enter into human history in the first place. A negative answer to the initial question of the divine's existence necessarily entails the conclusion that purported miracles such as Christ's Resurrection cannot be true.

Ehrman, too, recognizes that the philosophical question undergirds all the various debates between believers and those skeptical of the Bible. Indeed, at one point he says something that I could have mistaken as coming from the pen of Benedict had I not known otherwise:

The first thing to stress is that everyone has presuppositions, and it is impossible to live life, think deep thoughts , have religious experiences, or engage in historical inquiry without having presuppositions. The life of the mind cannot proceed without presuppositions. The question, though, is always this: What are the appropriate presuppositions for the task at hand?[17]

15. Ratzinger, "Relativism: The Central Problem for Faith Today," https://www .ewtn.com/library/CURIA/RATZRELA.HTM. In this same text Ratzinger adds: "My thesis is the following: The fact that many exegetes think like Hick and Knitter and reconstruct the history of Jesus as they do is because they share their same philosophy. It is not the exegesis that proves the philosophy, but the philosophy that generates the exegesis. If I know a priori (to speak like Kant) that Jesus cannot be God and that miracles, mysteries and sacraments are three forms of superstition, then I cannot discover what cannot be a fact in the sacred books. Let us look at this more precisely. The historical-critical method is an excellent instrument for reading historical sources and interpreting texts. But it contains its own philosophy, which in general—for example when I try to study the history of medieval emperors—is hardly important. And this is because in that case I want to know the past and nothing more. But even this cannot be done in a neutral way, and so there are also limits to the method."
16. Lewis, *Miracles*, 108.
17. Ehrman, *How Jesus Became God*, 144.

This is one of the questions that interests me most and which I think lies at the heart of the emeritus pontiff's statement that the debate in exegesis is at bottom a philosophical one. We can never completely suspend our biases, but we can at least do our best to remain conscious of their presence and engage in a self-critique that helps attune our thought with the breadth of knowledge we can gain from the sources available to us. While coming to a very different conclusion than Benedict, John Dominic Crossan puts this rather well when he says, "We cannot live without group ideology (or, if you prefer, theology), but we must be able to keep it in dialectic with public evidence."[18]

I believe that this is what lies at the heart of the pregnant line from Ratzinger's 1988 Erasmus Lecture in which he called for a self-criticism of the modern, historical-critical method of biblical interpretation. On the part of those involved in the craft of exegesis today, this self-criticism entails the effort to identify and purify the philosophical presuppositions we bring to our reading of the biblical text. In view of Ratzinger's envisioned critique, the pivotal question is: whose philosophical presuppositions best position us for an accurate understanding of the Bible and of the nature of things in general? This is an issue I will take up at the end of the book; at this moment I am concerned with the more basic task of identifying the foundational problem recognized by good thinkers on both sides of the religious-skeptical aisle.

Chapter Previews

Before embarking upon the volume's principal task of engaging biblical problems from within the discipline of critical exegesis, I pause in chapter 2 to consider the disputed question concerning the extent to which such an enterprise is justifiable for a Christian in the first place. Even a cursory overview of Benedict XVI's exegetical works reveals dramatic contrasts between his biblical scholarship and guiding magisterial principles of previous epochs. With appropriate reservations and criticisms, Benedict strongly advocates the use of modern scholarly methods—many of the same ones used by skeptics like Ehrman—to

18. John Dominic Crossan, *The Birth of Christianity: Discovering What Happened in the Years Immediately after the Execution of Jesus* (San Francisco: HarperSanFrancisco, 1998), 29.

help Christians better discern the face of Christ revealed in Scripture. In adopting many of these modern findings, it almost seems as if Benedict has forgotten principles enforced staunchly by the Magisterium less than a century earlier.

Though one may argue that the Church's stance on modern biblical scholarship bears only indirectly upon faith and morals, the issue remains timely today insofar as a divide persists in the Church concerning the extent to which it is appropriate to incorporate the tools and findings of modern exegesis in Catholic theology. Some, aligning themselves with a magisterial approach that once viewed modern scholarship with great skepticism, still doubt that historical-critical exegesis is reconcilable with the venerable traditions that preceded it.

The emeritus pontiff dedicated a significant portion of his scholarly life precisely to the endeavor of combatting the false dichotomy between the pre-conciliar and post-conciliar Church and to developing a balanced hermeneutic that takes seriously the presence of both continuity and discontinuity in Catholic doctrine throughout the ages. The aim of this second chapter is to face head-on patent discrepancies in the Church's approach to the Bible over the past century and, in so doing, offer the principles needed for a robust *apologia* of Catholicism's engagement with modern biblical scholarship. The principles needed for this account lie in Benedict's "hermeneutic of reform" and its central endeavor to discern the permanent theological core of Catholic magisterial teachings that have withstood the vicissitudes of history and the challenges of the modern scholarly world. As it turns out, the same hermeneutical maneuver put to work here on a question of Catholic doctrine will be applied in subsequent chapters to problems within the Bible itself.

Operating with the understanding that our enterprise of critiquing the critique "from within" is in keeping with the Catholic faith, in chapter 3 I spell out the core principles needed for this task. This chapter begins by surveying the principles detailed in Ratzinger's 1988 Erasmus Lecture, in particular the hermeneutical proposal in which Ratzinger called upon exegetes to develop a new, fuller hermeneutical method (Method C) that makes the truth of Scripture more evident by synthesizing the best of patristic-medieval exegesis (Method A) and historical-critical exegesis (Method B). For those who have read *Dark Passages of the Bible*, much of what is said at this point will be review with the addition of some new data that I have unearthed since that volume was composed. Although we will be working primarily at the level of Method B in this book, the Method A principles surveyed in this section undergird everything I will be arguing in later chapters.

Next, this chapter considers Ratzinger's exegesis in connection with medieval exegetes Thomas Aquinas and Bonaventure. In his early career, Ratzinger was critical of Thomistic neo-scholasticism, and in this period of his life there emerged a preference for Bonaventure which would guide his understanding of Scripture over the following decades. Ratzinger is, therefore, not a Thomist of the strict observance. With this initial caveat in place, there follows an overview of principles illustrating key points of contact in which Ratzinger connects—both implicitly and explicitly at points—his exegetical programme with that of Aquinas, whose exegesis offers a "counter-model" to deconstructive forms of modern exegesis.[19] By way of making these connections, Ratzinger certainly emends the tradition he inherited from Aquinas, but the dependence remains all the same.

Finally, the third chapter examines how the vision of the Erasmus Lecture has been received and carried forward at a very high level in the Church through the recent documents of the International Theological Commission and Pontifical Biblical Commission.

In the following chapters the import of the principles discussed in chapters 2 and 3 will become evident as we apply Benedict's hermeneutical proposal in the effort to make sense of some of the most difficult questions concerning the Gospels. The aim of these chapters is to provide a compelling alternative approach to the study of Jesus' life that eschews crucial pitfalls endemic to the hermeneutic of sus-

19. Note that I will be referring to the version of the Erasmus Lecture entitled "Biblical Interpretation in Conflict" from the volume *Opening Up the Scriptures*. This version of Ratzinger's text (there are three different published editions of the lecture in the English language alone) is interesting because it reveals more explicit connections with Thomas Aquinas than the original English version "Biblical Interpretation in Crisis" published in the volume *Biblical Interpretation in Crisis: The Ratzinger Conference on Bible and Church* (Grand Rapids, Mich.: Eerdmans, 1989).

picion typical of many modern scholars like Ehrman. Confronting the same troublesome biblical data as these thinkers, Benedict's approach is anything but naïve, yet it leads him to draw very different conclusions from those of Ehrman. We begin in chapter 4 by surveying Ehrman's approach. The point here is to clarify what precisely it is that a faithful exegete like Benedict is up against and to be challenged by the plausibility of Ehrman's approach, given his first principles. In chapter 5 we examine how Benedict addresses the same sort of issues. The respective conclusions of Benedict XVI and Ehrman follow from mutually incommensurable presuppositions about the Bible in relation to history and truth. For a Catholic, the question is whether the Christology that developed in the earliest days of the Church was the fruit of truthful and providential reflection upon the mystery of Jesus, or whether it was a misguided, delusional, desperate, or even conniving power play. In this chapter, we explore how Benedict XVI and the Pontifical Biblical Commission handle the same sort of—and indeed in many cases the very same—issues addressed by Ehrman. If there is one thing I hope the reader will take away from this chapter, it is my contention that Benedict's hermeneutic of faith offers a plausible and attractive alternative to Ehrman's agnostic approach to the Gospels, one that is every bit as scholarly and no more reliant on unprovable assumptions.

Building on Benedict XVI's approach to the life, death, and Resurrection of Christ discussed above, chapter 6 shows how the theology of the emeritus pontiff offers a robust hermeneutic for New Testament texts dealing with the end times, specifically the early Church's ostensibly failed expectation that Christ's second coming (*parousia*) would occur within the apostolic period. The question that arises from a reading of these texts is quite simple: Why has Christ not come back yet as he seemed to say he would? By searching out the intention of Scripture's sacred authors in relation to their expectation of an imminent *parousia*, Benedict offers a compelling alternative to the agnostic approach of Ehrman and others who look upon the early Church's eschatology as wishful thinking that never panned out. As above, I begin this chapter with a survey of the difficulty at hand through a frank engagement with the opposing view that calls into question Christian doctrine at its core. Then I examine problematic biblical and magisterial texts to further establish the parameters of the problem at hand, after which a solution will be advanced in light of magisterial texts and the corpus of Benedict XVI.

In the volume's concluding chapter I return to the book's point of departure and to a theme that runs throughout it. If the debate in modern exegesis is at bottom philosophical in nature, then we desperately need to carry out a criticism of the criticism, identifying and evaluating the philosophical presuppositions believers and nonbelievers alike bring to our reading of the biblical text. A major contention I make in this regard is that the impossibility of miracles is not something that can be proved, it can only be assumed. Indeed, I would say with Lewis that this agnostic assumption is held by faith rather than reason.

While in earlier chapters I remained content merely to offer Benedict's exegetical approach as a viable alternative to that of Ehrman, in this concluding chapter I offer some of my own reflections on the question why a person should be inclined to choose one over the other. To this end, I call into question the coherence of Ehrman's approach at its philosophical roots by challenging his position on the problem of evil, absolute moral norms, and human rationality itself. To this criticism of the criticism I add that there exist important positive reasons for accepting the Christian hypothesis and following Benedict's approach rather than Ehrman's. I argue that the testimony of religious experience (direct and indirect) ought to form an integral part of our evidence base when it comes to discussing the miraculous. As one who daily engages in the craft of historical-critical exegesis, I find Benedict XVI's comments on this subject refreshing and liberating. In contrast with what he calls a naturalist "ready-made philosophy" that precludes the possibility of such experience, Benedict urges us to approach the Bible with an "open philosophy" that refuses to exclude the possibility that God himself "can work in history and enter into it without ceasing to be himself, however improbable this might appear."[20] This posture, deeply rooted in the Catholic tradition with its conviction that the boundary of time and eternity is permeable, allows for the Bible to be what the Church has always claimed it to be: the word of God in human words.

20. Ratzinger, "Biblical Interpretation in Conflict," 22.

2

BENEDICT XVI AND MODERN BIBLICAL CRITICISM: A MAGISTERIAL ABOUT-FACE?

Before embarking upon our principal task of engaging biblical problems from within the discipline of critical exegesis, it is important first to consider the disputed question concerning the extent to which such an enterprise is justifiable for a Christian in the first place. Even a cursory overview of Benedict XVI's exegetical works reveals dramatic contrasts between his biblical scholarship and guiding magisterial principles of previous epochs. With appropriate reservations and criticisms, Benedict strongly advocates the use of modern scholarly methods—many of the same ones used by skeptics like Ehrman—to help Christians better discern the face of Christ revealed in Scripture. In adopting many of these modern findings, it almost seems as if Benedict has forgotten principles enforced staunchly by the Magisterium only a century ago.

Though one may argue that the Church's stance on modern biblical scholarship only indirectly bears upon faith and morals, the issue remains timely today insofar as a divide persists in the Church concerning the extent to which it is appropriate to incorporate the tools and findings of modern exegesis in Catholic theology. As I mentioned in chapter 1, Catholics today sometimes reject historical-critical scholarship out of hand, concluding that the approach itself is contrary to the faith since acquaintance with it sometimes does indeed lead people to lose their faith. Indeed, many still doubt that historical-critical exegesis is reconcilable with the venerable traditions which preceded it and, in particular, with a magisterial approach which once viewed modern scholarship with skepticism.[1]

The emeritus pontiff dedicated a significant portion of his scholarly life precisely to the endeavor of combatting the false dichotomy between the pre-conciliar and post-conciliar Church and to developing a balanced hermeneutic that takes seriously the presence of both continuity and discontinuity in Catholic doctrine through the ages. The aim of the present chapter is to face head-on patent discrepancies in the Church's approach to the Bible over the past century and, in so doing, to offer the principles needed for a robust *apologia* of Catholicism's engagement with modern biblical scholarship. The principles needed for this account lie in Benedict's "hermeneutic of reform" and its core endeavor to discern the permanent theological core of Catholic magisterial teachings that have withstood the vicissitudes of history and the challenges of the modern scholarly world. As it turns out, the same hermeneutical maneuver put to work here on a question of Catholic doctrine will be applied in subsequent chapters to problems within the Bible itself.

Leo XIII and Pius X: Rejection of Higher Criticism

To get a sense of the Magisterium's past attitude concerning the extent to which one can appropriate modern biblical scholarship, it is fitting to begin by examining the writings of two pontiffs who wrote at the height of the modernist controversy, Leo XIII and St. Pius X. In his 1893 encyclical *Providentissimus Deus*, Leo criticized the rise of modern biblical scholarship in no uncertain terms: "There has arisen, to the great detriment of religion, an inept method, dignified by the name of the 'higher criticism,' which pretends to judge of the origin,

1. At the opposite extremes of this divide we find those whom Benedict refers to as "progressivists" and "traditionalists" who disagree with today's Magisterium but agree with each other in viewing Catholic doctrine in the post-Vatican II Church as a rupture from what preceded it.

integrity and authority of each Book from internal indications alone."[2]
Leo's words are harsh but reasonable enough, for in the discipline
of history it is proper to be cautious of adjudicating issues concerning texts without any reference to the witness of how they have been
received and interpreted. Leo, however, goes farther than this: "It is
clear, on the other hand, that in historical questions, such as the origin
and the handing down of writings, the witness of history is of primary importance, and that historical investigation should be made with
the utmost care; and that in this matter internal evidence is seldom of
great value, except as confirmation."[3] Why is internal evidence prized
so little by Leo? With the rise of rationalism in his day, there was a
legitimate fear of a slippery slope, the fear that accepting the methods
and conclusions of modern criticism would lead to a loss of the sense
of the Bible's sacredness and, ultimately, to the loss of the Christian
faith itself:

> To look upon it in any other light will be to open the door to many evil con-
> sequences. It will make the enemies of religion much more bold and confi-
> dent in attacking and mangling the Sacred Books; and this vaunted "higher
> criticism" will resolve itself into the reflection of the bias and the prejudice
> of the critics. It will not throw on the Scripture the light which is sought, or
> prove of any advantage to doctrine; it will only give rise to disagreement and
> dissension, those sure notes of error, which the critics in question so plenti-
> fully exhibit in their own persons; and seeing that most of them are tainted
> with false philosophy and rationalism, *it must lead to the elimination from the
> sacred writings of all prophecy and miracle, and of everything else that is outside
> the natural order.*[4]

In the discussion of Benedict XVI's approach to higher criticism later
in this chapter, it will become clear that Benedict's observations a century later have confirmed the soundness of Leo's suspicions. Observing
the exegetical landscape in our day, Benedict is keenly aware of how
right Leo was in predicting the rise of "disagreement and dissension"
and the fact that biblical scholarship often represents nothing but "the
reflection of the bias and the prejudice of the critics." However, it will

2. Leo XIII, *Providentissimus Deus* (November 18, 1893), 17.
3. Ibid.
4. Ibid (emphasis added).

also become evident that Benedict stands in pointed contrast with Leo concerning the question of whether higher criticism can be successfully incorporated into Catholic practice or whether it will inevitably lead to the demise of the faith.

Touching more specifically on the central issues this chapter will treat is a 1907 *motu proprio* of Pius X. Prefacing his letter with a commendation of his predecessor Leo's encyclical, Pius lauded Leo for having "defended the divine character of [the sacred] books not only against the errors and calumnities of the rationalists but also against the false teachings of what is known as 'higher criticism'—something which the Pontiff most wisely exposed as nothing but the commentaries of rationalism derived from a misuse of philology and related disciplines."[5] Immediately after this Pius turns his attention to reinforcing the efforts of the Pontifical Biblical Commission (PBC) to stem the malignant tide of modern biblical scholarship:

We are pleased to note that the Pontifical Biblical Commission, after mature examination and the most diligent consultations, has issued a number of decisions that have proved very useful for the promotion and guidance of sound biblical scholarship in accordance with the established norms. But we have also observed that, although these decisions were approved by the Pontiff, there are some who have refused to accept them with the proper obedience, because they are both unduly prone to opinions and methods tainted by pernicious novelties and excessively devoted to a false notion of freedom—in fact, an immoderate license—which in sacred studies proves to be a most insidious and powerful source of the worst evils against the purity of the faith.

For this reason, we find it necessary to declare and prescribe, as we do now declare and expressly prescribe, that all are bound in conscience to submit to the decisions of the Biblical Commission, which have been given in the past and shall be given in the future, *in the same way as to the Decrees pertaining to doctrine, issued by the Sacred Congregations* and approved by the Sovereign Pontiff[6]

5. Pius X, *Praestantia Sacrae Scripturae* (November 18, 1907).

6. Ibid. In commenting on this document I have reproduced the translation found in Dean Béchard, *The Scripture Documents* (Collegeville, Minn.: The Liturgical Press, 2002), 320–21. The Latin text of the second paragraph reads: "Quapropter declarandum illud praecipiendumque videmus, quemadmodum declaramus in praesens expresseque praecipimus, universos omnes conscientiae obstringi officio sententiis Pontificalis Consilii de Re Biblica, sive quae adhuc sunt emissae, sive quae posthac edentur, *perinde ac Decretis Sacrarum Congregationum, pertinentibus ad doctrinam* probatisque a Pontifice, se subiiciendi."

This passage merits a number of observations, but prior to further discussion, it is important to know which decisions of the PBC are in question here. Between the years 1905 and 1933 the commission issued a series of sixteen *responsa* concerning deleterious views of Scripture reflected in the biblical scholarship emerging in that period. The decrees dealt with a variety of texts and centered on issues concerning the historical origin and interpretation of biblical books.[7] With regard to the overarching question of whether Catholics could embrace the conclusions of modern biblical scholarship in these matters, the response given by the PBC was on the whole "Negative." In this document Pius X manifests his will to "now declare and expressly prescribe" (*declaramus in praesens expresseque praecipimus*) that the PBC's findings are to be considered authoritative and binding on Catholic scholars, some of whom had hitherto lacked due obedience in their regard due to an attachment that confuses authentic freedom with "immoderate license" (*licentia intemperans*).

Pius's declaration was controversial even in its own day. In light of this chapter's broader argument it is significant to observe that, in addition to the official version of the above text published in *Acta Sanctae Sedis* on November 18, 1907, a variant unofficial draft was mistakenly printed shortly thereafter in *Civiltà Cattolica*, the Vatican's own newspaper. This version of the text reads:

We declare and prescribe that all are bound in conscience to submit to the decisions of the Biblical Commission *that pertain to doctrine*, which have been given in the past and shall be given in the future, in the same way as to the

7. The topics of the documents were as follows: implied quotations in Scripture (1905); historical narratives (1905); the Mosaic authorship of the Pentateuch (1906); the authorship and historicity of the Gospel of John (1907); the character and authorship of the Book of Isaiah (1908); the historicity of the first three chapters of Genesis (1909); the authorship and date of the Psalms (1910); the authorship, date, and historicity of Matthew (1911); the authorship, date, and historicity of Mark and Luke (1912); the Synoptic question (1912); the authorship and date of Acts (1913); the authorship, integrity, and date of the Pauline Pastoral Epistles (1913); the authorship and manner of composition of Hebrews (1914); the parousia in the letters of Paul (1915); certain added verses in the Vulgate (1921); and the false interpretation of Ps 16:10–11 and Mt 15 [16]:26 / Lk 9:25 (1933). This chapter will not examine all of these but rather will discuss a handful of representative positions with which Benedict XVI's exegetical principles and practice stand in clear tension. The document on the *parousia* will be treated later in this volume.

Decrees issued by the Sacred Congregations and approved by the Sovereign Pontiff.[8]

Although this text was replaced with the official one in the next printing of the paper, it reveals that Pius was aware of the need to phrase this document precisely and that said phrasing would have significant ramifications. Whereas the official version gives all PBC decrees the same authority as those concerning doctrine issued from other curial offices, this unofficial text appeared to limit the authority of the PBC by considering authoritative only its decisions pertaining to doctrine. On this point, however, the alternate text more closely resembles two later—also unofficial—statements issued by key curial figures.

Discussing this case in the appendix of *The Scripture Documents*, Dean Béchard relates that two "semi-official clarifications" of Pius's document were issued in conjunction with the final preparation of a newly revised edition of the *Enchiridion Biblicum* (1954). The statements appeared in separate journals in the form of review articles from no less important men than Athanasius Miller, OSB and Arduin Kleinhaus, OFM, secretary and sub-secretary of the PBC, respectively. Miller's text makes it quite clear that, contrary to the ostensible teaching of Pius X, the methods of modern biblical scholarship are appropriate so long as their conclusions do not contradict the Church's teaching on faith and morals.

However, as long as those decrees propose views that are neither immediately or mediately connected with the truths of faith and morals, it goes without saying that the interpreter of Sacred Scripture may pursue his scientific research with complete freedom and may utilize the results of these investigations, provided always that he respects the teaching authority of the Church.[9]

---

8. *Civiltà Cattolica* (November 27, 1907): 513-18. The Latin text of this alternate version includes a small but important variation on the official text: "Quapropter declarandum illud praecipiendumque videmus, quemadmodum declaramus in praesens expresseque praecipimus, universos omnes conscientiae obstringi officio sententiis Pontificalis Consilii de Re Biblica, *ad doctrinam pertinentibus*, sive quae adhuc sunt emissae, sive quae posthac edentur, perinde ac Decretis Sacrarum Congregationum a Pontifice probatis, se subiiciendi." This version limits the authority of PBC "sentences" to those pertaining to doctrine, whereas the official text indicates that *all* PBC decisions are to be followed in the same way one would heed decrees of other curial congregations pertaining to doctrinal matters.

9. Athanasius Miller, OSB, "Das neue biblische Handbuch," *Benediktinische Monat-*

Béchard comments that since the *responsa* dealt almost entirely with historical and literary issues rather than matters of faith and morals, it was clear that "biblical scholars are not bound by these earlier teachings, which addressed the particular needs of a historical situation happily no longer existent."[10] Further, he observes that the Magisterium of the time had ample opportunity to censure these men for their words, and that its silence concerning the two explanatory statements implies consent to their orthodoxy. Finally, Béchard adds to this the fact that "many highly respected Catholic exegetes, whose teaching and published research represent the practical outcome of this semi-official clarification, have since been appointed, in recent years, to serve as consultors or members of the PBC."[11] As if it were not enough to see this discrepancy between prior official papal teaching and the later semi-official statements of high-ranking PBC officials, in the twenty-first century an equally eminent president of the PBC would continue this trend—only this figure, whose writings would likely have been censured less than a century earlier, went on to become pope.[12]

Benedict XVI: A Divergent Appraisal of Modern Biblical Scholarship

This section will consider texts from Benedict XVI that convey in no uncertain terms the contrast he perceives between his own appraisal of modern biblical scholarship and that of his predecessors

---

schrift 31 (1955): 49–50. The translation reproduced here is in Dean Béchard, *The Scripture Documents*, 327. See also Arduin Kleinhaus, "De nova Enchiridii Biblici editione," *Antonianum* 30 (1955): 63-65.

10. Béchard, *The Scripture Documents*, 327-28.

11. Ibid., 328-29.

12. Of course, it is important to bear in mind the respective weight due to Benedict's various writings, which depends partly on whether he is speaking in his capacity as a private theologian or rather as pope or prefect of the CDF. As Benedict famously wrote in the foreword to his first volume on the person of Jesus, "It goes without saying that this book is in no way an exercise of the magisterium, but is solely an expression of my personal search 'for the face of the Lord.' Everyone is free, then, to contradict me. I would only ask my readers for that initial goodwill without which there can be no understanding." Benedict XVI, *Jesus of Nazareth: From the Baptism in the Jordan to the Transfiguration* (New York: Doubleday, 2007), xxiii–xxiv.

discussed above. Although many of the statements immediately below were made in his capacity as a theologian or as a curial official rather than as pope, the problem raised is that writings from the highest of Catholic officials today often appear to conflict directly with the binding pronouncements of the PBC in a time when it served as an official organ of the Magisterium.[13] In this regard it will also be helpful further below to see how Benedict maintained the same stance when he had occasion to write as a biblical theologian even after assuming the Chair of Peter.

There is no better place to begin a discussion of Benedict's biblical approach in relation to the PBC than to examine an address he gave as the commission's president on the occasion of its 100th anniversary. At the very outset of his talk, Cardinal Ratzinger gives us an indication of why he has devoted so much of his career to the delicate issue concerning the relationship of the Magisterium and exegesis, sharing that it was "one of the problems of my own autobiography."[14] He recounts the troubled story of one of his former professors, Friedrich Wilhelm Maier, whose flowering academic career had been dealt a sharp blow by the Magisterium in its 1912 Consistorial Decree *De quibusdam commentariis non admittendis.* The document forbade Maier to teach New Testament and required that the commentary into which Maier had been pouring all his energy had to be "altogether expunged from the education of the clergy." In his work Maier had defended the controversial two-source theory, which—as Ratzinger reminds his audience—is today "almost universally accepted" as an account of the synoptic problem.[15]

---

13. The discrepancy would not be nearly as significant if it were between a reigning pope and the PBC today. The commission was restructured by Paul VI in 1971 so that it acts no longer as an official organ of the Magisterium but rather as an advisory forum in which the Magisterium and expert exegetes to work together in the quest to illumine matters concerning Sacred Scripture.

14. Joseph Ratzinger, "Exegesis and the Magisterium of the Church," in *Opening Up the Scriptures*, 126. See also similar comments in Ratzinger's *Milestones: Memoirs 1927–1977* (San Francisco: Ignatius Press, 1998), 52–53.

15. Ratzinger, "Exegesis and the Magisterium of the Church," 127. As commonly articulated, the two-source hypothesis proposes that the Gospel of Matthew and the Gospel of Luke depended on common source material in Mark and an unidentified source, dubbed "Q" (the first letter of the German word for "source"). Ratzinger also mentions the figure of Maier in *Milestones*, 50–53.

Although the censured theologian was eventually permitted to resume his teaching, Ratzinger relates that "the wound that Maier had received in 1912 had never fully healed."[16] Indeed, Maier had told his student that he would probably not live to witness the full dawning of "the real freedom of exegesis of which he dreamed" and so yearned, "like Moses on Mount Nebo [in Deuteronomy 34], to gaze upon the Promised Land of an exegesis liberated from every shackle of magisterial surveillance."[17] Ratzinger spends the next part of his article in the effort "to climb Mt. Nebo with him, as it were, and to survey the country that we have traversed in the last fifty years," tracing out various milestones from the time of Pius XII forward as the Magisterium's relationship with modern exegesis approached its "Promised Land."[18] He reflects on Maier's situation with great sympathy, acknowledging, "It is perfectly understandable that, in the days when the decisions of the then Pontifical Biblical Commission prevented them from a clean application of the historical-critical method, Catholic theologians should cast envious glances at their Protestant colleagues."[19] As he would later state in one of his final public addresses as pope, Catholic exegetes prior to Vatican II "felt themselves somewhat—shall we say—in a position of inferiority with regard to the Protestants, who were making the great discoveries, whereas Catholics felt somewhat 'handicapped' by the need to submit to the Magisterium."[20] It is reve-

16. Ratzinger, "Exegesis and the Magisterium of the Church," 127.

17. Ibid., 127–28.

18. Ibid., 128. Ratzinger states, "The 1960s represent—to remain with our metaphor—the entrance into the Promised Land of exegetical freedom." Other pivotal moments in this process described by Ratzinger include the publication of *Divino Afflante Spiritu* (1943), the PBC's Instruction on the Historical Truth of the Gospels (1964), Vatican II's *Dei Verbum* (1965), the restructuring of the PBC by Paul VI's *Sedula Cura* in 1971, the 1971 appointment of Rudolf Schnackenburg (one of Friedrich Maier's prominent students) to the International Theological Commission, and the PBC's *The Interpretation of the Bible in the Church* (1994).

19. Ratzinger, "Exegesis and the Magisterium of the Church," 131.

20. Benedict XVI, Address to the Parish Priests and Clergy of Rome (February 14, 2013). Reflecting on his time at the Second Vatican Council, he wrote: "Even more hotly debated was the problem of Revelation. At stake here was the relationship between Scripture and Tradition, and it was the exegetes above all who were anxious for greater freedom; they felt themselves somewhat—shall we say—in a position of inferiority with regard to the Protestants, who were making the great discoveries, whereas Catholics felt

latory of just how much this point influenced his life that the pontiff returned to the same theme in one of his last public statements.

The extent to which Ratzinger was troubled by the early decisions of the PBC can be seen in multiple places throughout his corpus. Writing as prefect of the CDF, his introduction to *Donum Veritatis* (Instruction Concerning the Ecclesial Vocation of the Theologian) spoke of "the anti-modernistic decisions at the beginning of this century, especially the decisions of the Biblical Commission of that time."[21] His commentary on Vatican II had put the matter more bluntly, describing these decisions as symptomatic of an "anti-Modernistic *neurosis* which had again and again crippled the Church since the turn of the century."[22] As a result of this approach, he laments, the research of many scholars (like Maier above) was halted in its tracks and "much real wheat was lost along with the chaff."[23] He indicates that this same

---

somewhat 'handicapped' by the need to submit to the Magisterium. So a very concrete struggle was in play here: what sort of freedom do exegetes have? How does one properly read Scripture? What is the meaning of Tradition?"

21. Joseph Ratzinger, "On the 'Instruction Concerning the Ecclesial Vocation of the Theologian,'" in *The Nature and Mission of Theology: Approaches to Understanding Its Role in Light of the Present Controversy*, trans. Adrian Walker (San Francisco: Ignatius Press, 1995), 106.

22. Joseph Ratzinger, *Theological Highlights of Vatican II* (New York: Paulist Press, 1966), 11 (emphasis added); cf. ibid., 23. A bit later in the text Ratzinger sheds further revelatory reflections concerning his time at Vatican II: "The real question behind the discussion could be put this way: Was the intellectual position of 'anti-Modernism'—the old policy of exclusiveness, condemnation and defense leading to an almost neurotic denial of all that was new—to be continued? Or would the Church, after it had taken all the necessary precautions to protect the faith, turn over a new leaf and move on into a new and positive encounter with its own origins, with its brothers, and with the world of today?" Ibid., 44. For a lucid presentation of how Catholic scholarship "sank into a biblical winter" in this period, in the context of a sketch of the milestones in Ratzinger's writing on the nature of biblical scholarship, see Joseph T. Lienhard, SJ, "Pope Benedict XVI: Theologian of the Bible," *Homiletic and Pastoral Review* 110, 10 (2010): 66–78. For another sharp criticism of this anti-modernistic attitude that prevailed in the Church for more than a century, see Hans Urs von Balthasar, *The Office of Peter and the Structure of the Church* (San Francisco: Ignatius Press, 1986), 258–66.

23. Ratzinger, *Theological Highlights of Vatican II*, 21. Here, in stark contrast to the list of "milestones" discussed above, Ratzinger provides a brief but incisive history of the Church's "anti-modernistic" attitude. Pius IX's Syllabus of Errors, he observes, "undoubtedly went about this with excessively one-sided zeal. This development reaches its zenith in the various measures of Pius X against Modernism (the decree *Lamentabili* and

attitude was present even in the initial schema on divine revelation at Vatican II: "This document pursued once more the line of thought of Pius IX and Pius X. The schemata of the theological commission ... breathed this same spirit. The same cramped thinking, once so necessary as a line of defense, impregnated the text and informed it with a theology of negations and prohibitions."[24] Finally, in his PBC address discussed above, Ratzinger gets more specific as he defends faith's role in exegesis while simultaneously admitting:

> It remains correct that by making the judgments that we have mentioned, the Magisterium overextended the range of what faith can guarantee with certainty and that, as a result, the Magisterium's credibility was injured and the freedom needed for exegetical research and interrogation was unduly narrowed.[25]

It is striking to witness in this passage the humility and boldness of a Church official who recognizes that a frank appraisal of the limits of the Magisterium is a necessary step toward arriving at a deeper understanding of its nature and relationship to exegesis. The matter would be different if this had been written by a dissenting Catholic or an agnostic like Ehrman, but the fact is that it comes from the mouth of a man of the Church whose very vocation was devoted to defending

---

the encyclical *Pascendi* [1907], and, finally, the 'oath against Modernism' [1910]).... This historical perspective helps explain, then, that secret fear and mistrust of any theological expression of modern historical and philosophical thought. This same anxiety persisted until its last reverberation in the encyclical *Humani Generis* of Pius XII." Ibid. See also Ratzinger's commentary in which he states that tension between the Magisterium and modern exegesis "reached a new climax with the banning of professors at the Biblical Institute from teaching and with the exceptionally sharp polemic of Mgr. Romeo against modern Catholic exegesis." Quoted in Herbert Vorgrimler, *Commentary on the Documents of Vatican II* (New York: Herder and Herder, 1967), 3:157–58.

24. Ratzinger, *Theological Highlights of Vatican II*, 42–43. Ratzinger further recalls that "the problem of the historical dimension in theology which underlay the problems of revealed truth, scripture, and tradition" had "set off a most violent controversy" among the Vatican II Fathers debating these schemata. Elsewhere he describes the initial schema as composed in a "purely defensive spirit," with "the narrowest interpretation of inerrancy" and "a conception of the historicity of the Gospels that suggested that there were no problems." Vorgrimler, *Commentary on the Documents of Vatican II*, 3:159. If this original version had passed, "[t]he burden that this would have meant for the future course of Catholic theology was not easy to estimate: it would probably have been still more serious than the difficulties that resulted from the one-sided condemnations of modernism." Ibid., 159–60.

25. Ratzinger, "Exegesis and the Magisterium of the Church," 133.

the faith. This, then, begs the question: How does Ratzinger account for the discrepancy between his view of modern biblical scholarship and that of the Magisterium before him? Before answering this question, the following section will illustrate Ratzinger's convictions with concrete examples of how he adopts some of the very conclusions of modern scholarship which were forbidden by the PBC just decades earlier.

Apparent Contradiction between PBC Teaching and Ratzinger's Exegetical Practices

It is not only Ratzinger's statements *about* modern exegesis and the teaching of the past Magisterium that appear to stand in open contradiction to prior Church teaching; on a number of points Ratzinger's exegetical practice itself also plainly contradicts the views mandated to be held by Catholics according to the PBC's early decrees. For the sake of brevity, I will illustrate the problem with just a few among many possible examples covering a range of biblical books. Note that neither my nor Benedict's point here is to argue for a particular exegetical conclusion such as Markan priority (his position on this question will become quite clear in later chapters). Rather, here the concern is to address the larger question of what views a Catholic biblical scholar may hold and how to offer a robust *apologia* for the Church's change in stance regarding the same.

On the whole, the PBC decrees in question are carefully crafted so as to make their position known while avoiding categorical claims that could readily be falsified by later scholarly findings. For example, the 1908 decree *On the Character and Authorship of the Book of Isaiah* responds "Negative" to its third question:

Whether it may be admitted that ... the second part of the Book of Isaiah (chs. 40-66), in which the prophet addresses and consoles not the Jews contemporary with himself but, as one living among them, those mourning in the Babylonian exile, cannot have for its author Isaiah himself long dead, but must be attributed to some unknown prophet living among the exiles.[26]

26. Pontifical Biblical Commission, *On the Character and Authorship of the Book of Isaiah* (June 29, 1908). For this and all citations from PBC decrees, I have used the translation found in Dean Béchard, *The Scripture Documents*.

In various places Ratzinger demonstrates a conviction that the Book of Isaiah is the work, not of one author but rather of two or three, since he follows the standard scholarly convention of calling the author of Isa 40–66 as "Deutero-Isaiah."[27] But does this amount to saying that the later chapters of Isaiah "cannot have for its author Isaiah himself" and that the work "must" be attributed to someone else? The same applies in the case of the fourth and fifth questions of this PBC decree. Ratzinger seems to hold that there are multiple authors, but he does not insist upon what the fourth question rejects, namely, that "the philological argument ... is to be considered weighty enough *to compel* a serious and critical scholar ... to acknowledge for this book a plurality of authors."[28] Neither does he argue for what the fifth question rejects, that is to say, the claim that "there are solid arguments, even when taken cumulatively, *to prove* that the Book of Isaiah must be attributed not to Isaiah alone but to two or even more authors."[29] Ratzinger is a more careful thinker than that. Nevertheless, despite the fact that he does not technically contradict this PBC decree, it is clear that the two at least stand in deep tension.

The decree *On the Mosaic Authorship of the Pentateuch* provides more opportunity for reflection on this tension. Its first question reads:

Whether the arguments amassed by critics to impugn the Mosaic authenticity of the sacred books designated by the name Pentateuch are of sufficient weight ... to justify the statement that these books do not have Moses as their author but were compiled from sources for the most part posterior to the time of Moses.[30]

The answer to this question is, unsurprisingly, "Negative." Notice that the document does not expressly require one to maintain that Moses wrote the entire Pentateuch. In fact, the second question in this docu-

27. For just a couple of examples, see Joseph Ratzinger, *Introduction to Christianity* (San Francisco: Ignatius Press, 2004), 129–30, and *Eschatology: Death and Eternal Life* (Washington, D.C.: The Catholic University of America Press, 1988), 86.

28. Pontifical Biblical Commission, *On the Character and Authorship of the Book of Isaiah* (emphasis added).

29. Ibid. (emphasis added).

30. Pontifical Biblical Commission, *On the Mosaic Authorship of the Pentateuch* (June 27, 1906).

ment allows for the possibility that Moses entrusted his inspired work to another who, omitting nothing from what he received, composed it in a way faithful to Moses' own thought. The third question affirms that the authenticity of the Pentateuch would not be impugned if Moses had recourse to prior sources for its composition, while the fourth question allows for the possibility that certain alterations to the text were introduced over the centuries. At the same time, the fourth question permits this under the assumption that one grants "substantial Mosaic authenticity of the Pentateuch."

Rather than directly tackling the question of Mosaic authorship, Benedict's exegesis reflects the belief that more is going on in the redaction of the Pentateuch than mere additions to a text substantially produced at the time of Moses. This is especially evident in his treatment of the creation accounts in the set of homilies published under the title *In the Beginning*.[31] It also comes across in the various questions he addresses concerning creation in the interview book *God and the World*. In an interesting response contrasting the Bible and the Koran, he writes:

[The Bible] is mediated to us by a history, and even as a book it extends over a period of more than a thousand years. The question of whether or not Moses may have been a writer is one we can happily leave to one side. It is still true that the biblical literature grew up over a thousand year history and thus moves through quite different stages of history and of civilization, which are all reflected in it.... It becomes clear that God did not just dictate these words but rather that they bear the impression of a history that he has been guiding; they have come into being as a witness to that history.[32]

As is typical in his more informal works such as interviews or pastorally oriented documents aimed at a more popular audience, Ratzinger is careful not to take sides on the issue of who wrote the Pentateuch. What is noteworthy is that he says, "The question of whether or not Moses may have been a writer is one we can happily leave to one side." For the PBC this was certainly not a question that could remain

31. Joseph Ratzinger, *In the Beginning: A Catholic Understanding of the Story of Creation and the Fall* (Grand Rapids, Mich.: Eerdmans, 1995).
32. Joseph Ratzinger, *God and the World* (San Francisco: Ignatius Press, 2002), 151–52.

unanswered. Ratzinger thus entertains a position that is contrary to that of the PBC, yet this still does not amount to a direct contradiction. After all, the PBC decree simply required one to hold that the arguments of modern scholarship are not of sufficient weight "to impugn the Mosaic authenticity of the sacred books." It is not forbidden for Catholics today to hold substantial Mosaic authorship of the Pentateuch, so the language of the PBC decree checks out even though one can discern that Ratzinger's exegesis conflicts with what can be inferred from it.

A clearer example of contradiction concerns a text not typically mentioned in a discussion of problematic PBC statements, a 1933 decree *On the False Interpretation of Two Texts*. The first question of the text asks: "Whether it is permissible for a Catholic ... [to] interpret the words of Psalm 15 [16]:10–11 ... as if the sacred author was not speaking of the resurrection of our Lord Jesus Christ" and gives the answer "Negative."[33] As part of its argument, the document references the authoritative interpretation of "the two chief apostles" in Acts 2:24–33 and 13:35–37. The text reads:

> For David says concerning [Christ] ... "For thou wilt not abandon my soul to Hades, nor let thy Holy One see corruption. Thou hast made known to me the ways of life; thou wilt make me full of gladness with thy presence" [Ps 16:10]. Brethren, I may say to you confidently of the patriarch David that he both died and was buried, and his tomb is with us to this day. Being therefore a prophet, and knowing that God had sworn with an oath to him that he would set one of his descendants upon his throne, he foresaw and spoke of the resurrection of the Christ, that he was not abandoned to Hades, nor did his flesh see corruption. This Jesus God raised up, and of that we all are witnesses.[34]

Modern exegetes would question the New Testament's interpretation here on at least two points. The first concerns whether it is correct to assume that David composed this psalm, but that is not the issue here. More importantly, did the psalmist himself actually foresee the Res-

---

33. Pontifical Biblical Commission, *On the False Interpretation of Two Texts* (July 1, 1933).

34. Acts 2:25, 27, 30–32. Unless otherwise noted, all biblical citations will be taken from the Revised Standard Version.

urrection of Christ, as Acts maintains and the PBC mandated that Catholics hold? Benedict treats briefly of this question:

In the Hebrew version ["You do not give me up to Sheol, or let your godly one see the Pit ..."] the psalmist speaks in the certainty that God will protect him, even in the threatening situation in which he evidently finds himself, that God will shield him from death and that he may dwell securely: he will not see the grave. The version Peter quotes ["For you will not abandon my soul to Hades, nor let your Holy One see corruption ..."] is different: here the psalmist is confident that he will not remain in the underworld, that he will not see corruption.[35]

As Benedict observes, the version of the Old Testament typically used by the early Church was the LXX. In that version, the verbs "You will not abandon" and "Nor will you allow" of Psalm 16:10 occur in the future tense, describing a restoration from physical death after David's natural death occurs: "Here the psalmist is confident that he will not remain in the underworld, that he will not see corruption."[36] In the original Hebrew of Psalm 16, on the other hand, the sacred author has rescue from physical death in its sights. His use of the present tense—"You do not give me up"—reflects the hope that God would shield him from dying in the first place. Herein lies the ostensible contradiction between Benedict's exegesis of the psalm and that required by the PBC. The PBC requires one to affirm that the sacred (human) author was speaking of the Resurrection of Christ, whereas in the earliest version of the text the sacred author does not seem to have resurrection on his radar at all, let alone the Resurrection of Jesus.[37]

Another instance of tension between the requirements of the PBC and the New Testament exegesis of Benedict concerns the authorship of the Gospel of John. In a 1907 decree *On the Authorship and His-*

35. Benedict XVI, *Jesus of Nazareth: Holy Week: From the Entrance into Jerusalem to the Resurrection* (San Francisco: Ignatius Press, 2011), 255.

36. Ibid.

37. For a discussion of how the spiritual sense plays a role in the interpretation of Ps 16, see Matthew J. Ramage, *Dark Passages of the Bible: Engaging Scripture with Benedict XVI and Thomas Aquinas* (Washington, D.C.: The Catholic University of America Press, 2013), 269–73. Benedict adds a further potential wrinkle to the PBC argument in demonstrating an openness to the possibility that the speech of Acts 2 might not be that of Peter himself in the first place. See *Jesus of Nazareth: Holy Week*, 256.

toricity of the Fourth Gospel, the commission's first question considers "[w]hether … it is proved by such solid historical argument that the Apostle John and no other must be acknowledged as the author of the Fourth Gospel, and that the reasons brought forward by the critics against it in no wise weaken this tradition."[38] Although the PBC answers with an "Affirmative," Benedict's exegesis challenges this conclusion in an important way. According to Benedict:

> The evidence suggests that in Ephesus there was something like a Johannine school, which traced its origin to Jesus' favorite disciple himself, but in which a certain "Presbyter John" presided as the ultimate authority. The "presbyter" John appears as the sender of the Second and Third Letters of John…. He is evidently not the same as the Apostle, which means that here in the canonical text we encounter expressly the mysterious figure of the presbyter…. At any rate, there seem to be grounds for ascribing to "Presbyter John" an essential role in the definitive shaping of the Gospel.[39]

Benedict's conclusion stands in stark contrast to that arrived at by the PBC. However, it should be noted that he adds something which, while not completely eliminating the discrepancy, shows that he intends to say something similar to what the PBC said but in a more nuanced way. For Benedict, the contents of the Gospel go back "to an eyewitness, and even the actual redaction of the text was substantially the work of one of his closest followers."[40] As we will gather from the principles elucidated below, Benedict would likely say that his essential point was the same as that of the PBC—namely, to uphold the authoritative portrait of Jesus painted in the Gospel of John—even if certain assertions of the PBC would later stand in need of correction.

Perhaps the most obvious contradiction between Benedict's exegesis and the mandates of the PBC concerns the authorship, date, and mutual dependence of the synoptic Gospels—what is sometimes called the "synoptic problem." It so happens that this question is also the most germane to the concerns of the present volume, as will be seen in later chapters. Here I will offer illustrations from three different PBC docu-

---

38. Pontifical Biblical Commission, *On the Authorship and Historicity of the Fourth Gospel* (May 29, 1907).

39. Benedict XVI, *Jesus of Nazareth: From the Baptism in the Jordan to the Transfiguration*, 226.

40. Ibid., 227.

ments which speak to the same broader point and then discuss them in light of Benedict's thought. The first is the 1911 decree *On the Authorship, Date of Composition, and Historicity of the Gospel of Matthew.*[41] Its first question affirms that "it may and must be affirmed with certainty that Matthew, an apostle of Christ, is truly the author of the Gospel published under his name." Its fourth question is similar to the first:

Whether we may accept as probable the opinion of certain modern writers who assert that Matthew, strictly speaking, did not compose the Gospel as it has come down to us, but only composed a collection of the sayings and discourses of Christ, which a later anonymous author, whom they call the redactor of the Gospel, used as sources.

Answering "Negative," the PBC asserts as not "probable" the proposition that the Gospel of Matthew had its origin as a collection of Christ's sayings and discourses which were crafted into a literary whole by an author who lived later than the apostle Matthew. The sixth question goes further in responding "Negative to both parts" to the following suggestion:

Whether ... it may also be affirmed that the narratives of the deeds and words of Christ found in the Gospel have undergone certain alterations and adaptations under the influence both of Old Testament prophecies and of the more developed perspective of the Church, and that, in consequence, this Gospel narrative is not in conformity with historical truth.

This statement affirms that the Gospels must be acknowledged as representing the "historical truth" of Christ's life. It further insinuates that it would not be in conformity with said truth if the words and deeds of Christ's life had undergone certain alterations by the authors who wove them into their respective narratives.

The next source relevant to the synoptic problem is the 1912 decree *On the Authorship, Time of Composition, and Historicity of the Gospels of Mark and Luke.*[42] As in the case of Matthew above, this document's first question affirms that "the clear witness of the tradition ... compels us to affirm with certainty that Mark, the disciple and interpreter

---

41. Pontifical Biblical Commission, *On the Authorship, Date of Composition, and Historicity of the Gospel of Matthew* (June 19, 1911).

42. Pontifical Biblical Commission, *On the Authorship, Time of Composition, and Historicity of the Gospels of Mark and Luke* (June 26, 1912).

of Peter, and Luke the physician, the assistant and companion of Paul, were truly the authors of the Gospels respectively attributed to them." The fourth question requires Catholics to hold that the final verses of Mark are inspired and canonical. It additionally states that "the reasons by which some critics attempt to prove that the last twelve verses of the Gospel of Mark (Mk 16:9–20) were not written by Mark himself" fails to demonstrate that Mark was not the author of said verses. The fifth question concerning the chronological ordering of the Gospels states that it is not permitted "to abandon the claim ... that, after Matthew, who first of all wrote his Gospel in his own native dialect, Mark wrote second and Luke third."

Finally, the 1912 decree *On the Synoptic Question or the Mutual Relations Among the First Three Gospels* speaks to the same overarching problem and appears in stark contrast to the thought of Benedict XVI.[43] Its second question generates a pair of "Negative" responses:

> Whether we can consider what has been set forth above as observed by those who, without the support of any testimony of tradition or of any historical argument, easily embrace the hypothesis commonly known as the two-souce theory, which seeks to explain the composition of the Greek Gospel of Matthew and the Gospel of Luke mainly by their common dependence on the Gospel of Mark and a so-called collection of the sayings of the Lord; and, whether, in consequence, we can freely advocate this theory.

Thus it is not possible for a Catholic either to "easily embrace" or to "freely advocate" the two-souce theory, which considers the Gospels of Matthew and Luke to be the fruit of a synthesis between preexistent material from Mark and a separate collection of Jesus' sayings.[44]

Several works of Ratzinger exhibit fundamental disagreements with the aforementioned PBC conclusions. For example, in two works Ratzinger spoke of the two-souce theory as being "almost universally accepted" as an account of the synoptic problem.[45] In other works he

---

43. Pontifical Biblical Commission, *On the Synoptic Question or the Mutual Relations Among the First Three Gospels* (June 26, 1912).

44. This collection of "sayings" is commonly referred to as "Q," an abbreviated form of the German word *Quelle* or "source."

45. Ratzinger, "Exegesis and the Magisterium of the Church," 127; cf. *Milestones*, 50–51.

illustrates this conviction when, for example, he assumes that Mark's eschatology is oldest and that "the gospel of Matthew, composed contemporaneously with Luke's (or perhaps even later) contains an undiminished imminent eschatology which may even be described as heightened in comparison with Mark."[46] A speech by Cardinal Ratzinger presents us with a case in which he traces the titles of Jesus from the earlier title of "Christ" (seen in the confession of Mk 8:29) to "Christ, Son of the living God" (the parallel confession in Mt 16:16) to "Logos" (Jn 1).[47] However, in God and the World, he elaborates upon the synoptic problem more broadly and in a way that speaks to all of the above PBC decrees:

> With regard to the individual Gospels, today we assume that not Matthew but Mark is the oldest of the Gospels. Matthew and Luke have, so to speak, taken Mark as their basic framework and have enriched it with other traditional materials that were available to them. The Gospel of John, now, had a separate origin and development and is homogeneous. It is important that the first three Gospels were not just written by *one* writer in each case but were based on the transmission of material by the whole believing Church—a process, that is to say, in which material slowly crystallized in particular traditions that were finally brought together to form the text of the Gospels. In a certain sense, then, the question about particular people is secondary.... What is fundamental is that oral transmission came at the beginning, as is so characteristic in the Orient. That guarantees the close connection with the historical origin.[48]

46. Ratzinger, Eschatology, 37.

47. Joseph Ratzinger, "Christ, Faith, and the Challenge of Cultures," Speech given in Hong Kong to the presidents of the Asian bishops' conferences and the chairmen of their doctrinal commissions during a March 2–5, 1993 meeting.

48. Ratzinger, God and the World, 229. Elsewhere Ratzinger makes a similar point with a thought-provoking contrast with Protestantism and an allusion to Orthodoxy: "[A]n exclusive insistence on the *sola scriptura* of classical Protestantism could not possibly survive, and today it is in crisis more than ever precisely as a result of that 'scientific' exegesis which arose in, and was pioneered by, the Reformed theology. This demonstrates how much the Gospels are a product of the early Church, indeed, how the whole of Scripture is nothing other than tradition. So much so that a number of Lutheran scholars seem to converge with the view of the Eastern Orthodox: not sola scriptura but *sola traditio.*" Joseph Ratzinger and Vittorio Messori, The Ratzinger Report: An Exclusive Interview on the State of the Church (San Francisco: Ignatius Press, 1985), 160.

While well aware of the venerable tradition that considers Matthew the first of the Gospels, Ratzinger clearly accepts—with appropriate nuances and modifications—the standard suggestions held by modern scholars like Ehrman regarding the origin and relationship of the synoptic Gospels.[49] His findings thus directly contradict those of the earlier PBC to the effect that Matthew was the first of the Gospels and that he did not borrow from preexistent source material. Turning on its head the somewhat simplistic question of who wrote which Gospel and when, he focuses on the ecclesial nature of the Bible and wants to show that "the first three Gospels were not just written by *one* writer in each case but were based on the transmission of material by the whole believing Church." Earlier source material "slowly crystallized in particular traditions that were finally brought together to form the text of the Gospels." In this way, "the question about particular people is secondary," since the Gospels originated not simply with individual authors but rather in the heart of "the whole believing Church."[50]

In the same discussion Ratzinger adds further points that conflict with the PBC's declarations requiring Catholics to hold that the Apostles themselves wrote the Gospels after whom they were named:

According to the results of research, the texts of the three synoptic Gospels—Matthew, Mark, Luke—are intertwined with one another in some kind of close relationship and are interdependent. The question of how Matthew came to be written has been completely reopened. Nowadays the greater number of scholars are of the opinion that one cannot ascribe this Gospel to the apostle Matthew, that, on the contrary, it originated rather later and was written down toward the end of the first century in a Syrian Christian congregation. The origin and growth of the Gospels as a group now appears to us to be a very complex process. At the beginning there were probably collections of the sayings of Jesus, which were at first memorized and handed on

---

49. Ratzinger summarizes, "Earlier the Gospel of Matthew was held to be the oldest of the Gospels. A note by a second-century writer, Papias, says that Matthew first of all wrote this Gospel in Hebrew, and then it was translated into Greek.... Luke and Mark were also acceptable, but Matthew was held to be the oldest and the one that offered most, the one most immediately directed to the Church as far as her liturgy and her faith were concerned." Ratzinger, *God and the World*, 228.

50. For more of Ratzinger's thoughts on the origin of the canon in the heart of the Church, see Matthew J. Ramage, *Dark Passages of the Bible*, 62–68.

orally but quite soon were also written down in a set form.... In the beginning, then, there was oral tradition.[51]

Notice that Ratzinger does not go so far as forbid a Catholic to uphold the venerable tradition that the Apostle Matthew himself wrote the text attached to his name or that his was the first of the four Gospels. Rather, he is content to summarize the available scholarly evidence, the ancient tradition, and his own scholarly opinion. All the same, it is clear that, contrary to the early PBC, Ratzinger is fine with attributing the Gospels to authors other than the evangelists themselves, and he is comfortable accepting an ordering among the four that differs from the reckoning of the Church's more ancient tradition. He is even open to the presence of significant redactions to the biblical text from the second century, as when he overtly contradicts the PBC in stating, "In the second century, a concluding summary was added, bringing together the most important Resurrection traditions and the mission of the disciples to proclaim the Gospel to the whole world (Mk 16:9–20)."[52]

At the same time, Ratzinger is careful to maintain that the various evangelists and redactors, while re-forming the same basic material in view of their respective theological insights and purposes, "transmit the very same thing with slight variations."[53] To anticipate language that will become critically important further below in this chapter and in the book as a whole, "Even if the *details* of many traditions have been expanded in later periods, we can trust the Gospels *for the essentials* and can find in them the real figure of Jesus. It is much more real than the apparently reliable historical reconstructions."[54] The Gospels thus present us with a faithful portrait of the real historical Jesus. The evangelists, Ratzinger writes, "were practicing painstaking fidelity, but it was a fidelity that played a role in the formation process in the context of lived participation, though *without influencing the essentials.*"[55]

---

51. Ratzinger, *God and the World*, 229–30.

52. Benedict XVI, *Jesus of Nazareth: Holy Week*, 262.

53. Benedict XVI, *Light of the World* (San Francisco: Ignatius Press, 2010),, 174; cf. Joseph Ratzinger, *Daughter Zion: Meditations on the Church's Marian Belief* (San Francisco: Ignatius Press, 1983), 44.

54. Ratzinger, *God and the World*, 204 (emphasis added).

55. Benedict XVI, *Light of the World*, 174 (emphasis added).

Continuity and Discontinuity: Benedict's Hermeneutic of Reform

Up to this point I have been tracing the discrepancies between Benedict-Ratzinger's views and the views of the Magisterium of yesteryear vis-à-vis modern biblical criticism. However, the purpose of emphasizing this discontinuity becomes clear only when we examine how Benedict puts his critical observations to work, developing a hermeneutic capable of addressing many of the greatest challenges to the Magisterium's authority today. As we will see below, whether true reform will come about in the Church is bound up with our ability to understand and deal with two seemingly incompatible realities in the history of Catholic doctrine and practice.

In an important speech to the Roman curia in the first year of his pontificate, Benedict put the matter plainly concerning the proper implementation of Vatican II: "It is precisely in this combination of continuity and discontinuity at different levels that the very nature of true reform consists."[56] To understand what Benedict has in mind here, it is important to note that he is proposing not merely a "hermeneutic of continuity" as some have thought, but rather what he calls a "hermeneutic of reform." This term is fitting because Benedict's approach does not pretend that Catholicism has emerged utterly unchanged through the centuries, and so it is willing to come to terms with the elements of discontinuity we have witnessed in this chapter. At the same time, this hermeneutic maintains that over the course of history, "the one subject-Church ... increases in time and develops, yet always remaining the same."[57] Thus, in one brief statement, Benedict distances himself from both radical traditionalism, which refuses to accept the newness of the post-conciliar Church, and radical progressivism, which fails to realize that the Church today is the same Church that existed before Vatican II. He put this pointedly in an interview:

---

56. Benedict XVI, Christmas Address to the Roman Curia (December 22, 2005). For this principle and its application to the thorny issue of religious freedom, see Martin Rhonheimer, "Benedict XVI's 'Hermeneutic of Reform' and Religious Freedom," *Nova et Vetera* 9, no. 4 (2011): 1029–54.

57. Benedict XVI, Christmas Address to the Roman Curia (December 22, 2005).

It is impossible ("for a Catholic") to take a position for or against Trent or Vatican I. Whoever accepts Vatican II, as it has clearly expressed and understood itself, at the same time accepts the whole binding tradition of the Catholic Church, particularly also the two previous councils. And that also applies to the so-called "progressivism," at least in its extreme forms.... It is likewise impossible to decide in favor of Trent and Vatican I, but against Vatican II. Whoever denies Vatican II denies the authority that upholds the other two councils and thereby detaches them from their foundation. And this applies to the so-called "traditionalism," also in its extreme forms.... Every partisan choice destroys the whole (the very history of the Church) which can exist only as an indivisible unity.[58]

At the end of the day, both radical camps described above operate by what he has labeled a "hermeneutic of discontinuity and rupture," an approach that keeps them from accepting the Magisterium as the authoritative guardian of Christian orthodoxy still today. Regrettably, many Catholics today know only this popularized misinterpretation of Catholic history. According to Benedict, this is due in part to the fact that the hermeneutic of rupture "has frequently availed itself of the sympathies of the mass media."[59]

As an indication of how firmly he believes this, Benedict dedicated some of his final thoughts as pontiff to the variant interpretations of Vatican II, observing that "there was the Council of the Fathers—the real Council—but there was also the Council of the media" which also turned out to be the "accessible ... dominant ... more effective one."[60]

---

58. Ratzinger and Messori, *The Ratzinger Report*, 28–29. For further comments in this regard, see Avery Cardinal Dulles, SJ, "Benedict XVI: Interpreter of Vatican II," in *Church and Society: The Laurence J. McGinley Lectures, 1988–2007* (New York: Fordham University Press, 2008), 468–84.

59. Benedict XVI, Christmas Address to the Roman Curia (December 22, 2005). On the two interpretations of Vatican II, see also Ratzinger's *Salt of the Earth* (San Francisco: Ignatius Press, 1997), 75.

60. Benedict XVI, Address to the Parish Priests and Clergy of Rome (February 14, 2013). The pope further lamented, "We know that this Council of the media was accessible to everyone. Therefore, this was the dominant one, the more effective one, and it created so many disasters, so many problems, so much suffering: seminaries closed, convents closed, banal liturgy." At the same time, in this speech Benedict exuded a firm hope that the media's portrayal of Vatican II as a rupture will not be the final word and that the Church has great reason to rejoice in finally seeing the council bear the fruit it was designed to yield. As for the damage that occurred to the Church after Vatican II, Ratzinger had earlier stated, "I am convinced that the damage that we have incurred in these twenty

In various works he goes so far as to apply some of the same critical labels to this mentality that he did to the anti-modernist statements of the early twentieth century. Noting that even many Council Fathers entertained a problematic hermeneutic of the Council, Ratzinger described the ambience of the time as pervaded by an "almost naïve progressivist utopianism" and a "euphoria of reform" that "can only be called neurotic."[61] In a Wednesday catechesis on St. Bonaventure, he added:

> Indeed, we know that after the Second Vatican Council some were convinced that everything was new, that there was a different Church, that the pre-Conciliar Church was finished and that we had another, totally "other" Church, *an anarchic utopianism*! And thanks be to God the wise helmsmen of the Barque of St Peter, Pope Paul VI and Pope John Paul II, on the one hand *defended the newness of the Council, and on the other, defended the oneness and continuity of the Church*, which is always a Church of sinners and always a place of grace.[62]

Benedict notes that St. Bonaventure, while serving as Minister General of the Franciscan Order in his day, faced a problem similar to the one that the Church faces in the modern period. For the sake of unity within his order, Bonaventure made it a pastoral priority to combat the widespread "anarchic utopianism" that caused many to dissociate the search for authentic spirituality from the hierarchical structure of the Church. As indicated above, this is precisely the type of attitude we often witness today: a disregard of the hierarchical Church which takes its cue from the supposition that Vatican II is completely new and that it has fundamentally changed the nature of the rigid, pre-conciliar, hierarchical, institutional church. That said, in these passages Benedict

---

years is due, not to the 'true' Council, but to the unleashing within the Church of latent polemical and centrifugal forces; and outside the Church it is due to the confrontation with a cultural revolution in the West." *The Ratzinger Report,* 30. Ratzinger observed that historically any ecumenical council is typically followed by this sort of tumult, for which reason John Henry Newman spoke of the danger involved with convoking councils. Ibid., 39–40. This is a theme Ratzinger takes up elsewhere, as when he states, "And it cannot be denied that, from close by, nearly all councils have seemed to destroy equilibrium, to create crisis." *Principles of Catholic Theology* (San Francisco: Ignatius Press, 1987), 369.

61. Ratzinger, *Principles of Catholic Theology,* 227, 373.

62. Benedict XVI, General Audience (March 20, 2010) (emphasis added).

does indeed acknowledge a real "newness" and "discontinuity" in Vatican II. Indeed, in one place he even speaks of the pastoral constitution *Gaudium et Spes*, in conjunction with *Dignitatis Humanae* on religious liberty and *Nostra Aetate* on non-Christians, as a "countersyllabus" to that of Pius IX.[63] But if this speaks to the discontinuity side of Benedict's hermeneutic, it remains to be seen just how the aspect of continuity has its due place.

Discernment of the Essential: Key to Benedict's Hermeneutic of Reform

One of the central dimensions to Benedict's theology as a whole, and to his hermeneutic of reform in particular, lies in the endeavor to discern what he variously calls "the kernel," "essential," or "permanent" aspect of Catholic doctrine, which has remained unchanged through the centuries even amidst the vicissitudes of discontinuity and development described above.[64] The existence of this element is the linchpin that allows Benedict to grant the presence of both continuity and discontinuity in the Church throughout the ages. In what follows, I will be teasing out what he means by this concept and how he applies it to the problem of the Church's teaching concerning modern biblical scholarship.

Benedict's 2005 address to the Roman curia reveals the basis and aims of his thought concerning our subject. It is significant that Benedict incorporates the language of John Henry Newman when he affirms that a sound hermeneutic must admit the presence of discontinuity but must also firmly insist on the existence of a "permanent aspect" in the Church's teaching in such a way that at Vatican II "the continuity of principles proved not to have been abandoned."[65] Benedict's choice of the expression "continuity of principles" reflects verbatim Newman's second "note" for distinguishing a genuine doctrinal development from a "corruption," as it is expounded in his *Essay on*

---

63. Ratzinger, *Principles of Catholic Theology*, 381–82.

64. As we will see in later chapters, Benedict frequently employs these terms and other variations upon them when seeking to discern the principal affirmation of a problematic biblical text.

65. Benedict XVI, Christmas Address to the Roman Curia (December 22, 2005).

the Development of Christian Doctrine.[66] The pontiff's references to the essential or core dimension of Catholic teaching likewise reflect Newman's way of expressing that Catholic doctrine "has been in substance one and the same from the beginning."[67] These similarities, which are just a couple among many, are probably no coincidence given that Benedict not only beatified Newman but praised his theology elsewhere on various occasions. Reflecting on the "fruitful possibilities" for development of Newman's teaching on doctrinal development, he shares, "With this he had placed the key in our hand to build historical thought into theology, or much more, he taught us to think historically in theology and so to recognize the identity of faith in all developments."[68]

Throughout Benedict's corpus one can witness his endeavor to apply Newman's thought in a way that builds up the Church and lets the central truths of the faith shine forth. This comes across most explicitly when he is being interviewed about his personal vocation as a theologian.

66. John Henry Newman, *An Essay on the Development of Christian Doctrine* (Notre Dame, Ind.: University of Notre Dame Press, 1989), 178–85. Regarding the language of permanence used by Benedict, see ibid., 178, where Newman states, "Doctrines grow and are enlarged; principles are permanent." Among the other works of Newman that explore this theme, I would highlight his sermon "The Theory of Developments in Religious Doctrine" (1843) and his Letter to the Reverend Pusey (1865). See also the discussion of the parallels between Benedict and Newman in Gerald O'Collins, SJ, "Does Vatican II Represent Continuity or Discontinuity?" *Theological Studies* 73 (2012): 793.

67. Newman, Letter to the Reverend Pusey.

68. The context of this quotation is valuable to share at greater length: "Even deeper for me was the contribution which Heinrich Fries published in connection with the Jubilee of Chalcedon. Here I found access to Newman's teaching on the development of doctrine, which I regard along with his doctrine on conscience as his decisive contribution to the renewal of theology. With this he had placed the key in our hand to build historical thought into theology, or much more, he taught us to think historically in theology and so to recognize the identity of faith in all developments. Here I have to refrain from deepening these ideas further. It seems to me that Newman's starting point, also in modern theology, has not yet been fully evaluated. Fruitful possibilities awaiting development are still hidden in it. At this point I would only like to refer again to the biographical background of this concept. It is known how Newman's insight into the ideas of development influenced his way to Catholicism. But it is not just a matter of an unfolding of ideas. In the concept of development, Newman's own life plays a role. That seems to become visible to me in his well-known words: 'to live is to change, and to be perfect is to have changed often.'" Joseph Ratzinger, Presentation on the Occasion of the First Centenary of the Death of Cardinal John Henry Newman, April 28, 1990.

When asked whether there have in fact been "two Ratzingers" in his lifetime—one a progressive teenager and the other a resigned conservative ecclesial official—he responds:

I think I have already made the essential point, namely that the basic decision of my life is continuous.... I want to be true to what I have recognized as essential and also to remain open to seeing what should change.... I don't deny that there has been development and change in my life, but I hold firmly that it is a *development and change within a fundamental identity*.... Here I agree with Cardinal Newman, who says that to live is to change and that the one who was capable of changing has lived much.[69]

These comments are notable for a number of reasons. First, here again Ratzinger identifies with Newman in suggesting that the fullness of life in the Church—and in one's personal life as well—always entails a certain amount of change. Second, the terminology "essential point," "continuous," and "development and change within a fundamental identity" is typical of Newman and of writings throughout Ratzinger's corpus. Third, when traditionally minded Catholics are faced with Ratzinger's thought concerning the appropriateness of modern biblical scholarship, they sometimes point to the fact that many of his more controversial statements come from the time when he was a young progressive and writing as an individual rather than with the authority of the Magisterium. While it should certainly be granted that many of the relevant texts in this chapter are not stamped with the seal of magisterial authority, in this revealing application of hermeneutical principles to his own life Ratzinger has made it clear that his thought remained fundamentally one and the same throughout his career as a theologian and churchman. One cannot, as I have sometimes seen attempted, simply write off Ratzinger's earlier theology as that of "the young liberal Fr. Ratzinger."

Elsewhere in this same interview, Ratzinger sheds further light on the aim of his theology and the development of his thought:

---

69. Ratzinger, *Salt of the Earth*, 115–16 (emphasis added). In a different interview, Ratzinger was asked concerning his involvement in founding the international periodical *Concilium*, "What significance does this have for the man who was to become prefect of the former Holy Office? Was it a false step? A youthful transgression?" His reply was to the point: "It is not I who have changed, but others." Ratzinger, *The Ratzinger Report*, 18.

Although the constellations in which I have found myself—and naturally
also the periods of life and their different influences—have led to changes and
development in the accents of my thought, my basic impulse, precisely during
the Council, was always *to free up the authentic kernel of the faith from encrustations and to give this kernel strength and dynamism.* This impulse is the constant of my life.... Naturally the office gives an accentuation that isn't present
as such when you are a professor. But nonetheless what's important to me is
that I have never deviated from this constant, which from my childhood has
molded my life, and that I have remained true to it as the basic direction of
my life.[70]

The "encrustations" Ratzinger has in mind here are of various types,
but as we can gather from his comments in earlier portions of this
chapter, they certainly would include some of the writings of Leo XIII,
Pius X, and the PBC on the subject of modern biblical scholarship. It
is critical that Catholics not fall prey to "forced interpretations" for the
apparent contradiction in Church teaching on this or any other point.
Ratzinger states consolingly:

Doubt need not be immediately associated with a fall from faith. I can sincerely take up the questions that press upon me while holding fast to God,
holding to the essential core of faith. On the one hand, I can try to find solutions
for the seeming contradictions. On the other hand, I can also be confident
that, though I can't find them all, there are solutions even when I can't find
them. There are things that remain unsolved for the moment that should not
be explained by forced interpretations.[71]

---

70. Ratzinger, *Salt of the Earth*, 79 (emphasis added). In this same text Ratzinger
opens up about "the cost" of having to take on his ecclesiastical role and abandon full-
time scholarly inquiry. "For me [becoming Prefect of the Congregation for the Faith]
the cost was that I couldn't do full time what I had envisaged for myself, namely really
contributing my thinking and speaking to the great intellectual conversation of our time,
by developing an opus of my own. I had to descend to the little and various things pertaining to factual conflicts and events. I had to leave aside a great part of what would
interest me and simply serve and to accept that as my task. And I had to free myself from
the idea that I absolutely have to write or read this or that, I had to acknowledge that my
task is here." Ibid., 116–17. Though not stated explicitly here, it goes without saying that
part of the "accentuation" involved in taking on an ecclesiastical office is that one has to
be more careful in issuing theological opinions, since they all will be construed—rightly
or wrongly—as bearing authoritative weight. In this light, it is remarkable to see just
how much Ratzinger/Benedict pushed the envelope of theological development during
his tenure as prefect of the CDF.

71. Ratzinger, *Salt of the Earth*, 31 (emphasis added).

Fortunately for the Church, Ratzinger was not content with a forced interpretation that would offer a facile solution to the problem of how to deal with modern exegesis in the Church. "Holding to the essential core of faith," he puts his hermeneutical principles to work in the effort to offer a balanced account of continuity and discontinuity in the matter at hand. We will find in later chapters that this balance is invaluable in dealing with particular thorny issues within New Testament exegesis.

Application of Benedict's Method to the PBC Decrees

Having elucidated the two elements of Benedict's hermeneutic of reform and the pivotal operation that consists in seeking out the enduring essence of Catholic teachings, at last we are in a position to apply these principles to the problem of the Magisterium in relation to modern biblical scholarship. To this end, two texts are of particular relevance. The first is the text Ratzinger presented to the press upon the publication of the instruction *Donum Veritatis*. His comments on the document tie together the principles introduced above and add a note of solemnity, issued as they were by the cardinal-prefect of the CDF:

The text also presents the various forms of binding authority which correspond to the grades of the Magisterium. It states—perhaps for the first time with such candor—that there are *magisterial decisions which cannot be the final word* on a given matter as such but, *despite the permanent value of their principles*, are chiefly also a signal for pastoral prudence, a sort of *provisional policy*. Their *kernel* remains valid, but *the particulars determined by circumstances can stand in need of correction*."[72]

---

72. Ratzinger, "On the 'Instruction Concerning the Ecclesial Vocation of the Theologian,'" 106 (emphasis added). Among the texts Ratzinger has in mind here is the following portion of *Donum Veritatis* which discusses interventions of the Magisterium in the prudential order: "It could happen that some Magisterial documents might not be free from all deficiencies. Bishops and their advisors have not always taken into immediate consideration every aspect or the entire complexity of a question." The importance of this statement lies in the fact that it indicates certain aspects of magisterial utterances contain "deficiencies" which are not intended to be the comprehensive final word in response to their respective questions. In order to pursue his discipline well, the theologian must be competent in history in order to ascertain correctly the context in which dogmatic formulas arise and to be mindful of "the filtering which occurs with the passage of

This citation adds a pair of nuances germane to our endeavor. First, Ratzinger confirms that some magisterial decisions are intended to be not definitive but rather "provisional" determinations of pastoral prudence. Second, in keeping with the terminology we have already examined, he indicates that such statements have a kernel that remains valid throughout history, while certain "particulars" or accidental features "can stand in need of correction" by later formulations.[73]

Ratzinger offers two examples to illustrate the aforementioned point. "In this connection," he writes, "one will probably call to mind the pontifical statements of the last century regarding freedom of religion and the anti-Modernist decisions of the then Biblical Commission."[74] The second of these examples is the very issue at the heart of this chapter. Having already established immediately prior to this the principle that magisterial statements have both a permanent core as well as particulars that may stand in need of correction over time, he now adds that, "*as warning calls* against rash and superficial accommodations, they remain perfectly legitimate," for "the anti-Modernist decisions of the Church performed the great service of saving her from foundering in the bourgeois-liberal world."[75] Thus, from our privi-

---

time." While the document is careful to ensure that this statement not be construed as "a relativization of the tenets of the faith," it proceeds to add these poignant words: "The theologian knows that some judgments of the Magisterium could be justified at the time in which they were made, because while the pronouncements contained true assertions and others which were not sure, both types were inextricably connected. Only time has permitted discernment and, after deeper study, the attainment of true doctrinal progress." Congregation for the Doctrine of the Faith, *Donum Veritatis*, 24.

73. Early in his pontificate Francis reiterated this same distinction in so many words: "Exegetes and theologians help the church to mature in her own judgment. Even the other sciences and their development help the church in its growth in understanding. There are ecclesiastical rules and precepts that were once effective, but now they have lost value or meaning. The view of the church's teaching as a monolith to defend without nuance or different understandings is wrong." Quoted in Francis and Antonio Spadaro, SJ, "A Big Heart Open to God," *America* (September 30, 2013).

74. Ratzinger, "On the 'Instruction Concerning the Ecclesial Vocation of the Theologian,'" 106.

75. Ibid. Among the things the PBC intended to save us from was what Ratzinger calls a "ready-made philosophy" which uses historical criticism to draw false and destructive conclusions from the premise that God cannot intervene in history and reveal himself to man. Ratzinger tells us that such a being "is not the God of the Bible." Ratzinger, "Biblical Interpretation in Conflict: On the Foundations and the Itinerary for Exegesis

leged vantage point a century later, we can see that the principal goal or core of the PBC decrees did not consist in their assertions concerning such things as when and by whom particular biblical books were composed. Rather, the substance of what the Magisterium intended to convey at the time, and which remains true today, is the need to safeguard the authority of the Scriptures, the historicity of Jesus, and the Church's divine foundation in the wake of deconstructive intellectual currents which would undermine the faith. Be that as it may, immediately following these words concerning the important pastoral role played by the PBC's early decrees, Ratzinger soberly acknowledges, "Nevertheless, with respect to particular aspects of their content, they were *superseded* after having fulfilled their pastoral function in the situation of the time."[76]

Today," 23. In another work, he adds that modern scholarship sometimes reveals more about the presuppositions of the scholar than about the person of Jesus: "I must admit the more I hear about these efforts of source research, the less confidence I feel in the plethora of hypotheses it has thrown up.... I think all these attempts are reconstructions in which we can always see the face of the architect.... All these constructions have been undertaken with one guiding idea: There can be no such thing as God made man." Ratzinger, *God and the World*, 203. See also *The Ratzinger Report*, 143–44, in which we are exhorted to beware of an uncritical acceptance of a *weltanschauung* that tries "to find a message that represents what we already know, or at any rate what the listener wants to hear." For this reason, a "criticism of the criticism" or a "self-critique of historical exegesis" is needed in order to evaluate the claims and limits of modern scholarship in a way "that both carries on and modifies Kant's critiques of reason." Ratzinger, "Biblical Interpretation in Conflict," 8. For more on historical-critical exegesis revealing the face of the interpreter just as much as the face of Jesus, see Dale Allison, *The Historical Christ and the Theological Jesus*: "There is the Jesus of Tom Wright, a Jewish prophet and almost, it seems, orthodox Christian. There is the Jesus of Marcus Borg, a religious mystic who dispensed perennial wisdom. There is the Jesus of E. P. Sanders, a Jewish eschatological prophet à la Albert Schweitzer. There is the Jesus of John Dominic Crossan, a Galilean but Cynic-like peasant whose vision of an egalitarian kingdom and non-violent God stood in stark contrast to the power politics of Roman domination. One could go on.... [T]he portraits, which serve different constituencies in the marketplace, are to a large degree not complementary but contradictory." Even regarding his own work Allison writes, "I would be deceiving myself were I to imagine that my Jesus was nothing but the product of brutal historical honesty." Reflecting on a rough period in his life during which he wrote a book on Jesus, Allison admits that the Jesus he presented there was "probably the Jesus I needed at the time." Allison, *The Historical Christ and the Theological Jesus*, 17.

76. Ratzinger, "On the 'Instruction Concerning the Ecclesial Vocation of the Theologian,'" 106 (emphasis added).

Benedict employs similar language in his 2005 Christmas address to the Roman curia, underscoring the need to distinguish "permanent" from "contingent" dimensions of magisterial teaching:

In this process of innovation in continuity we must learn to understand more practically than before that *the Church's decisions on contingent matters—for example, certain practical forms of liberalism or a free interpretation of the Bible—should necessarily be contingent themselves, precisely because they refer to a specific reality that is changeable in itself. It was necessary to learn to recognize that in these decisions it is only the principles that express the permanent aspect,* since they remain as an undercurrent, motivating decisions from within. On the other hand, *not so permanent are the practical forms that depend on the historical situation and are therefore subject to change.* Basic decisions, therefore, continue to be well grounded, whereas the way they are applied to new contexts can change.[77]

77. Benedict XVI, Christmas Address to the Roman Curia (December 22, 2005) (emphasis added). For an informative discussion of the historical condition that affects magisterial decisions, see the Congregation for the Doctrine of the Faith's 1973 declaration *Mysterium Ecclesiae*. At the beginning of a pivotal section entitled "The Notion of the Church's Infallibility Not to Be Falsified," it indicates that we should seek to "define exactly the intention of teaching proper to the various formulas." However, difficulties arise in this domain for two reasons: first from the fact that God's mysteries so transcend the human intellect that they remain "wrapped in darkness" in this life, and second from "the historical condition that affects the expression of revelation." Spelling out what is meant by this "historical condition," the CDF argues that "the meaning of the pronouncements of faith depends partly upon the expressive power of the language used at a certain point in time and in particular circumstances. Moreover, it sometimes happens that some dogmatic truth is first expressed incompletely (but not falsely), and at a later date, when considered in a broader context of faith or human knowledge, it receives a fuller and more perfect expression." When one attends to these contexts, we see that the Church "usually has the intention of solving certain questions or removing certain errors" and that "all these things have to be taken into account in order that these pronouncements may be properly interpreted." Ever affirming that the truths of the faith are not dependent upon "the changeable conceptions of a given epoch," the document acknowledges that "it can sometimes happen that these truths may be enunciated by the Sacred Magisterium in terms that bear traces of such conceptions." In light of the foregoing points, the document concludes that, while the Church's ancient dogmatic formulas "maintain ... completely the same meaning" and "remain forever suitable" when interpreted correctly, "it does not however follow that every one of these formulas has always been or will always be so to the same extent." *Mysterium Ecclesiae*, 5. On the continuity of meaning in dogmatic formulas over the centuries, see the First Vatican Council constitution *Dei Filius*, ch. 4: "Hence, too, that meaning of the sacred dogmas is ever to be maintained which has once been declared by Holy mother Church, and there must never be any abandonment of this sense under the pretext or in the name of a more profound understanding." See also the discussion of this formula in Charles Journet, *What*

Here the pontiff situates decisions regarding "a free interpretation of the Bible" within the realm of "decisions on contingent matters" that are "subject to change." As seen in the document above, so here he maintains that decrees like those of the PBC have a "permanent aspect" that remains valid even if the "practical forms" of decisions are "not so permanent" due to the changing landscape of the Church's situation in history. To many Catholics the use of such language in relation to magisterial statements may understandably come across as jarring. However, if we understand the expression properly within the context of principles addressed in this chapter, it is right at the heart of Ratzinger's brilliant solution to the thorny problem of the Magisterium in relationship to modern biblical scholarship—a solution which he arrives at only by courageously facing difficulties head-on.

How are we to explain Benedict's pointed language and the about-face in the Church's attitude toward the modern historical-critical method today? Why did the PBC issue these decrees which to many people today seem so plainly incorrect? Ratzinger offers a vivid comparison to illustrate:

The process of intellectual struggle over these issues that had become a necessary task can in a certain sense be compared with the similar process triggered by the Galileo affair. Until Galileo, it had seemed that the geocentric world picture was inextricably bound up with the revealed message of the Bible, and that champions of the heliocentric world picture were destroying the core of Revelation. It became necessary fully to reconceive the relationship between the outward form of presentation and the real message of the whole, and it required a gradual process before the criteria could be elaborated ... Something analogous can be said with respect to history. *At first it seemed as if the ascription of the Pentateuch to Moses or of the Gospels to the four individuals whom tradition names as their authors were indispensable conditions of the trustworthiness of Scripture and, therefore, of the faith founded upon it.* Here, too, it was necessary for the territories to be re-surveyed, as it were; the basic relationship between faith and history needed to be re-thought. This sort of clarification could not be achieved overnight.[78]

Is Dogma? (San Francisco: Ignatius Press, 2011), 20, 98. For the rejection of any form of "evolutionism" in the Church, see also Pius X's *Lamentabili Sane* (1907) as well as his *Pascendi Dominici Gregis* (1907), 26–28 and "Oath against Modernism" (1910)

78. Ratzinger, "Exegesis and Magisterium of the Church," 134. Benedict XVI reflected on this dimension of the Galileo affair in a poignant speech about Vatican II near

In this passage Ratzinger sheds insight into the reason certain features of the PBC decrees in question stood "in need of correction." Those who crafted the statements had assumed that the trustworthiness of Scripture—and thereby the faith itself—would be undermined if the Church entertained findings of modern scholarship that contradicted ancient traditions concerning such matters as the authorship and dating of biblical books.

To offer just one illustration of this concern, some understandably fear dating the Gospel of Matthew later than Mark because this opens the door to the claim that the papal institution narrative in Matthew 16 was a tradition invented by the early Church rather than spoken by Jesus. However, I would counter by arguing that, even if Matthew does not represent a precise transcript of Jesus' words, one who approaches the text from the perspective of faith will see Matthew's work as not an invention but rather a reflection of a Petrine primacy found already in the earliest stratum of the Christian faith. On this point Ratzinger observes, "The play on the word 'rock' ... does not work with complete success in Greek, where it is now necessary to switch gender from Petros to Petra: we can thus hear even through this pun the Aramaic word *kepha* and perceive the voice of Jesus himself."[79] According to Ratzinger, the "substance of what Matthew says" is echoed throughout the entire New Testament, a unity that "can be explained only is what is recounted in Matthew originates in Jesus himself."[80]

---

the end of his pontificate: "And we knew that the relationship between the Church and the modern period, right from the outset, had been slightly fraught, beginning with the Church's error in the case of Galileo Galilei; we were looking to correct this mistaken start and to rediscover the union between the Church and the best forces of the world, so as to open up humanity's future, to open up true progress." Benedict XVI, Address to the Parish Priests and Clergy of Rome (February 14, 2013).

79. Joseph Ratzinger, *Called to Communion: Understanding the Church Today* (San Francisco: Ignatius, 1996), 60.

80. Ibid, 58. Additionally, if we hold all of the Scriptures to be inspired, then to me it is nonsensical to reject the theological developments we find in later Gospels simply on the grounds that they are later. Ratzinger explains, "[F]or one who is in the faith of the Church reads the Bible as the word of God, the validity of a given statement does not depend upon the historical hypotheses concerning its most ancient form and source.... It is valid because Holy Scripture is valid and because Scripture presents it to us as an utterance of Jesus. Said in other terms: the guarantee of its validity does not result from

Conclusion

While it is understandable to fear a certain "slippery slope" once one becomes acquainted with the undeniable presence of discontinuity in certain areas of Catholic teaching, thankfully the Church offers guidance for how to navigate through these difficulties. Indeed it is critical—and relieving for a Catholic—to realize that the Church recognizes various levels of magisterial teaching which command correspondingly different types of assent. Among the various doctrines of the Church, the CDF indicates that many require "irrevocable assent," since of their own nature they are "irreformable."[81] These teachings form the *substance* of the Catholic faith, which cannot change. Writing as head of the PBC, Ratzinger offered some examples of teachings which, in contrast with the PBC decrees examined in this chapter, could never be altered as the result of modern biblical scholarship: the birth of Jesus by the Virgin Mary, the institution of the Eucharist by Jesus, and Jesus' bodily Resurrection from the dead. Concerning this last point, he tells us that Jesus' bodily Resurrection "is the *meaning* of the empty tomb," as if to preempt any objectors who would claim that the essence of the empty tomb lay in a spiritual experience of the

---

hypothetical constructs, however well founded they might be, but from inclusion in the canon of Scripture, which in turn the faith of the Church avouches as the Word of God." Ratzinger, *Called to Communion*, 58–59.

81. Congregation for the Doctrine of the Faith, "Doctrinal Commentary on the Concluding Formula of the *Professio Fidei*" (1998), 5, 8. The CDF teaches that a Catholic may never withhold assent to a divinely revealed truth, such as the articles of the Creed, Marian dogmas, the inerrancy of Scripture, and papal infallibility. Likewise, a Catholic may never refuse to accept "those teachings belonging to the dogmatic or moral area, which are necessary for faithfully keeping and expounding the deposit of faith, even if they have not been proposed by the Magisterium of the Church as formally revealed." Among many doctrines that fall within the scope of this statement, the CDF reminds us of the illicitness of euthanasia, the legitimacy of saint canonizations, and the reservation of priestly ordination only to men, to name only a few examples. For a delineation of these levels, along with examples of doctrines that have an "irrevocable character," see ibid., 11. That said, with this the CDF has not intended to provide a complete list of truths which Catholics are bound to hold as irreformable. Indeed, it even elucidates a third category of teachings "which either the Roman Pontiff or the College of Bishops enunciate when they exercise their authentic Magisterium." Even if these are not proclaimed "by a definitive act," the document indicates that they nevertheless require "religious submission of will and intellect" on the part of the faithful. Ibid., 10.

apostles and not a direct encounter with the Son of God in his glori-
fied flesh. In short, Ratzinger emphasizes that the Christian faith is
bound up with certain accidental features, but it requires us to profess "that Jesus—in all that is essential—was effectively who the Gospels reveal him to be."[82] This point will be of paramount importance
in later chapters as we explore the figure of Jesus through the eyes of
Benedict in his *Jesus* trilogy.

In this way, despite his frank criticisms of certain aspects of past
magisterial pronouncements, Ratzinger's hermeneutical approach
is worlds apart from an attitude that would conclude from such observations that the Magisterium has erred in an essential matter and
thereby abdicated its authority to teach Christians today. For, while
he does not shy away from facing the most alarming challenges to the
Magisterium's teaching authority, he writes, "Yet, neither do we lightly
condemn the past, even if we see it as a necessary part of a process
of knowing."[83] We must therefore regard as illegitimate the moves of
those who, believing themselves to be ahead of the curve in matters of
doctrinal development, dissent from today's Magisterium on the hypothetical grounds that its teaching *might* change some day and that
at any rate their views do not deny anything "irreformable."[84] Indeed,
given what was said above, features some consider essential to the faith
in theory could be shown to be accidental, but the CDF rightly reminds us that individual Catholics are in no position to play the role
of Magisterium in these matters. What are we to do in the meantime?
Benedict offers this wise counsel in the context of an interview:

Of course we always need to ask what are the things that may once have been
considered essential to Christianity but in reality were only expressions of
a certain period. What, then, is really essential? This means that we must
constantly return to the gospel and the teachings of the faith in order to see:
First, what is an essential component? Second, what legitimately changes with the

82. Ratzinger, "Exegesis and the Magisterium of the Church," 134 (emphasis added).
83. Ratzinger, *Theological Highlights of Vatican II*, 20, 136.
84. In this regard it is important to recall that the CDF commentary is not exhaustive. Even if it does not explicitly identify certain erroneous teachings or practices, the
Magisterium's mind on these matters has often been made manifest in myriad other
ways which call for the "religious submission" of the Catholic's will and intellect.

changing times? And third, what is not an essential component? In the end, then, the decisive point is always to achieve the proper discernment.[85]

Once again, for Benedict the key to properly assessing the presence of discontinuity in Catholic teaching over the centuries lies in a hermeneutic of reform and the crucial endeavor to distinguish what is essential in the faith from what "were only expressions of a certain period" or what "legitimately changes with the changing times."

One final text from an interview sheds unique light into the person of Ratzinger-Benedict as he turns the thorny problems addressed by the PBC on their head. Rather than letting the myriad challenges of modern biblical scholarship trouble one's faith, he invites the believer to see the complicated process of the Bible's composition as the work of divine providence:

He must learn that *the complicated history of the genesis of biblical texts does not affect the faith as such.* What shines through this history is something different and greater. Through this complicated historical genesis, which, by the way, is always hypothetical, one can see, on the contrary, how statements and realities, which are not simply invented by man, impress themselves upon his consciousness. *I believe that precisely when one comes to know the human factors of biblical history, one also sees all the more clearly that it is not just a case of human factors, but that another is speaking here.*[86]

For Ratzinger, the fruit of modern biblical scholarship presents a picture of the Bible's origin that gives even more glory to the divine providence at work in the early Church than it would if we could rest consoled in knowing that Matthew was the first Gospel, that the Beloved Disciple wrote John, or that the Pentateuch could be substantially attributed to Moses.

At the same time, throughout his career Ratzinger has shown that he no more believes in the validity of all modern biblical scholarship than he believes that the past decrees of the PBC provide an accurate

85. Benedict XVI, *Light of the World*, 141. In another interview, Ratzinger addressed the problem of ecumenism in like terms: "We can only humbly seek *to essentialize our faith,* that is, to recognize what are really the essential elements in it—the things we have not made but have received from the Lord—and in this attitude of turning to the Lord and to the center, to open ourselves in this *essentializing* so that he may lead us onward, he alone." Ratzinger, *God and the World*, 453 (emphasis added).

86. Ratzinger, *Salt of the Earth*, 32 (emphasis added).

analysis of the Bible's origins.[87] Rather, Ratzinger's biblical project aims to offer a balanced synthesis of the best of ancient and modern thought, taking into account the strengths and shortcomings of each. He therefore takes seriously the greatest fruits and challenges of modern scholarship but in a way that enables us to see more clearly the person of Jesus Christ. This is put best by Benedict himself on the subject of his *Jesus of Nazareth* trilogy:

> What you might call the high point of my book was the demonstration that the Jesus in whom we believe is really also the historical Jesus and that his figure, as portrayed in the Gospels, is much more realistic and credible than the numerous alternative portraits of Jesus that are paraded before us in constant succession.... The important point is this: The only real, historical personage is the Christ in whom the Gospels believe, and not the figure who has been reconstituted from numerous exegetical studies.[88]

---

87. We will see this especially in his famous call for a "criticism of the criticism" discussed in the next chapter. One example of Benedict's balanced approach can be seen in how he responds to an interviewer whose question seemed to exhibit a very negative view of modern biblical criticism as such. Benedict grants his point regarding the limits of said scholarship, but he adds, "I would put things more cautiously and say that research on points of detail remains important and useful, even though the excess of hypotheses eventually leads to absurdity. It is clear that the Gospels also reflect the concrete situation of the transmitters of the tradition and that they are clothed directly in the flesh in faith." Benedict XVI, *Light of the World*, 172–73. For an in-depth treatment of Ratzinger's project of exegetical synthesis, see Ramage, *Dark Passages of the Bible*, chapter 2.

88. Benedict XVI, *Light of the World*, 173. Approaching the matter from a different angle but with what I take to be a substantially similar upshot, Francis Watson writes, "Jesus is known only through the mediation of his own reception. There is no access to the singular, uninterpreted reality of a 'historical Jesus' behind the reception process.... Reception is original rather than secondary: there can be no giving without a corresponding receiving, and both together constitute the completed event in which Jesus acts out his calling. In consequence, no prior space is available for Jesus to enact a reality exclusively his own, recoverable by stripping away everything that may be attributed to the early church. There is nothing in the gospel that may *not* be attributed to the early church; for the story that is told speaks of a gift received rather than an object abstracted from this communicative context and accessible as it is in itself." Francis Watson, *Gospel Writing: A Canonical Perspective* (Grand Rapids, Mich.: Eerdmans, 2013), 606. I think that this perspective is helpful for adjudicating any number of debates in New Testament exegesis. Because we cannot say that a given text is either exclusively from Jesus or from the Church, then the provenance of a passage such as Mt 16:17–19 is a moot question. For the Petrine primacy was, of course, something both given by Jesus and already mediated by the Church in the text that Matthew presents us.

This text from Benedict also reflects the ultimate goal of the present volume: to build up the Church through a sincere engagement with modern problems that would call into question our warrant for believing in Christ. The beauty and power of Benedict's exegetical vision is that it offers a compelling reason to believe that Christians today have access to the true person of Jesus and the essence of his saving message presented in the Gospels. And the key is that Benedict achieves this conviction not by ignoring but precisely by embracing what the historical-critical approach has to offer. Although he draws different conclusions from this observation, the matter has been put well by Ehrman in lamenting that the best of modern biblical scholarship is not made more widely available to intelligent Christians: "That's a pity," he says, "because historical criticism can have serious theological payoffs, and these should be embraced and proclaimed."[89] It is my hope and conviction that engaging modernity in this volume will yield great dividends for the reader interested in the quest for a synthesis of faith and reason in biblical studies today.

89. Ehrman, *Jesus, Interrupted,* 272.

3

BENEDICT XVI'S "METHOD C"
EXEGETICAL VISION

In the previous chapter, I addressed the fundamental question of how a Catholic like Ratzinger may faithfully engage modern biblical criticism while remaining grounded in a tradition that was for so long inimical to it. Operating with the understanding that our enterprise of critiquing the critique "from within" is in keeping with the Catholic faith, we are now in a position to spell out the key principles needed for this task.

This chapter begins by surveying these principles as detailed in Ratzinger's 1988 Erasmus Lecture, in particular the hermeneutical proposal in which Ratzinger called upon exegetes to develop a new, fuller hermeneutical method (Method C) that makes the truth of Scripture more evident by synthesizing the best of patristic-medieval exegesis (Method A) and historical-critical exegesis (Method B). For those who have read *Dark Passages of the Bible*, most of what is said in this initial part will be review, but with the addition of some new material I have unearthed since that volume was composed. Although we will be working primarily at the level of Method B in this book, the Method A principles surveyed in this section undergird everything I will be arguing throughout.

Next, the chapter considers Ratzinger's exegesis in connection with medieval exegetes Thomas Aquinas and Bonaventure. In his early career, Ratzinger was critical of Thomistic neo-scholasticism, and in this period of his life there emerged a preference for Bonaventure that would guide his understanding of Scripture over the following decades. Ratzinger is, therefore, not a Thomist of the strict observance. With this initial caveat in place, there follows an overview of principles illustrating key points of contact in which Ratzinger connects—both implicitly and explicitly at points—his exegetical programme with that of Aquinas, whose exegesis offers a "counter-model" to deconstructive forms of modern exegesis.[1] By way of making these connections, Ratzinger certainly emends the tradition he inherited from Aquinas, but the dependence remains all the same.

Finally, this chapter examines how the vision of the Erasmus Lecture has been received and carried forward at a very high level in the Church through the recent documents of the International Theological Commission and the Pontifical Biblical Commission.[2]

Ratzinger's "Method C" Proposal

At the conference following his 1988 Erasmus Lecture, the then-prefect of the Congregation for the Doctrine of the Faith argued convincingly that today's exegetes must have recourse to both ancient and modern methods of interpretation if they are to make sense of the problems in Scripture. He called upon exegetes to develop a new, fuller hermeneutical method that makes the truth of Scripture more

1. Note that I will be referring to the version of the Erasmus Lecture entitled "Biblical Interpretation in Conflict" from the volume *Opening Up the Scriptures*. This version of Ratzinger's text (there are three different published editions of the lecture in the English language alone) is interesting because it reveals more explicit connections with Thomas Aquinas than the original English version published in the volume *Biblical Interpretation in Crisis*.

2. I describe this reception as being at a "very high level" since neither Benedict XVI's exegetical works written during his pontificate nor the documents of the Roman curia are binding magisterial documents. Indeed, Benedict tells us in the foreword to *Jesus of Nazareth* that it is "not a work of the Magisterium" but rather of his personal search "for the face of the Lord." Ibid., xxiii. Nevertheless, they represent the highest level of authoritative engagement with modern exegesis over the past half-century and are therefore rightly regarded as guides for how to move forward with our endeavor.

evident by synthesizing the best of ancient (patristic-medieval) and modern (historical-critical) exegesis:

> You can call the patristic-medieval exegetical approach Method A. The historical-critical approach, the modern approach ... is Method B. What I am calling for is not a return to Method A, but a development of a Method C, taking advantage of the strengths of both Method A and Method B, but cognizant of the shortcomings of both.[3]

Benedict's programme aims to incorporate insights from both the patristic-medieval method, which tends to emphasize the unity and truth of Scripture, and the historical-critical method, which often observes development, diversity, and apparent contradictions therein. My previous work *Dark Passages of the Bible* expounded at length upon the constitutive principles of these two methods, especially the Method A realities of inspiration, inerrancy, the canon, and the interpretive guidelines handed on to the Church by *Dei Verbum*. All of these traditional magisterial principles are assumed here. But in order to ground the task that will be carried out in later chapters of this book, in what follows I will review a few central points discussed in more detail in my previous volume.[4]

---

3. Benedict's words are taken from a summary and transcript of the discussion following his lecture. See Paul T. Stallsworth, "The Story of an Encounter," in *Biblical Interpretation in Crisis*, 107–8. Benedict's lecture "Biblical Interpretation in Crisis: On the Question of the Foundations and Approaches of Exegesis Today" is printed in ibid., 1–23. As Gregory Vall observes, "Strictly speaking, we are dealing not with two specific 'methods' but two general approaches. A series of basic principles unites the work of exegetes as diverse as Origen and Chrysostom, Bernard of Clairvaux and Thomas Aquinas, so that we may speak of a single dominant patristic-medieval approach to exegesis, which Cardinal Ratzinger has labeled 'Method A.' When we turn to consider those biblical commentators whose work falls under the umbrella of 'historical-critical' exegesis, the diversity of specific methodologies is perhaps even greater. But in this case too, fundamental principles of exegesis shared by these scholars may be identified, justifying the label 'Method B.'" Gregory Vall, "Psalm 22: *Vox Christi* or Israelite Temple Liturgy?" *The Thomist* 66 (2002): 175–200.

4. Much of what follows in this next section is found in Ramage, *Dark Passages of the Bible*, ch. 2.

A Potential Weakness of Method A and the Principles of Method B's Response

Despite all the strengths of patristic and medieval exegesis, at times those who employ the traditional method tend to emphasize the unity and inerrancy of Scripture and its spiritual sense to the neglect of its literal sense with the evidence apparent contradictions observable through a serious engagement with it.[5] For historical-critical scholars, this remains a continual source of skepticism with regard to traditional exegesis. Benedict XVI's work stands on a solid middle ground between the excesses of certain Method A exegetes and the skepticism typical of Method B. He typically gives a positive but sober assessment of patristic spiritual exegesis, as we witness in his treatment of the parables of the Good Samaritan and the Prodigal Son.[6] For Benedict,

5. For instance, in his *On First Principles* Origen employs a helpful image to describe sacred Scripture as having a "body" (historical sense) and "soul" (spiritual sense). However, at times in his exposition he dismisses the importance of the literal sense and goes so far as to say that it sometimes does not even exist. Ibid., 4.12. On the other hand, Matthew Lamb contrasts Thomas Aquinas with many medieval allegorists who "seemed more interested in detours than in the intended route." Aquinas paid painstaking attention to the literal sense as the one sense which is present in all the verses of Scripture. Says Lamb: "By far, the greatest service which St. Thomas performed in regard to exegetical presuppositions was to assert plainly the sufficiency of the literal meaning. The literal is the only sense on which theological arguments can be based. St. Augustine and others had counseled that arguments must be adduced from 'plain testimonies,' but never would they have dreamt of identifying these exclusively with the literal sense." Thomas Aquinas, *Commentary on Saint Paul's Epistle to the Ephesians*, trans. Matthew Lamb (Albany, N.Y.: Magi Books, 1966), 15.

6. Concerning the Good Samaritan, he writes: "The Church Fathers understood the parable Christologically. That is an allegorical reading, one might say—an interpretation that *bypasses the text*. But when we consider that in all the parables, each in a different way, the Lord really does want to invite us to faith in the Kingdom of God, which he himself is, then a Christological exposition is *never a totally false* reading. In some sense it reflects an inner potentiality in the text and can be a fruit growing out of it as from a seed." Benedict XVI, *Jesus of Nazareth: From the Baptism to the Transfiguration*, 199 (emphasis added). The pope proceeds to meditate on the parable's various features over a span of several pages. Of particular interest here is how he views the Fathers' interpretation of the man who was stripped and beaten, wounded and left half dead. He notes that the Fathers interpreted this particular man's sufferings as an allegory of mankind's twofold alienation due to sin—which has "stripped" us of the grace we had received and "wounded" us in our nature. Benedict explains (200): "Now, that is an instance of

successful spiritual exegesis can go beyond the text of Scripture only after it has gone *through* the text by dealing with its literal sense. This is not an easy task to achieve, for even the most brilliant Fathers of the Church themselves struggled with it.

If a hallmark of Method A is that it views Scripture from a spiritual perspective and is able to discern the voice of Christ within it, then a strength of Method B is that it attends to Scripture's literal meaning and desires to hear the voice of Scripture's human authors at work therein. Method B does not so much approach Scripture as God's word but instead operates according to the principle that it ought to bracket out the question of faith and study these words insofar as they are human words of a past context, a definite cultural milieu with its own language and mindset. In the foreword to the *Baptism* volume of his *Jesus* trilogy, Benedict gives the parameters of historical-critical work: "It attempts to identify and to understand the past—as it was in itself—with the greatest possible precision, in order then to find out what the author could have said and intended to say in the context of the mentality and events of the time."[7] It employs all the scientific tools at the disposal of modern man, not limited to but including a broader knowledge of history, recent discoveries in archaeology and the various natural sciences, and an increased competence in Semitic languages, in view of attaining to the original meaning of the texts.

The "critical" attitude is not necessarily critical in the way many people initially think. For example, concerning his attempt to ascer-

---

allegory, and *it certainly goes far beyond the literal sense. For all that, though, it is an attempt to identify* precisely the two kinds of injury that weigh down human history." Notice the pope's language here. He states that the allegorical patristic interpretation "bypasses the text" (*also eine Auslegung am Text vorbei*) and "certainly goes far beyond the literal sense (*die sicher weit über den Wortsinn hinausgeht*)."

Similar language can be found in Benedict's dealings with the parable of the Prodigal Son. Noting the difficulty involved in the effort to locate the figure of Jesus in this parable when it is read allegorically, he asks (207): "Where does Jesus Christ fit into all this? Only the Father figures in the parable. Is there no Christology in it? Augustine *tried* to work Christology in where the text says that the Father embraced the son (Lk 15:20). The arm of the Father is the Son.'" The pope comments, "This is a very evocative exposition, but it is still an 'allegory' that clearly goes *beyond the text* (*die ganz klar über den Text hinausgeht*)."

7. Ibid., xvi.

tain whether the New Testament's understanding of expiation is one that we can accept today, Benedict writes:

Naturally this will require of us a readiness not only to form a "critical" assessment of the New Testament, but also to learn from it and to let ourselves be led by it: not to dismantle the texts according to our preconceived ideas, but to let our own ideas be purified and deepened by his word.[8]

According to Benedict, historical criticism does not of its own nature seek to dismantle or criticize the faith, and it is compatible with the Christian faith so long as we approach the Bible with a willingness to be led by it. At the same time, it does entail a willingness be purified by asking questions—and entertaining corresponding answers—that faithful Christians of previous ages did not tend to raise.

Method B's Weaknesses

Of course, modernity's willingness to question traditional Christian assumptions about Scripture is not always accompanied by a desire to build up the faith. Traditionally minded Christians are well aware that those belonging to the historical-critical school at times have sought to undermine central tenets of the faith, especially when it comes to the figure of Jesus. The pope goes so far as to insinuate the presence of a demonic element in certain areas of historical-critical scholarship.[9] According to Benedict, the Antichrist wants to show that

8. Benedict XVI, *Jesus of Nazareth: Holy Week*, 120.

9. Benedict XVI, *Jesus of Nazareth: From the Baptism to the Transfiguration*, 35–36. With respect to this subversive element present in the work of some exegetes, Scott Hahn and Benjamin Wiker have recently undertaken to show that "[t]he development of the historical-critical method is fully intelligible only as part of the broader project of secularization in the West over the past seven centuries." Hahn and Wiker, *Politicizing the Bible: The Roots of Historical Criticism and the Secularization of Scripture, 1300–1700* (New York: Crossroad Publishing Company, 2013), 9. Specifically, the authors argue that the originators of the method developed it as a means of producing beliefs that accord with modern secular political aims. Additionally, the authors find it highly significant that in the work of Descartes, Hobbes, and Spinoza, nature was redefined as mathematical and mechanical: "Perhaps most important, the politicization of Scripture took place within a radically redefined cosmos, a mathematical-mechanical view of nature that was in continual antagonism to the Judeo-Christian cosmology.... It soon became apparent that, since this universe was an entirely law-governed, self-contained, and self-sustaining machine, the active, living, creating, and redeeming God of the Old and New Testament would either have to be redefined (by being subsumed into nature via pantheism),

Scripture's teaching is false and that its spiritual meaning is a mere human invention, a fundamentalist's abuse of the text. He wants to have
us believe that an "objective" reading of the biblical text is one done
with the caveat that the spiritual and the material are incompatible,
that God could never enter into human history and disclose himself.
Benedict has noted that in the present age these philosophical tenets
of some biblical critics have grown to the stature of academic dogmas,
to the point that criticizing them at all is considered tantamount to
sacrilege.[10] Because of this bias, scholars and others committed to
creedal Christianity have rightly been taken aback by many of the
presuppositions of critical scholars.[11] In light of these circumstances,

---

relieved of the power to control and sustain his creation (thereupon standing outside of
nature as an entirely dispassionate and detached watchmaker), or simply rejected." Hahn
and Wiker, *Politicizing the Bible*, 544.

For another pointed survey of modern criticism's origins, see N. T. Wright, *Jesus
and the Victory of God* (Minneapolis: Fortress Press,1996), 1–124. On the great iconoclast
Reimarus (1694–1768), who has been credited with inaugurating the "Old Quest" for the
historical Jesus, Wright notes: "His aim seems to have been to destroy Christianity (as he
knew it) at its root, by showing that it rested on historical distortion or fantasy. Jesus was
a Jewish reformer who became increasingly fanatical and politicized. His cry of derelic-
tion on the cross signaled the end of his expectation that his god would act to support
him. The disciples fell back on a different model of Messiahship, announced that he had
been 'raised,' and waited for their god to bring the end of the world. They too were disap-
pointed, but instead of crying out in despair they founded the early Catholic church....
The 'Quest' began as an explicitly anti-theological, anti-Christian, anti-dogmatic movement. Its initial agenda was *not* to find a Jesus upon whom Christian faith might be
based, but to show that the faith of the church (as it was then conceived) could not in fact
be based on the real Jesus of Nazareth." Ibid., 16–17.

10. Benedict XVI, "Biblical Interpretation in Crisis," 21. Cf. Francis Martin, "Joseph
Ratzinger, Benedict XVI, on Biblical Interpretation: Two Leading Principles," *Nova et
Vetera* 5 (2007): 285–314. Among the achievements of Martin in this article, he appropriates Benedict's criticism of reductionist modern cognitional theories. This criticism of
the criticism and its "scholarly dogma" that "we know Jesus couldn't have thought such
things" is echoed powerfully in N. T. Wright, *The Challenge of Jesus*, 93. Undoubtedly
Benedict's critique of this "dogma" has as its background Rudolf Bultmann's well-known
claim, "It is impossible to use electric light and the wireless and to avail ourselves of modern medical and surgical discoveries, and at the same time to believe in the New Testament world of spirits and miracles." Bultmann, "New Testament and Mythology," in
Rudolf Bultmann, Hans Werner Bartsch, and Reginald H. Fuller, *Kerygma and Myth: A
Theological Debate* (New York: Harper and Row, 1961), 5.

11. By employing the term "creedal Christianity" one includes not only Catholics but
all Christians who profess faith in the revelation of the triune God as expounded in the

Benedict argues that if historical criticism is to play a role in the exegesis of believers today, there must take place a "criticism of criticism," as he described it in his Erasmus lecture.[12]

Benedict's critique helps us to see that, despite its capacity to challenge longstanding assumptions of exegetes who profess the Christian faith, Method B's fundamental strength turns out also to constitute its principal weakness: its willingness to ask radical questions of Scripture and its ability to provide a scientific analysis of Scripture often lead to excess of regard for its own competence and lack of regard for Christ. But aside from its excesses, there is a more fundamental problem often present in historical-critical exegesis. Since faith is a not a fundamental component of Method B exegesis, those who employ this method sometimes miss the ultimate end, the very *raison d'être* of Scripture: the opportunity to encounter the living God who teaches man through his sacred word. As Benedict puts it, "Approaches to the sacred text that prescind from faith might suggest interesting elements on the level of textual structure and form, but would inevitably prove merely preliminary and structurally incomplete efforts."[13] When exegetes thus fail to rise up to appreciate the divine teaching in Scripture and remain solely at the level of Scripture as a collection of texts, it is impossible for them to see its inspired unity:

[The historical-critical] method is a fundamental dimension of exegesis, but it does not exhaust the interpretive task for someone who sees the biblical writings as a single corpus of Holy Scripture inspired by God.... The unity of all of these writings as one "Bible" is not something it can recognize as an immediate historical datum.[14]

Church's early creeds. The term "Chalcedonian Christianity" is also frequently used by scholars of various denominations to articulate their shared belief in the nature of God and his revelation in Jesus Christ. For more on the subject of scholars ruling out the possibility of God's self-disclosure in human history, see also Benedict's "Biblical Interpretation in Crisis" as well as the more recent *Verbum Domini* (cited hereafter as *VD*) §36, where he elucidates the simple rule: "In applying methods of historical analysis, no criteria should be adopted which would rule out in advance God's self-disclosure in human history."

12. "Biblical Interpretation in Crisis," 6. In *Light of the World*, also, he argues (171): "What is needed is not simply a break with the historical method, but a self-critique of the historical method; a self-critique of historical reason."

13. *VD* §29.

14. Benedict XVI, *Jesus of Nazareth: From the Baptism to the Transfiguration*, xvi–xvii.

For the emeritus pontiff, what we call the Bible is not truly the Bible unless we see it "as a single corpus of Holy Scripture inspired by God." Method B exegesis can examine lines of development and the growth of traditions in Sacred Scripture, yet it cannot make the further step of seeing them as a unity. For Method A, on the other hand, the many books of Scripture have a unity precisely inasmuch as they participate in the economy of salvation. Accordingly, to the extent that historical criticism disavows the possibility of an economy of salvation, it denies Scripture its unifying principle. For Benedict, it would be a travesty not to accept the Method A principles, which enlighten and heal the defects in Method B and which alone enable Scripture to be experienced as God's holy word.

Both Approaches Are Needed for the Method C Project

In light of the "criticism of criticism" initiated by Benedict, Method B exegetes must be attentive if they are to ensure that their efforts do not neglect the role of faith and ultimately end up bankrupt. The pontiff counsels that exegetes today take the further step of acknowledging faith as a hermeneutic:

> If it wishes to be theology, [exegesis] must take a further step. It must recognize that the faith of the Church is that form of "sympathia" without which the Bible remains a *closed* book. It must come to acknowledge this faith as a hermeneutic, the space for understanding, which does not do dogmatic violence to the Bible, but precisely allows the solitary possibility for the Bible to be itself.[15]

Contrary to the tenets of those who approach Scripture with a hermeneutic of suspicion, Benedict understands that Method A's herme-

---

15. Benedict XVI, "Biblical Interpretation in Crisis," 22–23; cf. *VD* §§51–52. Ratzinger elsewhere writes, "[H]istorical-critical exegesis does not bring the Bible to today, to my current life.... The problem of exegesis is connected, as we have seen, with the problem of philosophy. The indigence of philosophy, the indigence to which paralyzed, positivist reason has led itself, has turned into the indigence of our faith. The faith cannot be liberated if reason itself does not open up again. If the door to metaphysical cognition remains closed, if the limits of human knowledge set by Kant are impassable, faith is destined to atrophy: It simply lacks air to breathe." Joseph Ratzinger, "Relativism: The Central Problem for Faith Today," https://www.ewtn.com/library/CURIA/RATZRELA .HTM.

neutic of faith is in reality the key to unlocking the true meaning of Scripture, without which it remains "a closed book."

Lest one assume that Benedict's proposed exegetical synthesis is solely a theoretical affair, it is important to emphasize that he has long been instantiating it in his work, especially in his *Jesus of Nazareth* trilogy. In the foreword to his third and final installment treating the life of Jesus, he insists on this very method:

> I am convinced that good exegesis involves two stages. Firstly one has to ask what the respective authors intended to convey through their text in their own day—the historical component of exegesis. But it is not sufficient to leave the text in the past and thus relegate it to history. The second question posed by good exegesis must be: is what I read here true? Does it concern me? If so, how? With a text like the Bible, whose ultimate and fundamental author, according to our faith, is God himself, the question regarding the here and now of things past is undeniably included in the task of exegesis. The seriousness of the historical quest is in no way diminished by this: on the contrary, it is enhanced.[16]

In the foreword to the second volume of *Jesus*, Benedict likewise speaks to the necessity of synthesizing the "historical hermeneutic" (Method B) and "faith hermeneutic" (Method A) and his own attempt to do so in his work on Jesus:

> If scholarly exegesis is not to exhaust itself in constantly new hypotheses, becoming theologically irrelevant, it must take a methodological step forward and once again see itself as a theological discipline, without abandoning its historical character. It must learn that the positivistic hermeneutic on which it has been based does not constitute the only valid and definitively evolved rational approach; rather, it constitutes a specific and historically conditioned form of rationality that is both open to correction and completion and in need of it. It must recognize that a properly developed faith-hermeneutic is appropriate to the text and can be combined with a historical hermeneutic, aware of its limits, so as to form a methodological whole. Naturally, this combination of two quite different types of hermeneutic is an art that needs to be constantly remastered.[17]

---

16. Benedict XVI, *Jesus of Nazareth: The Infancy Narratives* (New York: Image, 2012), xi.

17. Benedict XVI, *Jesus of Nazareth: Holy Week*, xiv–xv.

Here Benedict warns that scholarly exegesis will become an endless, "theologically irrelevant" maze of hypotheses unless it takes a "methodological step forward." It must continue its patient attentiveness to the historical nature of Scripture, but this must be at the service of theology. "A faith-hermeneutic" helps correct and complete the historical method. The two methods can be "combined ... so as to form a methodological whole." However, he notes that "this combination of two quite different types of hermeneutic is an art that needs to be constantly remastered." The Church is therefore constantly working *toward* an adequate approach to Scripture and learning the *art* of balancing two very different exegetical methods. Our efforts toward a synthesis will necessarily remain imperfect, but their goal is always the same: an encounter with the Lord. Writing as a theologian rather than in his capacity as the Roman pontiff, he humbly confesses:

> I would not presume to claim that this combination of the two hermeneutics is already fully accomplished in my book. But I hope to have taken a significant step in that direction. Fundamentally this is a matter of finally putting into practice the methodological principles formulated for exegesis by the Second Vatican Council (in *Dei Verbum* 12), a task that unfortunately has scarcely been attempted thus far.... In the combination of the two hermeneutics of which I spoke earlier, I have attempted to develop a way of observing and listening to the Jesus of the Gospels that can indeed lead to personal encounter and that, through collective listening with Jesus' disciples across the ages, can indeed attain sure knowledge of the real historical figure of Jesus.[18]

The pope concludes that the Method C synthesis he is searching for is ultimately a matter of "finally putting into practice the methodological principles formulated for exegesis by the Second Vatican Council." The council's teaching demands that exegetes have recourse to the strengths of both the faith hermeneutic (Method A) and historical hermeneutic (Method B) if they wish to plumb the depths of Scripture. Each method on its own is insufficient for this endeavor and eventually leads to problems.[19]

Benedict certainly acknowledges the many problems prevalent in

---

18. Ibid., xv, xvi–xvii.

19. In point of fact, in *Verbum Domini*, the pope goes so far as to claim that the two levels of exegesis "exist only in reciprocity." *VD* §35.

Method B exegesis, but he is very clear that the historical-critical approach may not be discarded any more than Method A may be. In fact, as he writes in the first volume of *Jesus*, "The historical-critical method —specifically because of the intrinsic nature of theology and faith—is and remains an indispensable dimension of exegetical work. For it is of the essence of biblical faith to be about real historical events."[20] As the pontiff explains, God has really entered into human history in his revelation to Israel and with the coming of Christ, and for this reason historical-critical exegesis must be carried out in order that the historical dimension of Scripture might be more greatly penetrated. Moreover, although Method B has the weakness of sometimes thinking it can arrive at a pure and perfect understanding of Sacred Scripture devoid of all reference to its role within the Church, the implementation of this method nevertheless keeps one from the opposite extreme view of paying heed to ecclesiastical traditions while neglecting discoveries in the field of critical scholarship. Thus he says, "There should be no particular need to demonstrate that on the one hand it is useless to take refuge in an allegedly pure, literal understanding of the Bible. On the other hand, a merely positivistic and rigid ecclesiasticism would not do either."[21] In other words, one's adherence to the pronouncements of the Magisterium in matters of biblical interpretation ought not to be done in a positivistic manner, that is to say, in such a way that one closes the door to modern findings without considering the possibility

20. Benedict XVI, *Jesus of Nazareth*, xv. He also reiterates the teaching in *VD* §32: "Before all else, we need to acknowledge the benefits that historical-critical exegesis and other recently-developed methods of textual analysis have brought to the life of the Church. For the Catholic understanding of sacred Scripture, attention to such methods is indispensable, linked as it is to the realism of the Incarnation." Benedict's words also corroborate what Pius XII wrote in *Divino afflante Spiritu*, §38, §40; cf. Pontifical Biblical Commission, *Sancta Mater Ecclesia* §4.

21. Benedict XVI. "Biblical Interpretation in Crisis," 6; Cf. *VD* §44, which quotes the Pontifical Biblical Commission's *The Interpretation of the Bible in the Church*: "'The basic problem with fundamentalist interpretation is that, refusing to take into account the historical character of biblical revelation, it makes itself incapable of accepting the full truth of the incarnation itself. As regards relationships with God, fundamentalism seeks to escape any closeness of the divine and the human ... for this reason, it tends to treat the biblical text as if it had been dictated word for word by the Spirit. It fails to recognize that the word of God has been formulated in language and expression conditioned by various periods.'"

that Scripture's mysteries might be more deeply penetrated with their help. Likewise, this means that Catholics should be cautious in theorizing about the nature of biblical inspiration and inerrancy while they lack a firm grasp of the Bible's sometimes quite problematic content. As was noted in the introduction, this situation has unfortunately led many Catholics to write off modern biblical scholarship without ever having honestly considered its claims and evidence.[22]

Spelling out the interplay between patristic-medieval and historical-critical exegesis, Benedict writes that there are two exegetical "operations" pertinent to the examination of any given text of Scripture from a Method C perspective:

> Certainly texts must first of all be traced back to their historical origins and interpreted in their proper historical contexts to the extent possible. But the second exegetical operation is that they must also be examined in the light of the total movement of history and in the light of history's central event, our Lord Jesus Christ. Only the *combination* of *both* these methods will yield understanding of the Bible.[23]

22. Apropos of those who still doubt that historical-critical exegesis is reconcilable with the venerable traditions which preceded it, I could do no better than to recall the words of N. T. Wright: "When Christianity is truest to itself, however, it denies precisely this dichotomy—uncomfortable though this may be for those of us who try to live in and speak from and to both communities simultaneously. Actually, I believe this discomfort is itself one aspect of a contemporary Christian vocation.... I am someone who believes that being a Christian necessarily entails doing business with history and that history done for all it's worth will challenge spurious versions of Christianity, including many who think of themselves as orthodox, while sustaining and regenerating a deep and true orthodoxy, surprising and challenging though this will always remain.... It simply will not do to declare this question out-of-bounds, to say that the Church's teaching will do for us, thank you very much, so we do not need to ask historical questions.... The skeptics can and must be answered, and when we do so we will not merely reaffirm the traditions of the Church.... We will be driven to reinterpret them, discovering depths of meaning within them that we had never imagined." Wright, *The Challenge of Jesus*, 16–18. Also in need of careful consideration are these pointed words from Wright: "[T]he way to Christian growth is often to allow oneself to be puzzled and startled by new apparent complexity. There is great simplicity at the heart of this picture, but it is costly. The price it demands is sustained attention to the specific, and to us strange and perhaps even repellent, first-century ways of thinking that characterized Jesus. Is it after all Jesus we want to discover and follow, or would we prefer an idol of our own making?" Wright, 93.

23. Benedict's words are cited in Stallsworth, "The Story of an Encounter," 107. He repeats this theme in various works. For example, in *Feast of Faith: Approaches to a Theology of the Liturgy* (San Francisco: Ignatius Press, 1986), he states (58): "The whole

The first operation, examining the historical origins and contexts of biblical texts, is the prerogative of Method B. In a Method C hermeneutic that incorporates the goods of both Method A and Method B, this comes first in the order of execution and provides ground for the subsequent operation of Method A spiritual exegesis.[24] It is important to know as much as possible about the realities signified by the words of a text (the literal sense) if one is to correctly grasp any signification these realities might themselves have (their spiritual sense). Meanwhile, just as grace perfects man by building on nature, so Method A's spiritual encounter with Scripture perfects Method B's exegetical operation by placing the texts of Scripture within the total movement of history and understanding them in light of Christ as history's central event.[25] Benedict makes this same point in so many words:

[T]he inner nature of the [historical-critical] method points beyond itself and contains within itself an openness to complementary methods. In these

---

Old Testament is a movement of transition to Christ." In *Eschatology* he likewise examines how this second exegetical operation of examining events in light of Christ played out in the nascent Church (113): "The risen Lord became the canon within the canon, the criterion in whose light tradition must be read. In the illumination which he brought, the internal struggles of the Old Testament were read as a single *movement* towards the One who suffered, was crucified, and rose again" (emphasis mine).

As regards the topic of tracing texts back to their historical origins, Pius XII penned these words: "What is the literal sense of a passage is not always as obvious in the speeches and writings of the ancient authors of the East, as it is in the works of our own time. For what they wished to express is not to be determined by the rules of grammar and philology alone, nor solely by the context; the interpreter must, as it were, go back wholly in spirit to those remote centuries of the East and with the aid of history, archaeology, ethnology, and other sciences, accurately determine what modes of writing, so to speak, the authors of that ancient period would be likely to use, and in fact did use." *Divino afflante Spiritu* §35.

24. In reality, of course, the ordinary Christian's canonical reading of Scripture is not necessarily concerned with historical-critical questions and therefore comes "before" Method B's academic treatment. However, here I am trying to describe the order that is necessary in order to ensure a warranted rather than arbitrary canonical reading, and this is achieved with the help of Method B.

25. Constitutive of this "perfection" wrought by Method A exegesis is the fact that it does not negate, but rather preserves, the text's original meaning ascertained through Method B. For a Method C exegete, the spiritual sense apprehended through praying biblical texts over the centuries makes the most sense when it is seen in continuity with the historical events that gave rise to it.

words from the past, we can discern the question concerning their meaning for today; a voice greater than man's echoes in Scripture's human words; the individual writings [*Schrifte*] of the Bible point somehow to the living process that shapes the one Scripture [*Schrift*].[26]

Method B exegesis may therefore come first in order of execution, but it is not first in an absolute sense. What is first absolutely is something the historical-critical method can only examine on a material level and thus point toward—the reality of Scripture as God's word, and the end of Scripture, which is to encounter God teaching through his word (both of which are principles of Method A).[27] In other words, Method A gives the exegete the real reason for his investigation because it gives him God's word, whereas Method B by itself does not formally study Scripture as God's word; it examines only its material components and therefore "does not transmit the Bible to today, into my present-day life."[28] Method B's investigation of the human dimension of Scripture must therefore be done with a view toward showing the inherent openness of its words to a reality which transcends them and which they serve to make present. Its operation should serve the reader by making it easier for him to achieve what Method A seeks: an encounter with Christ, who is not a mere figure of the past but is present teaching the reader of Scripture today.[29] Method A does not negate Method B but rather presupposes and builds upon it.

26. Benedict XVI, *Jesus of Nazareth*, xviii.

27. As Benedict will write with regard to his own historical-critical work in *Jesus of Nazareth*, "[T]his book presupposes historical-critical exegesis and makes use of its findings, but it seeks to transcend this method and to arrive at a genuinely theological interpretation of the scriptural texts." *Jesus of Nazareth: Holy Week*, 295. For Benedict, historical criticism is not an end in itself but rather an aid to our encounter with Christ through "a genuinely theological interpretation of the scriptural texts."

28. Benedict XVI, *Truth and Tolerance: Christian Belief and World Religions*, trans. Henry Taylor (San Francisco: Ignatius Press, 2004), 133.

29. Benedict has described this interplay between the operations of Method A and Method B in various other ways throughout his corpus of work. He often uses different terms to describe the two exegetical methods from different angles. He may speak of "Method A" versus "Method B" at one moment and "historical hermeneutic" versus "faith hermeneutic" in another; he has also referred to "scholarly" and "scientific" exegesis in contradistinction to *lectio divina*. In an *Angelus* address delivered during the 2008 bishops' synod on God's word, he taught Christians how to encounter Christ in Scripture in the following manner: "Scientific exegesis and *lectio divina* are therefore both

The upshot of Benedict's work is that, when employing the tools of Method B, the Method C exegete will be such only to the extent that his Method B operation (investigating the origins and the literal sense of Scripture) remains faithful to the principles of Method A exegesis (e.g. sacred Tradition, the Magisterium, inspiration, inerrancy, the spiritual sense, etc.). In other words, even before he attempts to carry out Method A's operation of spiritual exegesis, the Method C exegete already begins his Method B operation in accordance with the rule of faith adhered to by Method A. This will be clearly seen when we examine how Benedict instantiates his method in later chapters of this volume.

In this way, it really is possible for the Method C exegete to incorporate Method B into his work: he is able to set aside the accidental features or assumptions of particular exegetical "traditions" without abandoning the principles of sacred tradition as a source of revelation. For Pope Benedict, faith does not require that Christians espouse all patristic-medieval assumptions, for example the ancient belief that Matthew was the earliest gospel. The Method C exegete can remain completely committed to the faith while asking questions and accepting answers never entertained by exegetes of previous ages, and he can do this because his work stands in accord with the principles of the Christian faith—not the least among which is the belief that greater knowledge of the historical dimension of Scripture leads to greater knowledge of Christ.

It is appropriate to conclude this section with some of Benedict's most recent comments in *Light of the World*. In this book-length inter-

---

necessary and complementary in order to seek, through the literal meaning, the spiritual meaning that God wants to communicate to us today." Benedict XVI, *Angelus*. October 26, 2008. This quote concisely encapsulates the goal of the pope's twofold exegetical approach. "Scientific exegesis" (Method B) ascertains the literal meaning of Scripture, but it is when the Christian turns to the prayer of *lectio divina* (a feature of Method A's approach) that he discovers the biblical text has a spiritual meaning relevant to his own life. According to Benedict, this spiritual sense is arrived at "through" the literal. It is significant that Benedict dedicated a section of *Verbum Domini* not only to the theory behind *lectio divina* but also to teaching Christians how to practice it today. As is frequently the case, here we have Benedict not only laying out theoretical principles for Christians but also offering guidance for instantiating them in real life. Cf. *VD* §§86–87.

view, he once again reiterates the importance of historical-critical exegesis and the need to establish a synthesis between critical and faith-based approaches to Scripture. Writing more than twenty years after the Erasmus Lecture in which he introduced his Method C proposal, the pope provides the following summary of its main principles:

The application of the historical method to the Bible as a historical text was a path that had to be taken. If we believe that Christ is real history, and not myth, then the testimony concerning him has to be historically accessible as well. In this sense, the historical method has also given us many gifts. It has brought us back closer to the text and its originality, it has shown us more precisely how it grew, and much more besides. *The historical-critical method will always remain one dimension of interpretation.* Vatican II made this clear. On the one hand, it presents the essential elements of the historical method as a necessary part of access to the Bible. *At the same time, though, it adds that the Bible has to be read in the same Spirit in which it was written.* It has to be read in its wholeness, in its unity. And that can be done only when we approach it as a book of the People of God *progressively advancing toward Christ.* What is needed is not simply a break with the historical method, but a self-critique of the historical method; a self-critique of historical reason that takes cognizance of its limits and recognizes the compatibility of a type of knowledge that derives from faith; *in short, we need a synthesis between an exegesis that operates with historical reason and an exegesis that is guided by faith.* We have to bring the two things into a proper relationship to each other. That is also a requirement of the basic relationship between faith and reason.[30]

It is once again clear that for Benedict the historical-critical method plays a key role in exegesis. At the same time, he quotes Vatican II in explaining that Scripture "has to be read in its wholeness, in its unity." The only way to achieve this is to read it as the story of "the People of God progressively advancing toward Christ." It would difficult to find a better endorsement of the hermeneutic of the divine pedagogy than what Benedict has here. He likewise reiterates the call for a "synthesis

---

30. Benedict XVI, *Light of the World*, 171–72 (emphasis added). See also Benedict's recent comments in *VD* §34: "The Synod Fathers rightly stated that the positive fruit yielded by the use of modern historical-critical research is undeniable. While today's academic exegesis, including that of Catholic scholars, is highly competent in the field of historical-critical methodology and its latest developments, it must be said that comparable attention need [sic] to be paid to the theological dimension of the biblical texts, so that they can be more deeply understood in accordance with the three elements indicated by the Dogmatic Constitution *Dei Verbum.*"

between an exegesis that operates with historical reason and an ex-egesis that is guided by faith." For Benedict, the truth and unity of Scripture cannot be reconciled in the face of modern challenges unless exegetes have recourse to the tools of both Method A and Method B exegesis. Grappling with the greatest of problems within Scripture, in light of Benedict's plan for exegesis, will lead Christians to a deeper encounter with the mystery of Christ as well as to a better under-standing of the nature of Scripture itself.

Benedict, Aquinas, and Bonaventure

Having summarized the broad strokes of Ratzinger's exegetical vi-sion, I will now flesh out in more detail the basis for carrying out his programme that is found in the Method A theology of St. Bonaven-ture and St. Thomas Aquinas. Even though these connections will not be made explicitly in later chapters, the principles articulated below undergird Benedict's exegesis through and through.

Ratzinger's Early Critiques of Neo-scholasticism and Preference for Bonaventure

Although what follows will focus primarily on commonalties be-tween the exegetical projects of Ratzinger and Aquinas, a word is in order concerning the former's critical stance toward scholasticism in the form it had assumed within the century prior to Vatican II. In the interview book *Salt of the Earth*, Ratzinger sums up his view at the time of the council:

I was of the opinion that scholastic theology, in the form it had come to have, was no longer an instrument for bringing faith into the contemporary dis-cussion. It had to get out of its armor; it also had to face the situation of the present in a new language, in a new openness. So a greater freedom also had to arise in the Church.[31]

Instances of such criticism abound in Ratzinger's reflections published after the council in the volume *Theological Highlights of Vatican II*. Here he relates that the council's preparatory schema on revelation, framed upon the basis of a "cramped" neo-scholastic theology with an "exces-

31. Ratzinger, *Salt of the Earth*, 73.

sively one-sided zeal," was imbued with the same "anti-Modernistic neurosis which had again and again crippled the Church since the turn of the century."[32]

Young Fr. Ratzinger was critical of scholasticism broadly speaking, but in a few places it emerges that he had difficulty relating with Thomas Aquinas specifically. Reflecting on his seminary experience at Freising, he writes, "I had difficulties in penetrating the thought of Thomas Aquinas whose crystal-clear logic seemed to me to be too closed in on itself, too impersonal and ready-made."[33] Ratzinger traces the cause of this difficulty to his experience with a certain Thomist professor who "presented us with a rigid, neo-scholastic Thomism that was simply too far afield from my own questions.... [I]t seemed that he himself no longer asked questions but limited himself to defending passionately, against all questions, what he had found."[34]

Fr. Ratzinger struggled to relate with the thought of Aquinas early in his career, but he found a like-minded partner in Bonaventure. He indicates in his *habilitation* thesis on Bonaventure's theology of history, "For the questions with which I was concerned, Bonaventure was naturally a more likely subject for study than Aquinas."[35] Bonaventure dealt more directly than Aquinas with the themes that interested Ratzinger—specifically, questions at the intersection of divine revelation, history, and metaphysics. Moreover, while Bonaventure did not target Thomas himself in his critiques of contemporary Aristotelianism, it is likely that what Ratzinger describes as an "anti-Thomism" in Bonaventure exerted its influence upon him insofar as Bonaventure was wary of a theology that would rely too heavily upon the thought of Aristotle.[36]

While Bonaventure's lesser reliance on Aristotle had its appeal for Ratzinger, the latter acknowledges that neither Bonaventure nor Aquinas discussed the nature of divine revelation in the sense it has been understood within fundamental theology in the modern period. As one

32. Ratzinger, *Theological Highlights of Vatican II*, 41–42, 27; cf. *Theological Highlights*, 23, 219.

33. Ratzinger, *Milestones*, 44.

34. Ibid., 14.

35. Joseph Ratzinger, *Theology of History in St. Bonaventure* (Chicago: Franciscan Herald Press, 1971), xii.

36. Ratzinger, *Theology of History*, 136–38.

finds in the treatise on prophecy in the *Summa* (II-II, qq. 171–74), the theologians of the Middle Ages were more concerned with the nature of "revelations" than with the objective reality or content of "revelation" as such.[37] Ratzinger elaborates:

[In the High Middle Ages] "revelation" is always a concept denoting an act. The word refers to the act in which God shows himself, not the objectified result of this act. And because this is so, the receiving subject of revelation is always also part of the concept of "revelation." Where there is no one to perceive "revelation," no re-*vel*-ation has occurred, because no *veil* has been removed.[38]

Meanwhile, Bonaventure's understanding of revelation referred to the unveiled spiritual sense of Scripture rather than its letter. This had a profound impact on Ratzinger's theology of revelation as evinced in writings spanning his entire career. Following Bonaventure, Ratzinger does not view Scripture as being revelation per se but rather the "essential witness" or "testimony" to a revelation that precedes and exceeds it.[39] This perspective has profound implications for how Benedict deals with problems concerning the life of Christ brought to light by modern New Testament scholarship.

Aquinas and Benedict: Points of Contact

Notwithstanding young Fr. Ratzinger's criticisms of neo-scholastic thought, from both what was stated above and from what he states elsewhere in his corpus it is clear that Ratzinger's problem was not

37. Ibid., 57.

38. Ratzinger, *Milestones*, 108.

39. Ratzinger, *Theology of History*, 62. On the subject of Scripture not being revelation per se but rather the "essential witness" or "testimony" to a revelation that precedes and exceeds it, see *Milestones*, 109 and 127; Karl Rahner and Joseph Ratzinger, *Revelation and Tradition* (New York: Herder, 1966), 35; Benedict XVI, *VD* §§17–18. Peter Enns, an important popular evangelical author, speaks in very similar terms which may strike one as quite surprising coming as they do from the pen of a Protestant: "The Bible is not, never has been, and never will be the center of the Christian faith.... As theologians tell us, the Bible, in various and complex ways, 'bears witness' to Christ. That is the Bible's role, to encourage the faithful to live in its pages in order to look up from the pages and, by the power and love of the Spirit of God, see Jesus. The Bible doesn't say, 'Look at me!' It says, 'Look through me.' The Bible, if we are paying attention, decenters itself." Peter Enns, *The Bible Tells Me So: Why Defending Scripture Has Made Us Unable to Read It* (San Francisco: HarperOne, 2014), 237.

with Thomas himself so much as with the overly rigid presentation of Aquinas common in preconciliar theology. The following will tease out several points of contact between the thought of Aquinas and Ratzinger implied by the latter's suggestion that Thomas's exegesis offers an antidote to secularist forms of modern exegesis.

Benedict and Aquinas's "Open Philosophy"

On a number of occasions Benedict has made plain his conviction that Aquinas's example provides a powerful basis for countering modern challenges to the Bible. After explaining that his *Jesus of Nazareth* is not a "Life of Jesus" or a "Christology," he explicitly states that Aquinas's treatise on the life of Christ in the *Summa* is "closer to my intention" and that with this work "my book has many points of contact."[40] Though privy to modern scholarly tools in a way Aquinas was not, Benedict identifies with the latter in his patient attentiveness to God's word and his desire to put believers in touch with the mystery of Jesus, his "figure and message."[41]

In the section of his Erasmus Lecture entitled "Basic Elements of a New Synthesis," Benedict expounds at some length on the importance of Thomas's thought for helping believers encounter Christ through his word. In contrast with a Kantian "ready-made philosophy," Aquinas's "open philosophy" is "capable of accepting the biblical phenomenon in all its radicalism" by admitting that a real encounter of God and man is witnessed in history—and made possible today—by the Scriptures.[42] For Benedict, a "critique of the critique" requires a rejection of the false presuppositions of those who would exclude *a priori* God's ability to speak through human words. Aquinas's exegesis, deeply rooted in the Catholic tradition with its conviction that the boundary of time and eternity is permeable, allows for the Bible to be

---

40. Benedict XVI, *Jesus of Nazareth: Holy Week*, xvi.

41. Ibid.

42. Benedict XVI, "Biblical Interpretation in Conflict," 23. Elsewhere Ratzinger contrasts a proper hermeneutic with this closed, Kantian, "ready-made" approach: "In short, in the revelation of God, he, the living and true One, bursts into our world and also opens the prison of our theories, with whose nets we want to protect ourselves against God's coming into our lives." Ratzinger, "Relativism: The Central Problem for Faith Today."

what the Church has always claimed it to be: the word of God in human words. This point will prove crucially important later as we present Benedict's hermeneutical engagement with modern scholarship as an alternative to the mainstream skeptical view found in Ehrman.

The Literal Sense, Assertions, and "the Essential Point"

One important point of contact between Aquinas and Benedict is not explicated by the latter but is nonetheless evident in the way he instantiates his own principles by attempting to determine the "essential point" asserted according to the literal sense concrete biblical texts. Benedict demonstrates keen awareness that certain texts seem plainly to contradict what is stated in other texts:

> It is because faith is not set before us as a complete and finished system that the Bible contains contradictory texts, or at least ones that stand in tension to each other.[43]

> It follows straightaway that neither the criterion of inspiration nor that of infallibility can be applied mechanically. It is quite impossible to pick out one single sentence and say, right, you find this sentence in God's great book, so it must simply be true in itself.[44]

---

43. Benedict XVI, *God and the World*, 152; cf.: "The problem of dating Jesus's Last Supper arises from the contradiction on this point between the Synoptic Gospels, on the one hand, and Saint John's Gospel, on the other." Benedict XVI, *Jesus of Nazareth: Holy Week*, 106.

44. Benedict XVI, *God and the World*, 153; cf. Benedict XVI, Address to Participants in the Plenary Meeting of the Pontifical Biblical Commission (May 2, 2011): "Lastly, I would only like to mention the fact that in a good hermeneutic it is not possible to apply mechanically the criterion of inspiration, or indeed of absolute truth by extrapolating a single sentence or expression. The plan in which it is possible to perceive Sacred Scripture as a Word of God is that of the unity of God, in a totality in which the individual elements are illuminated reciprocally and are opened to understanding." See also this thought-provoking text from James Tunstead Burtchaell, *Catholic Theories of Biblical Inspiration since 1810: A Review and Critique* (Cambridge: Cambridge University Press, 1969), 299, 303–4: "Both by those who accept these claims [of inerrancy and infallibility] and by those who reject them, they have been imagined as some sort of flawless, eternal ownership of the truth, expressed in formulas that might from time to time need a little translating, but never need replacing. In this sense, there has probably never been an inerrant declaration uttered or book written, nor need we look forward to one. But if inerrancy involve wild, and sometimes even frightening movement, if it mean being pulled to the right and to the left, being tempted constantly to deviate, yet always managing somehow to regain the road, then it begins to sound rather like what the Church has been

The problem of admitting the presence of contradictory biblical texts, of course, lies in squaring these with the doctrine of inerrancy as it is articulated in *Dei Verbum*: "Therefore, since *everything asserted by the inspired authors or sacred writers must be held to be asserted by the Holy Spirit*, ..."[45]

As Germain Grisez has noted, it is a great mistake to read the above sentence as saying that everything in Scripture is asserted by the Holy Spirit: "Scripture contains not only many sentences expressing no proposition, but many sentences that express propositions not asserted by their human authors."[46] In a helpful footnote in which he offers illustrations from Aquinas to support his claim, Grisez adds that the Council Fathers would have been well aware of the difference between a mere statement on the one hand and an assertion or teaching on the other.[47] Brian Harrison, OS, in an essay which critiques a view similar to that advanced by Grisez, offers a further helpful specification. According to the Council *relator* of *Dei Verbum* 11, Harrison notes, the word teach (*docere*) refers to those things which are truly affirmed (*asseruntur*) in Scripture.[48] Harrison cites an important text from Raúl Cardinal Silva Herínquez to clarify:

about.... In sum, the Church does find inerrancy in the Bible, if we can agree to take that term in its dynamic sense, and not a static one. Inerrancy must be the ability, not to avoid all mistakes, but to cope with them, remedy them, survive them, and eventually even profit from them. In a distinct selection of faith-leavings from a distinct epoch of faith-history, we have the archives of the process by which our ancestral faith began from nothing, involved itself in countless frustrating errors, but made its way, lurching and swerving, 'reeling but erect,' somehow though never losing the way, to climax in Christ."

45. *Dei Verbum*, §11 (emphasis added). The text continues: "... it follows that the books of Scripture must be acknowledged as teaching solidly, faithfully and without error that truth which God wanted put into sacred writings for the sake of salvation."

46. Germain Grisez, "The Inspiration and Inerrancy of Scripture," in St. Paul Center for Biblical Theology, *For the Sake of Our Salvation: The Truth and Humility of God's Word* (Steubenville, Ohio: Emmaus Road Publishing, 2010), 186.

47. Ibid., 186n15. Grisez states that "[t]he distinction between what is asserted and what is said without being asserted is one that Thomas uses regularly." Examples he provides from the *Summa theologiae* include II-II, q. 110, a. 3, ad 1; I, q. 77, z. 5 ad 3; q. 100, a. 2, ad 2.

48. *Acta synodalia Sacrosancti Concilii Oecumenici Vaticani II* (Rome: Typis Polyglottis Vaticanis, 1970-), vol. 4, pt. 5, 709; Brian Harrison, "Restricted Inerrancy and the 'Hermeneutic of Discontinuity'" within the volume *For the Sake of Our Salvation*, 244. In another piece, Harrison pointedly criticizes certain "recent Catholic authors" who "have

[T]he doctrine of biblical inerrancy is better expressed by the formal criterion of *teaching*, since it is according to that criterion that no error can be
found. For in another sense, that is, the material sense, it is possible for expressions to be used by the sacred writer which are erroneous in themselves,
but which, however, he does not wish to teach.[49]

As Harrison proceeds to observe, the *relator* informed the Council Fathers that Herínquez's above proposal had been accepted "substantially" by the doctrinal commission. Thus Harrison affirms Herínquez's
clarification as "a guide to what the Council means."[50]

In contrast with Grisez, Harrison argues that the key distinction
in the cardinal's text is not between "affirmations" and "teachings" on
the one hand and "statements" on the other.[51] Rather, for him the di-

---

tried to reconcile [the teaching of *Dei Verbum* 11] with the supposed occurrence of errors
in Scripture by charging that the errors they have in mind are never in fact *affirmed* by
either the divine or human authors." Harrison describes such a maneuver as a "contorted
hermeneutic" which "unreasonably attempts to determine what is being affirmed in a
given text in Scripture by appealing to content rather than form—subject matter rather
than syntax ... but this procedure—trying to identify an author's assertions by looking
at *what* he is talking about instead of *how* he talks about it—violates basic, common-
sense principles of verbal communication. Brian Harrison, "Does Vatican Council II Allow for Errors in Sacred Scripture?" *Divinitas*, LII, 3 (2009): 279–304. The text cited here
is from an updated version of the article available at http://www.rtforum.org/lt/lt145-6.
html. This is a helpful critique, but it does not negate the importance of distinguishing
statements from assertions as Grisez does. This fundamental endeavor to distinguish
nonaffirmed statements from core assertions in the biblical text can be seen in the exegesis of Joseph Ratzinger throughout his career. But unlike the unnamed authors whom
Harrison critiques, Ratzinger's exegesis by no means neglects the syntax or *how* a biblical
author wishes to assert his point. On the contrary, his patient attentiveness to this reality is what makes his hermeneutic so powerful.

49. *Acta Vaticani II*, vol. 3, pt. 3, 799.
50. Harrison, "Restricted Inerrancy," 245.
51. It is helpful to compare what Harrison writes in the above piece to another
work in which he provides a helpful clarification of his view: "[S]ome biblical affirmations—above all, those that are *per se* less directly concerned with salvation—may be
only approximations, or it may be that they express certain truths only in simple, popular
language rather than in precise or technical terminology. For since the formal object of
Sacred Scripture is to teach us God's plan of salvation for the human race, and not profane history, natural science, or other forms of merely worldly knowledge *for their own
sakes*, one should not expect or demand, as a condition of the Bible's freedom from error,
when it touches upon these subjects, the same standards of accuracy and clarity in description and terminology as we would expect and demand in works (especially modern
academic works) whose formal object is these 'secular' branches of knowledge.... [W]e

chotomy is to be found in contrasting what is formally "taught" with what is merely "used" (*adhiberi*) by the sacred writers in making their assertions. The category of what is merely used, Harrison concludes, may include expressions (*locutiones*) that are "materially" erroneous.[52] It is worth noting that here we have a Thomistically inspired distinction between material and formal error leveraged in order to make sense of the Scriptures. As Aquinas himself indicates in his *Commentary on the Sentences*, some biblical statements pertain to the substance of the faith (*ad substantiam fidei*), while others pertain to the faith only accidentally (*per accidens*). With respect to Genesis, we will see later that Aquinas thus states that the doctrine of creation belongs to the substance of the faith, but how and in what order the world was made (*quo autem modo et ordine factus sit*) pertain to the faith only accidentally.[53]

Paul Synave and Pierre Benoit make a similar distinction, following the contours of Aquinas's discussion of prophecy in the *Summa*:

Truth is the *adequatio rei et intellectus*. It exists only in the judgment. And by "judgment" we obviously do not mean every proposition made up of subject, verb, and predicate, but the formal act by which the intellect affirms its conformity (*adequatio*) to the object of knowledge.... An [inspired] author does

---

should not set the bar unreasonably high in deciding what is *to count* as truth, as opposed to error, when the sacred writers make statements about secondary matters that are only indirectly linked to the Bible's principal and overall purpose." Harrison, "Does Vatican Council II Allow for Errors in Sacred Scripture?"

52. Harrison, "Restricted Inerrancy," 245. Harrison's way of speaking, though perhaps jarring to some, has ancient precedent. Origen, after observing that there are many points on which the Gospels' narratives do not agree, added, "I do not condemn [the Evangelists] if they even sometimes dealt freely with things which to the eye of history happened differently, and changed them so as to subserve the mystical aims they had in view; so as to speak of a thing which happened in a certain place, as if it had happened in another, or of what took place at a certain time, as if it had taken place at another time, and to introduce into what was spoken in a certain way some changes of their own. They proposed to speak the truth where it was possible both materially and spiritually, and where this was not possible it was their intention to prefer the spiritual to the material. The spiritual truth was often preserved, as one might say, in the material falsehood." Origen, *Commentary on the Gospel of John*, in *Ante-Nicene Fathers*, Vol. 9, ed. Allan Menzies (Buffalo, N.Y.: Christian Literature Publishing Co., 1896), Book X, 4. On the possible existence of material error (or imperfection) in Scripture, in contrast with the impossibility of formal errors in Scripture, see Matthew Ramage, *Dark Passages of the Bible*, 131–46.

53. Aquinas, *In II Sent.*, dist. 12, a. 2.

not speak of everything in an absolute way.... He tells the truth or he is mistaken only within the limits of the field of vision which he has established for himself and in which he forms his judgment.... We must therefore respect the varying degrees of his assent, rather than take all his sentences as categorical affirmations.[54]

Abbot Denis Farkasfalvy speaks in similar terms:

Divine inspiration does not imply that each passage and sentence of the biblical text must be found free of error from every conceivable point of view.... But such a realization does not prove that God's word *asserts* error. Rather, it only means that God's message is expressed, at one or another point of salvation history, with the imperfections characteristic of human existence.[55]

One might expand upon Farkasfalvy's point by explaining that any apparent errors in Scripture are in reality material imperfections rather than formal errors, since the biblical text still conveys "the human author's concretely defined purpose and its divine author's salvific purpose," in such a way that "every passage expresses the truth which it is supposed to express according to God's salvific will."[56]

Matthew Lamb, in his translation and notes on Aquinas's *Commentary on Ephesians*, makes a similar point from an angle that also accounts for the divine pedagogy discussed above:

---

54. Paul Synave and Pierre Benoit, *Prophecy and Inspiration* (New York: Desclée, 1961), 134–35. Cf. ibid., 142: "[God] certainly cannot prevent [the sacred author] from using in one way or another these erroneous views and, consequently, from letting them show through in his text. For example, no one will deny that the biblical authors had now outmoded cosmological ideas in which they believed, and that they employed them in their writings because they were unable to think apart from contemporary categories. But they do not claim to be teaching them *for their own sakes*; they speak of them for a different purpose, e.g. to illustrate creation and divine providence."

55. Denis Farkasfalvy, *Inspiration and Interpretation: A Theological Introduction to Sacred Scripture* (Washington, D.C.: The Catholic University of America Press, 2010), 232. Farkasfalvy's explanation has many resonances with the following text of C. S. Lewis. Writing on the subject of the Psalms, the latter observes: "The human qualities of the raw materials show through. Naïveté, error, contradiction, even (as in the cursing psalms) wickedness are not removed. The total result is not 'the word of God' in the sense that every passage, in itself, gives impeccable science or history. It carries the word of God; and we ... receive that word from it not by using it as an encyclopedia or an encyclical but by steeping ourselves in its tone or temper and so learning its overall message." C. S. Lewis, *Reflections on the Psalms* (London: Harvest Books, 1964), 111–12.

56. Farkasfalvy, *Inspiration and Interpretation*, 232.

We tend to regard a truth as either clearly and explicitly revealed or not revealed at all. But for St. Thomas man's knowledge of the faith grows; truths
are revealed slowly over a period of time. The Bible communicates this or-
ganic development of salvation-history to men up to its definitive apex in the
revelation of the Word Incarnate himself. The whole of the Bible must be
approached with faith; this does not mean that every sentence is a definable
dogma.[57]

As Lamb relates, it is not as if one can find a definable dogma in every sentence of Scripture; indeed, Scripture never claims this about
itself. The reason for this is that the authors of Scripture understood
and taught revealed truth with varying degrees of clarity depending on
their place within the course of salvation history. To discern dogmatic
content within Scripture thus requires careful attention to the inten-
tions of its authors and to the broader role of a particular text within
the development of the canon as a whole. This also requires overcom-
ing the assumption that something is "revealed" only if it is perfectly
reflective of God's own knowledge, or else it is not revealed at all.

For his part, Benedict assesses concrete problems in a way that is
compatible with and builds on the above understanding of inspiration
and revelation. Throughout his corpus the pontiff often seeks to reconcile apparently erroneous biblical texts by inquiring into their "substance" or "essential point," that is to say, by asking what message the
human and divine authors intend to teach or assert in a given text.
In the chapters that follow, we will examine many instances in which
Benedict makes this exegetical move.

Yet, although Benedict follows the Thomistic tradition regarding
the importance of ascertaining the intention or assertion of thorny
biblical texts, Aaron Pidel, SJ, astutely observes that the pontiff "re-
tools the neo-Thomist notion of intention in several important ways."[58]
Whereas the neo-scholastic instrumental model of inspiration is able
to qualify the inerrancy of Scripture only through the "strained effort" to nail down the individual biblical author's judgment, Ratzinger

57. Lamb (trans.), in Aquinas's *Commentary on Saint Paul's Epistle to the Ephesians*,
256n17.

58. Aaron Pidel, SJ, "Joseph Ratzinger and Biblical Inerrancy," *Nova et Vetera* 12.1
(2014): 308.

"transfers the locus of intention and affirmation from the human authors of Scripture to Scripture itself."[59] And Ratzinger can make this move "because he conceives of Scripture (*qua* revelation) as text-plus-living-subject."[60]

Ratzinger's major innovation here is to emphasize that individual biblical authors were embedded within the community of faith.[61] Thus in the foreword to his *Jesus of Nazareth: Baptism* volume, Benedict envisions not two (divine and human) but three "interlocking subjects" of Scripture. First, there is the individual author who wrote the text. Here it is noteworthy that he makes room for the possibility of a "group of authors" for a given text, presumably intending by this to account for redaction and for books like Isaiah which most likely have multiple authors writing during different historical epochs. Second, the People of God is the "collective subject" who is now identified as "actually the deeper 'author' of the Scriptures." Third, as affirmed by the scholastic tradition, God himself is "at the deepest level the one speaking" through men and their humanity.[62]

In calling attention to the complex layers of this corporate intentionality, Ratzinger is able to countenance the existence of biblical *errata* in a way his neo-scholastic forebears were not. On the eve of Vatican II, Ratzinger wrote:

[A]ccording to a practically irrefutable consensus of historians there definitely are mistakes and errors in the Bible in profane matters of no relevance for what Scripture properly intends to affirm.... The true humanity of Scripture, behind which the mystery of God's mercy arises all the more, is now finally dawning on our awareness; namely that Scripture is and remains inerrant and beyond doubt in everything that it properly intends to affirm, but this is not necessarily so in that which accompanies the affirmation and is not part of it.[63]

As Pidel puts it, from Ratzinger's perspective not to concede the Bible's historical infelicities is "to baptize stubborn fideism and to consign the Church to an intellectual ghetto."[64] But this admission is made pos-

59. Ibid., 310–11, 314.   60. Ibid., 318.
61. Ibid.
62. Benedict XVI, *Jesus of Nazareth: From the Baptism to the Transfiguration*, xx–xxi.
63. Jared Wicks, "Six Texts by Prof. Joseph Ratzinger as Peritus before and during Vatican Council II," *Gregorianum* 89 (2008): 280.
64. Pidel, "Joseph Ratzinger and Biblical Inerrancy," 312–13.

sible because Ratzinger makes an important move: he considers all
individual biblical texts in light of their place within the entire plan of
salvation culminating in Christ. Thus Pidel remarks that for Benedict
the canonical books are surely inerrant, "but only to the extent that
they bear upon the intention of the whole—the mystery of Christ."[65]
Accordingly, Scripture's inerrant content is not to be equated with
what individual human authors intended to affirm, but rather with the
requirements of the Church's faith in Christ.[66]

Benedict instantiates these principles with a crucial distinction
he makes in various ways throughout his corpus. A number of these
emerge in his essay "Farewell to the Devil?" to which we will return
later in this volume. According to Ratzinger, if we wish to know
whether geocentrism or the existence of the devil is *de fide*, then we
have to distinguish "the doctrinal message of the Bible" from "what
may be only the temporary contingent vehicle for its real theme."[67] We
must separate the core "content" of Scripture from its shell or "form."[68]
It is critical to discern "what is and is not necessary for a profession
of faith" and make it clear "where faith ends and where world view
begins."[69] In a wonderfully evocative image, he states that we have to
learn again and again, with the changing of the times, how to distinguish between "fixed stars" and "planets," between "permanent orien-
tation" and "transient movement."[70] Of course, even with Ratzinger's
trifold understanding of biblical authorship, it remains very difficult
to ascertain what in a given passage is essential to the faith and what
is accidental. For this reason, and in keeping with his emphasis upon
the people of God as Scripture's collective intending subject, Ratz-

65. Ibid., 330.
66. Ibid., 329.
67. Ratzinger, "Farewell to the Devil?" in *Dogma and Preaching* (San Francisco: Ignatius Press, 2011), 198. A concise summary of Ratzinger's argument in this essay can be
found in my piece by the same title, "Farewell to the Devil?" for the *Gregorian Institute*
blog (October 25, 2013).
68. Ratzinger, "Farewell to the Devil?" 199.
69. Ibid.
70. Ibid. For other instances of Ratzinger applying these distinctions, see his "Zum
Problem der Entmythologisierung Des Neuen Testamentes," *Religionsunterricht an
höheren Schulen* 3 (1960): 2–11 and Pidel's discussion of it in "Joseph Ratzinger and Biblical Inerrancy," 324ff.

inger affirms that knowledge of what is revelation and what is only its shell is ultimately discernible only by the living community of faith.[71] The three realities of Scripture, tradition, and Magisterium "are not static entities placed beside each other, but have to be seen as one living organism of the word of God, which from Christ lives on in the Church."[72]

Donum and Usus of Prophecy

Related to the issue of discerning an author's intention, Matthew Lamb draws attention to another facet of Aquinas's theology that is particularly helpful for reconciling the presence of apparently erroneous texts within Scripture with the doctrine of biblical inspiration. This involves the discovery that Aquinas's treatment of inspiration takes place within the context of the Holy Spirit's gift of prophecy. As Lamb says of the saint, "He lived in an age when the Bible was still considered within the total context of the prophetic mission exercised by the people of God. Scripture was not seen as the end product of this mission but as a means of continuing it."[73] According to Paul Synave and Pierre Benoit, commentators on Aquinas whom Lamb discusses and at certain points critiques, the Angelic Doctor offers a corrective for the Christian who might otherwise have a one-dimensional understanding of revelation. As I alluded to above, Christians are often tempted to identify "revelation" with "revelations" or discrete infallible propositions channeled to man by God above. In Thomas's view, however, the divine light infused when an inspired prophet receives a revelation does not necessarily involve the perfect communication of a particular supernatural idea. Simply put, due to the limitations inherent within man's darkened intellect and weakened will, not every idea presented on the sacred page reflects God's own knowledge of the universe.

71. Ratzinger, "Zum Problem der Entmythologisierung Des Neuen Testamentes," 11.
72. Jared Wicks, "Six Texts by Prof. Joseph Ratzinger," 276–77. For Ratzinger one of the key principles that has been deployed in this community over time is the recognition that an Old Testament passage is "not directly true, in its bare literal meaning," but rather problematic passages within it are "valid insofar as they are part of the history leading up to Christ." Ratzinger, "Farewell to the Devil?" 200.
73. Lamb, in the Introduction to Aquinas's Commentary on Ephesians, 7.

As Lamb explains, the key here rests on Aquinas's distinction between the *donum* and the *usus* of the gift of prophecy. Aquinas writes:

The use of any prophecy is within the power of the prophet.... Hence, one could prevent himself from using prophecy; the proper disposition is a necessary requirement for the correct use of prophecy since the use of prophecy proceeds from the created power of the prophet. Therefore, a determinate disposition is also required.[74]

Thus even if the Holy Spirit inspires a sacred author-prophet, this does not guarantee that this particular author has the requisite disposition to use the prophetic gift properly.

This is by no means to say that an error has been committed when a particular sacred author fails to make perfect use of the *donum* he has received from God. On the contrary, when considering questions of biblical inspiration it is critically important that we not isolate individual authors and texts from the entire order of divine revelation wisely established in God's providence. Thus, says Lamb, "[T]he emphasis is shifted from isolated individuals to God's control of the whole process in which the Bible was formed. The pre-required dispositions [of the Bible's authors] were arranged for within the scope of this special Providence."[75] That is to say, the very defects we observe in Scripture turn out to be a most significant clue for grasping its true purpose. If the reader will permit me to indulge in another quotation from C. S. Lewis, "[T]he value of the Old Testament may be dependent on what seems its imperfection."[76]

Condescension and the Divine Pedagogy

Returning more directly to Ratzinger's own remarks in the Erasmus Lecture, we find that another point of contact between Benedict and Aquinas involves the recognition of how essential it is to grasp the

---

74. Thomas Aquinas, *De veritate*, q. 12, a. 4. Translation by Matthew Lamb in Aquinas's *Commentary on Ephesians*, 258. Lamb provides references to many other places in Aquinas's corpus in which he distinguishes the prophetic *donum* and *usus*; cf. ibid., 258n20. For a more thorough discussion of inspiration and prophecy in Aquinas from which many insights in this chapter were drawn, see Matthew Ramage, *Dark Passages of the Bible*, 118–42.

75. Lamb, Introduction to Aquinas's *Commentary on Ephesians*, 9.

76. Lewis, *Reflections on the Psalms*, 114.

Christological teleology of salvation history. For Ratzinger, Thomas serves as a salutary "counter-model" in the field of exegesis today, for he presupposes the action of divine providence guiding salvation history to its destination in Christ. Christ is thus for Benedict "the unifying principle" of history "which alone confers sense on it," and God's action gradually leading his people towards Christ is "the principle of the intelligibility of history."[77]

Aquinas's Christological teleology helps us answer certain questions which arise in light of the foregoing argument: Why did divine providence permit Scripture's authors to sometimes have imperfect dispositions with regard to the gift of prophecy, and how does this imperfection contribute to the value of the Old Testament? The inner intelligibility of God's decision to permit certain defects in Scripture is found within his choice to ennoble human beings as secondary or instrumental causes of its authorship. While God is the primary author of Scripture, *Dei Verbum* affirms the Patristic tradition that he "condescended" so as to achieve his purpose by means of human instruments who functioned as true authors.[78] Thus the literal—or perhaps better, literary—sense of Scripture is that which was intended by Scripture's human authors, who, by means of their literary craft, used various forms and devices within a particular genre.

Yet Aquinas reminds us that the literal sense of Scripture must be approached not only bearing in mind the literary peculiarities of a given work, but also with attention to how this work fits into the canon of Scripture, which developed over a period of more than a thousand years. Aquinas's critical insight here lies in his consideration of the divine pedagogy, the gradual teaching method by which God gradually prepared his people over the centuries for the coming of Christ in the flesh. As Matthew Lamb observes, for Thomas the Spirit's prophetic gift is likened to divine education: "Aquinas holds that education is a process in which the teacher actualizes the potentialities of the stu-

---

77. Ratzinger, "Biblical Interpretation in Conflict," 24n37. Benedict here is citing Maximino Arias Reyero, *Thomas von Aquin als Exeget: Die Prinzipien seiner Schriftdeutung und seine Lehre von den Schriftsinnen* (Einsiedeln: Johannes Verlag, 1971), 106; cf. "Biblical Interpretation in Conflict," 23n35.

78. Second Vatican Council, *Dei Verbum*, 11.

dents as regards knowledge and virtue."[79] In *De veritate*, a text referenced by Lamb at various points in his notes, Thomas develops his divine pedagogy hermeneutic by comparing the education of the whole human race in divine things to the education of an individual: "Just as there is a progress in the faith of an individual man over the course of time, so there is a progress in faith for the whole human race. This is why Gregory says that divine knowledge has increasingly grown over the course of time."[80] In the same way that an individual believer slowly appropriates the truths of the faith into his life, so too the people of God gradually appropriates divine knowledge over the course of salvation history.

As Aquinas proceeds to explain, God had to hand on the faith to men in piecemeal form, not because he is an inept teacher, but because this is the only way men can digest its content: "Man acquires a share of this learning, not indeed all at once, but little by little, according to the mode of his nature."[81] Israel, God's pupil, could not perfectly appropriate the divine teaching immediately because she assimilated this teaching according to the mode of our weak human nature. As Aquinas astutely observes, Scripture itself likens the state of the people of Israel in the Old Testament to spiritual childhood before God the Father:

> The master, who has perfect knowledge of the art, does not deliver it all at once to his disciple from the very outset, for he would not be able to take it all in, but he condescends to the disciple's capacity and instructs him little by little. It is in this way that men made progress in the knowledge of faith as time went on. Hence the Apostle (Galatians 3:24) compares the state of the Old Testament to childhood.[82]

For Thomas, as for St. Paul, whose theology he invokes, God's firstborn son Israel gradually made progress in knowledge of him in accordance with the divine Teacher's most wise pedagogy. God condescended and taught man in accordance with the way he learns best,

---

79. Lamb, in Aquinas's *Commentary on Ephesians*, 261n29.
80. Thomas Aquinas, *De veritate*, q. 14, a. 11.
81. Thomas Aquinas, *Summa theologiae*, II-II, q. 2, a. 3. See also Matthew Ramage, *Dark Passages of the Bible*, 101.
82. Thomas Aquinas, *Summa theologiae*, II-II, q. 1, a. 7, ad 2.

which is "little by little." Ultimately, through the life and ministry of Jesus Christ, man attained the perfection of divine knowledge.

Aquinas explores this divine teaching method elsewhere in commenting on the text from St. Paul just cited. He argues that God's teaching was perfectly suited to the needs and ability of the people of God at every stage of divine revelation, taking into account the fact that the people would not always fully grasp what he wished to convey. In the words of Thomas:

Nothing prevents a thing being not perfect simply, and yet perfect in respect of time: thus a boy is said to be perfect, not simply, but with regard to the condition of time. So, too, precepts that are given to children are perfect in comparison with the condition of those to whom they are given, although they are not perfect simply. Hence the Apostle says (Gal 3:24): "The Law was our pedagogue in Christ."[83]

For Thomas, God was not unable or unwilling to teach Israel himself; rather, it was precisely because of his knowledge of frail human nature that he used tangible and even transitory means like the Law. Thus he is able to say that "nothing prevents a thing being not perfect simply, and yet perfect in respect of time." In other words, the reality is that God knew the Law was imperfect and did not contain the fullness of truth. However, given man's frail intellect and hard heart it was "perfect in respect of time," meaning that God adapted his teaching to the needs of his disciple Israel at every moment throughout the course of divine revelation. Herein lies the import of C. S. Lewis's words cited above: the very value of the Old Testament depends upon a certain imperfection which God permitted within it so as to reveal himself in a way that respects and ennobles our human nature.

The importance of what Aquinas and Lewis are saying here comes into full relief if one steps back to observe just how often Benedict XVI has insisted upon a hermeneutic of divine pedagogy over the past two decades. His *Verbum Domini* is particularly significant because it has a section entitled "The 'Dark' Passages of the Bible," in which the pontiff does this, though without precisely the same vocabulary. Benedict states that instances of violence and immorality in the Bible can be adequately

83. Ibid., I-II, q. 98, a. 2, ad 1.

addressed only if Catholics take seriously the fact that "God's plan is manifested *progressively* and it is accomplished slowly, *in successive stages* and despite human resistance." He explains that God patiently and gradually revealed himself in order to "guide and educate ... training his people in preparation for the Gospel." Since "revelation is suited to the cultural and moral level of distant times," it narrates certain things "without explicitly denouncing the immorality of such things," a fact that "can cause the modern reader to be taken aback." What is needed for correct interpretation, therefore, is "a training that interprets the texts in their historical-literary context [another way of saying Method B] and within the Christian perspective [Method A] which has as its ultimate hermeneutical key 'the Gospel and the new commandment of Jesus Christ brought about in the paschal mystery.'"[84]

The above text itself echoes the words of *Dei Verbum* and the later *Catechism of the Catholic Church*, which eloquently states: "The divine plan of revelation ... involves a specific divine pedagogy: God communicates himself to man gradually. He prepares him to welcome by stages the supernatural revelation that is to culminate in the person and mission of the incarnate Word, Jesus Christ."[85] This patristically based hermeneutic of divine pedagogy articulated by Benedict and the *Catechism* is precisely the bridge that enables one to reconcile the unity of Scripture traditionally emphasized by Christian exegetes with the development, diversity, and apparent contradictions observed by modern scholars. For the hermeneutic of divine pedagogy affirms that Scripture has a unity in light of the fact that it proceeds from God's one wise educational plan for mankind and communicates God himself to man. At the same time, this hermeneutic is comfortable with diversity and apparent contradictions in Scripture since it sees these within the greater context of their progression toward Christ.[86]

---

84. Benedict XVI, *VD* §42 (emphasis original); cf. §§11 and 20 for Benedict's use of the term "divine pedagogy."

85. *Catechism of the Catholic Church*, §53. I have cited the *Catechism* here because of its clarity and conciseness, but the *Catechism* itself is summarizing the Second Vatican Council constitution *Dei Verbum*, §15. For other magisterial statements of the divine pedagogy, see Pius XI, *Mit Brennender Sorge*, §15 and *Lumen Gentium*, §9, which explain Israel's relationship with God in terms of gradual instruction."

86. "The Bible is the condensation of a *process of revelation* which is much greater and

To further draw out the implications of this suggestion, I would like to sample some more texts that illustrate the importance Benedict places on a hermeneutic that takes seriously the divine pedagogy. In his *In the Beginning*, he describes the Bible as the story of a twofold struggle: God's struggle to "make himself understandable to them over the course of time," and the people of God's struggle to "seize hold of God over the course of time." This familiarization between God and man was a journey of faith, and "only in the process of this journeying was the Bible's real way of declaring itself formed, step by step." The message of the Bible becomes clearer as salvation history progresses and man acquires an increasing ability to penetrate the divine mysteries. Ultimately, however, the whole Old Testament is "an advance toward Christ," and as such its real meaning becomes clear only in light of him who is its end. Benedict therefore argues that exegetes interpret individual texts correctly only when they "see in the text where this way is tending and what its inner direction is."[87]

Benedict's revealing interview *God and the World* is also illuminating, especially given the question concerning how the Christian Scriptures apparently implicate God in evil in a way that seems comparable with the Koran's portrait of God. It is noteworthy that in this work Benedict treats precisely the issue of whether the Scriptures exhibit development. Contrasting Islam's belief that the Koran was dictated directly to Muhammad by God, he observes that the books of the Bible "bear the impression of a history that [God] has been guiding," since they were composed and developed over a thousand years, mediated by "quite different stages of history and of civilization."[88] As in the texts just discussed, so here he explains, "The Bible is not a text-

---

inexhaustible.... It is then part of a living organism which, through the vicissitudes of history, nonetheless *conserves its identity*." Benedict XVI, "Sources and Transmission of the Faith," *Communio* 10 (1983): 28.

87. Benedict XVI, *In the Beginning*, 10–11. See also Benedict's *Jesus of Nazareth: From the Baptism to the Transfiguration*, where he explains that the process of the Bible's formation was "not linear ... but when you watch it unfold in light of Jesus Christ, you can see it moving in a single overall direction." According to Benedict and his "Christological hermeneutic," Christ is "the key to the whole" of Scripture. Benedict, *Jesus of Nazareth: From the Baptism to the Transfiguration*, xix.

88. Benedict XVI, *God and the World*, 151–52 (emphasis added).

book about God and divine matters but contains images with percep-
tions and insights in the course of development, and through these
images, slowly and step by step, a historical reality is coming into existence."[89] As Ratzinger stated on the eve of Vatican II's solemn inauguration, this feature of biblical revelation is precisely what distinguishes the Bible from the religious texts of other great world religions:
"[T]hese are taken to be timeless divine dictations, whereas the Bible
is the result of God's historical dialogue with human beings and only
from this history does it have meaning and significance."[90]

But if the Christian cannot turn to a given page of the Bible for
the fullness of revealed truth, then where can he find it? Ratzinger answers, "The level on which I perceive the Bible as God's Word is that
of the unity of God's history.... In our Christian reading of it, we are
more than ever convinced, as we said, that the New Testament offers
us the key to understanding the Old."[91] The idea I wish to convey by
sampling these works of Benedict on the importance of a divine pedagogy hermeneutic is summarized well in a final work, *Introduction to
Christianity*, in which he states quite simply, "Anyone who wishes to
understand the biblical belief in God must follow its historical development from its origins with the patriarchs of Israel right up to the
last books of the New Testament."[92]

89. "Let us compare Holy Scripture with the Koran, for example. Moslems believe
that the Koran was directly dictated by God. It is not mediated by any history; no human
intermediary was needed; it is a message direct from God. The Bible, on the other hand,
is quite different. *It is mediated to us by a history, and even as a book it extends over a period
of more than a thousand years.* The question of whether or not Moses may have been a
writer is one we can happily leave to one side. It is still true that the biblical literature
grew up over a thousand-year history and thus moves through quite different stages of
history and of civilization, which are all reflected in it. In the first three chapters of Genesis, for instance, we meet with a quite different form of culture from what came later, in
the exilic literature, or in the wisdom literature, and then finally in the literature of the
New Testament. It becomes clear that God did not just dictate these words but rather
that *they bear the impression of a history that he has been guiding; they have come into being
as a witness to that history.*" Ibid. (emphasis added)

90. In Jared Wicks's "Six Texts by Prof. Joseph Ratzinger," 280.

91. Benedict XVI, *God and the World*, 153 (emphasis added). Benedict again goes on
to speak of the "process of collective development" and the "many stages of mediation" by
which the biblical books gradually were able to "bring the history of God's people and of
God's guidance to verbal expression."

92. Benedict XVI, *Introduction to Christianity*, 116. It is illuminating to read the

The Spiritual Sense

Another connection between Benedict and Aquinas concerns their agreement about the need for a rich doctrine of the senses of Scripture. While I believe that the principles already articulated are sufficient to account for certain troublesome biblical texts from an apologetics perspective, Benedict also identifies spiritual exegesis as an essential component of his programme. Indeed, it is here that the word of God achieves its end of taking flesh in our human lives and becoming truly a "living" word. In *Verbum Domini*, Benedict draws on Aquinas, himself citing Augustine, to emphasize the importance of the spiritual sense. In reality "it is impossible for anyone to attain to knowledge of that truth unless he first have infused faith in Christ" since "the letter, even that of the Gospel, would kill, were there not the inward grace of healing faith."[93] In the Erasmus Lecture Benedict speaks to this at greater length:

> To discover how each given historical word intrinsically transcends itself, and thus to recognize the intrinsic rightness of the rereadings by which the Bible progressively interweaves event and sense, is one of the tasks of objective interpretation. It is a task for which suitable methods can and must be found. In this sense, the exegetical maxim of Thomas Aquinas is much to the point: "The task of the good interpreter is not to consider words, but sense."[94]

In contrast with those whose methodologies focus solely on the "words" of Scripture, Benedict shares with Aquinas the conviction that the words of Scripture were meant to be "re-read" over time, to point beyond themselves to a reality revealed through them but which transcends them.[95] In this way, their rich teaching on the senses of Scripture, while giving due attention to its words, also points beyond the words so as to show that even Scripture's most problematic pas-

---

entire chapter from which this citation is taken, as in it Benedict traces the roots of Israel's monotheism such as it developed throughout the Old Testament period.

93. *VD* §29; cf. *ST* I-II, q. 106, a. 2.

94. Benedict XVI, "Biblical Interpretation in Conflict," 26 (emphasis added), citing Thomas Aquinas, *In Matthaeum*, XXVII, n. 2321 (ed. R. Cai [Turin/Rome: Marietti, 1951], 358). Cf. *VD* §37. He cites Aquinas three times in this work.

95. For the reality of revelation being broader than the Bible, see Benedict's "Biblical Interpretation in Conflict," 26, and *VD* §16.

sages may put believers in touch with Christ. The text in its wholeness, Benedict says, must become *Rabbenu*, "our teacher."[96] Method A
exegesis indicates that the texts of Scripture signify something in addition to their human authors' original intended meaning: realities in
the lives of believers of all ages who meditate on these texts in order to
gain the knowledge and strength they need to live a life in Christ. As
Benedict indicates, Christians may be privy to the fullness of revelation in a way our Old Testament forefathers were not, but the ancient
truths taught therein "are of course valid for the whole of history, for
all places and times" and "always need to be relearned."[97]

A Word on Sobriety with Respect to Aquinas

As Ratzinger famously stated in his Erasmus Lecture, however,
simply retreating to past thinkers like Aquinas is not a viable path
out of our modern exegetical problems. Lest one take away from this
chapter an overly romanticized view of Thomas's theology of inspiration, it is worth recalling that Thomas himself did draw out the full
implications of his own principles. Lamb observes:

> St. Thomas was aware of a certain growth or development in the revelation
> of supernatural mysteries, even though he could scarcely perceive the histori-
> cal dimensions of such an evolution. Any reflections on the Bible's inerrancy
> must take this development into account. Truth in God undergoes no change,
> but man's apprehension of the truth does.[98]

In other words, notwithstanding the integrity of Aquinas's principles, the exegetical horizon of his day did not allow him to perceive

---

96. "Biblical Interpretation in Conflict," 27. This dimension of the divine pedagogy is eloquently described by the Pontifical Council for Interreligious Dialogue: "[The
Church] takes her lead from divine pedagogy. This means learning from Jesus himself,
and observing the times and seasons as prompted by the Spirit. Jesus only progressively
revealed to his hearers the meaning of the Kingdom, God's plan of salvation realized in
his own mystery. Only gradually, and with infinite care, did he unveil for them the implications of his message, his identity as the Son of God, the scandal of the Cross. Even his
closest disciples, as the Gospels testify, reached full faith in their Master only through
their Easter experience and the gift of the Spirit. *Those who wish to become disciples of
Jesus today will pass through the same process of discovery and commitment.*" Dialogue and
Proclamation, §69 (emphasis added).

97. Benedict XVI, *God and the World*, 154.

98. Lamb, in his Introduction to Aquinas's *Commentary on Ephesians*, 10.

the extent of historical development within the Scriptures which we now recognize thanks to modern exegesis. A theology of inspiration grounded in Aquinas alone is thus impossible; as I insisted above, the only way out of the modern exegetical quagmire is to march boldly through it. For our emeritus pontiff Benedict XVI, this effort entails synthesizing the tools and findings that modern criticism has to offer with the best of the Christian exegetical tradition. And in Benedict's view, Aquinas' theology of inspiration contains principles which ought to play an important role in such a synthesis.

Conclusion: The Reception of Benedict's Vision in Recent Curial Documents

In the final section of this chapter, we turn our attention from Benedict's appropriation of the tradition to some comments on how Benedict's approach has been received in three recent curial documents. This reception of Benedict's exegetical vision at a very high level within the Church reveals that it is not something unique to him but rather an authentic appropriation of *Dei Verbum* in the Church today. In its 2011 *Theology Today: Perspectives, Principles and Criteria*, the International Theological Commission (ITC) echoes the vision of Vatican II and Benedict in identifying the task of exegesis as that of ascertaining "what God has wished to communicate to us."[99] Further, echoing Ratzinger and the *Catechism*, it bids the interpreter to bear in mind the entirety of sacred tradition, cognizant that Christianity is not primarily a "religion of the book" but rather of the living Word, the person Jesus Christ. Echoing language employed by Ratzinger throughout his career, it teaches that the Scriptures are "witnesses of faith" and "testify" to the Gospel revelation which is something greater within which the Bible finds its proper context.[100]

99. Second Vatican Council, *Dei Verbum*, 12; International Theological Commission, *Theology Today: Perspectives, Principles and Criteria*, 21–22.

100. This terminology appears a number of times within the document. For example, see *Theology Today*, 7, 26, and 30: "The gospel of God is fundamentally testified by the sacred Scripture of both Old and New Testaments.... Tradition is the faithful transmission of the Word of God, witnessed in the canon of Scripture by the prophets and the apostles and in the *leiturgia* (liturgy), *martyria* (testimony) and *diakonia* (service) of the Church." Ibid., 7. For a more thorough discussion of how the Scriptures witness or

In the course of its 2014 *God the Trinity and the Unity of Humanity*, the ITC offers principles to reconcile the many Old Testament texts in which God ostensibly acts against his own nature by commanding deeds such as the slaughter of men, women, and children.[101] While this theme is not the central focus of this volume, it is important to make a couple observations. First, the ITC follows Benedict in acknowledging the incompatibility of violence with the nature of God such as we understand it through reason.[102] Second, like Benedict the ITC emphasizes that the Christian must interpret the entire Old Testament in light of its gradual progression toward Jesus Christ, what above was described in terms of the divine pedagogy. The document describes the Old Testament's redaction in terms of an evolutionary dynamic (*dinamica evolutiva*) wherein the faith of ancient Israel was gradually purified through a reconfiguration of memory (*riconfigurazione della memoria*). The ITC argues that it is from the retrospective vantage point of the fullness of faith that the entire antecedent process of divine revelation ought to be evaluated.[103]

---

attest to revelation, see my *Dark Passages of the Bible*, especially 7n8 and 65–66. See also Ratzinger's comments on the eve of Vatican II's solemn inauguration: "Then it is clear that revelation itself is always more than a formulated witness in Scripture; for revelation is the living reality that surrounds Scripture and expands it." "Six Texts by Prof. Joseph Ratzinger," 271–72.

101. ITC, *God the Trinity and the Unity of Humanity*, 26.

102. Ibid., 24. Since there currently exists no official English text of this work in English, translations used in this volume are mine.

103. Ibid., 27. Whereas the ITC speaks here of developments within the Bible in evolutionary terms, John Henry Newman sees good reason not to describe the phenomenon precisely in this way. See his *Essay on the Development of Christian Doctrine*, where he argues for the distinction between development and evolution, based on the Church's profession that the substance of the faith has not changed over time, as would be implied if one adopted the evolutionary paradigm of species change. In this same paragraph the ITC draws a parallel between the progressiveness of divine revelation and development of doctrine within the Church. Here it is Newman again who sees such an analogy when he writes: "The prophetic Revelation is, in matter of fact ... a process of development: the earlier prophecies are pregnant texts out of which the succeeding announcements grow; they are types. It is not that first one truth is told, then another; but the whole truth or large portions of it are told at once, yet only in their rudiments, or in miniature, and they are expanded and finished in their parts, as the course of revelation proceeds." Newman, *Essay*, 64. Newman has the correct intuition that there exists an underlying "Idea" behind revelation itself which was clarified gradually over time as Israel grew in her ability to apprehend the Lord's teaching. Indeed right after the passage just cited he says, "The

Most significantly for our purposes, in 2014 the Pontifical Biblical Commission (PBC) issued a document that bears directly upon our quest in this volume. *The Inspiration and Truth of Sacred Scripture* admirably executes the exegetical vision outlined in Vatican II's *Dei Verbum* and Benedict XVI's *Verbum Domini*, works upon which it explicitly draws. To begin, the PBC follows Benedict in unabashedly confronting the problems raised by modern scholarship and recognizing the threat they pose to Christian belief:

The whole value for the life and mission of the Church depends on their inspiration and truth.... Nevertheless, the truth present in the sacred texts is not always easily recognizable. At times, there are at least apparent contrasts between what is read in the biblical accounts and the findings of the natural and historical sciences. These sciences appear to contradict what the biblical writings affirm and place their truth in doubt.[104]

The PBC remains convinced that eliminating problematic passages from our Bible study or from the public reading of Scripture in the liturgical assembly will not do, even as its members remain cognizant of "contradictions of a geographical, historical, and scientific nature, which are rather frequent in the Bible."[105] Here again, the only way out of these apparent contradictions is to be found by tackling them head-on: "[W]e cannot eliminate any passage from the narrative; the exegete must strive to find the significance of every phrase in the context of the narrative as a whole."[106]

In agreement with the ITC and Benedict's vision discussed above, the PBC affirms that a guiding hermeneutical principle necessary for this task involves the effort to ascertain the intention underlying a thorny biblical text. But here this intention is discussed in greater detail:

In the Bible, we encounter many and various themes. An attentive reading, however, shows that *the primary and dominating theme* is God and his salvific plan for human beings. The truth which we find in Sacred Scripture *essen-*

---

whole Bible, not its prophetical portions only, is written on the principle of development" and "It is certain that developments of Revelation proceeded all through the Old Dispensation down to the very end of our Lord's ministry." Newman, *Essay*, 65, 67–68

104. Pontifical Biblical Commission, *The Inspiration and Truth of Sacred Scripture* (Collegeville, Minn.: The Liturgical Press, 2014), xiii.

105. Ibid., 163, 167.

106. Ibid., 124.

tially concerns God and his relationship with his creatures.... To respond to the questions that arise in the interpretation of these difficult texts, it is necessary to study them carefully, taking into account the findings of the modern sciences and, simultaneously, *the main theme* of the texts, namely, God and his plan of salvation. Such an approach shows how the doubts raised against their truth and origin in God can be resolved.[107]

In other words, addressing believers' doubts concerning the truth of Scripture requires making it clear that the essence or main theme (in other words, the guiding intention) of the Scriptures is to reveal God and his plan for our salvation. All other, problematic material within the canon must be viewed in light of this purpose. Closely echoing Benedict's understanding of the divine pedagogy, the PBC goes on to affirm that troublesome passages ultimately make sense only in light of their progression toward Jesus Christ: "The other definitions of God in the biblical writings are oriented toward the Word of God made man in Jesus Christ. This incarnate word becomes the key to their interpretation."[108]

Another crucial section from the PBC's document bears the title "Multiform Truth." Here the commission reminds us that the principle of unity within multiplicity has always been recognized by the Church.[109] Echoing the teaching laid out in Benedict's *Verbum Domini*, it is argued that not all biblical authors convey the same message for the very reason that they lived in completely different epochs and cultural contexts:

The span of time encompassed by the literature of the Bible is without doubt very extensive, since it goes beyond a millennium; it necessarily reveals the legacy of concepts tied to a particular era, of opinions which are the fruit of experience or concerns characteristic of a particular epoch of the People of

---

107. Ibid., xiv (emphasis added).

108. Ibid. Fascinatingly, at this point the commission weighs in emphatically on the question of restricted or unrestricted biblical inerrancy: "It is obvious that these considerations do not resolve all the difficulties, but it is undeniable that *Dei Verbum*, with the expression 'the truth ... for the sake of our salvation' *restricts biblical truth* to divine revelation which concerns God himself and the salvation of the human race." Ibid., 125. It is not my purpose here to weigh in on this debate, but it is noteworthy that a document containing this claim received the *nihil obstat* of the prefect of the Congregation for the Doctrine of the Faith.

109. Ibid., 158.

God.... The duty of the interpreter is to avoid a fundamentalist reading of Scripture so as to situate the various formulations of the sacred text in their historical context, according to the literary genres then in vogue.[110]

The upshot of this principle is that certain Old Testament texts will reflect the culture in which they were written as much as they reflect God's own mind about how we are to go about our daily lives. To be sure, salvation history "does not exist without a historical nucleus," but that does not amount to requiring a "fundamentalist reading" wherein every deed of a biblical patriarch happened precisely as recorded and ought to be emulated today.[111]

But the PBC does not stop there: "This multiform manifestation of divine truth should not be restricted to the literature of the Old Testament." Unity within diversity is a principle applicable also and especially in the case of the Gospels on which the present volume focuses. Thus, what is written in the Gospel according to Luke, for example, "should be respected and supported, even if it does not coincide exactly with what Mark or John say."[112] This extension of multiform truth to the text of the New Testament is an important point that is essential to get right if the Christian is to have any hope of a serious engagement with modern biblical criticism. The reason for this is that historical-critical scholarship is unanimous in recognizing a diversity of voices within the New Testament. A serious Bible student who is also a believer must find a way to acknowledge this diversity while seeing within it an expression of *truth* with an underlying unity that reflects the divine wisdom. Ironically, the agnostic and the fundamentalist concur in rejecting the coexistence of this truth with diversity, but the Catholic Church insists that the two belong together. The question we will need to address in later chapters is *how* the two coexist.

That said, the PBC is quite clear in affirming that this inspired unity within diversity is a first principle that cannot be proven by reason alone. Describing its own purpose, the document states:

In this document, then, the PBC does not intend to demonstrate the fact of the inspiration of the biblical writings, which is a task for fundamental theol-

---

110. Ibid., 164–65.
112. Ibid., 164.

111. Ibid., 124.

ogy. We begin, rather, from the truth of faith according to which the books of Sacred Scripture are inspired by God and communicate his Word; our contribution will be only to clarify their nature, as it appears from the testimony of the writings themselves.[113]

In the conclusion to our volume we will return to this important point on the role of first principles within our exegetical debates. But by way of concluding this summary of the PBC's recent work, I would like to recall just one more point about what the PBC saw as its purpose in drafting the piece:

The brevity of the treatment may not always be satisfactory, but the hermeneutical principles set forth here should prove helpful, as should some points on specific questions…. [W]hat is formulated here is a possible hermeneutical strategy with the intention of provoking further reflection in dialogue with other interpreters of the sacred text.[114]

The same could be said both with regard to the present volume and to *Dark Passages of the Bible* that preceded it. The two texts take up challenging passages from the Old and New Testaments and attempt to explain them in light of the Church's authoritative interpretive principles. But even if there turns out to be much wanting in my argument about a given passage here and there, I am convinced that the vision of Benedict XVI to which I am pointing is something that the Church needs to receive in earnest if we are to have any hope of engaging influential biblical critics like Ehrman inside and outside the academy today.[115]

---

113. Ibid., 3.

114. Ibid., 168.

115. This vision is also pregnant with important ramifications beyond the field of biblical studies: "This polyphony of sacred voices is offered to the Church as a model so that she might acquire, in the present, the same capacity to combine the unity of the message to be transmitted to humanity, with the necessary respect for the multiform varieties of individual experiences, cultures, and gifts bestowed by God." Ibid., 164.

4

THE LIFE, DEATH, AND RESURRECTION OF CHRIST: BART EHRMAN

As we saw at the end of the last chapter, the International Theological Commission and the Pontifical Biblical Commission have been putting into practice key aspects of Benedict's exegetical vision in their recent documents. Recourse to divine pedagogy, the effort to determine authorial assertions, and the recognition of a multiform truth within Scripture are all constitutive features of this endeavor. In the following chapters the import of these principles will become evident as we apply Benedict's hermeneutical proposal in the effort to make sense of some of the most difficult questions concerning the Gospels. The aim will be to provide a compelling alternative approach to the study of Jesus' life that eschews crucial pitfalls endemic to the hermeneutic of suspicion typical of many modern scholars like Ehrman. Confronting the same troublesome biblical data as these thinkers, Benedict's approach is anything but naïve, yet it leads him to draw very different conclusions from those of Ehrman. We will begin here in this chapter by surveying Ehrman's approach; in the next chapter we will examine how Benedict addresses the same sort of issues.

In chapter 1 of this book, I made a few brief notes in the introduction regarding Ehrman's position on the divinity and Resurrection of Jesus. In the present chapter, arguments from a few of his books will be explored in greater depth, so as to show that their gravity beckons more than a superficial apologetic response on the part of the Christian faithful. My aim in this chapter will be achieved if by the end of it the reader feels significantly challenged while also being able to identify certain areas in which Ehrman's approach ought to be challenged.

Misquoting Jesus

In this book Ehrman is concerned with the question of how we got the Bible. In the author's own words, the text's overarching theses are as follows:

- We do not have the originals of any of the books of the New Testament.
- The copies we have were made much later, in most instances many centuries later.
- We have thousands of these copies, in Greek—the language in which of all the New Testament books were originally written.
- All of these copies contain mistakes—accidental slips on the part of the scribes who made them or intentional alterations by scribes wanting to change the text to make it say what they wanted it to mean (or thought that it did mean).
- We do not know how many mistakes there are among our surviving copies, but they appear to number in the hundreds of thousands. It is safe to put the matter in comparative terms: there are more differences in our manuscripts than there are words in the New Testament.
- The vast majority of these mistakes are completely insignificant, showing us nothing more than that scribes in antiquity could spell no better than most people can today.
- But some of the mistakes matter—a lot. Some of them affect the interpretation of a verse, a chapter, or an entire book. Others reveal the kinds of concerns that were affecting scribes, who sometimes altered the text in light of debates and controversies going on in their own surroundings.
- The task of the textual critic is both to figure out what the author of a text actually wrote and to understand why scribes modified the text (to help us understand the context within which scribes were working).
- Despite the fact that scholars have been working diligently at these tasks for three hundred years, there continue to be heated differences of opinion. There are some passages where serious and very smart scholars disagree about what the original text said, and there are some places where we will probably never know what the original text said.[1]

---

1. The bullet points above are Ehrman's own summary of *Misquoting Jesus* as found in its sequel, *Jesus, Interrupted*, 183–84. Ehrman argues further that the Bible, in addition

According to Ehrman, the conservative response to his arguments in *Misquoting Jesus* has generally been to claim that the variants in extant biblical manuscripts have no bearing on what the texts mean or on the theological conclusions one draws from them.

Ehrman argues that just the opposite is the case. Some of the biblical manuscript variants, he says, really matter when it comes to important questions like the following:

Was Jesus an angry man? Was he completely distraught in the face of death? Did he tell his disciples that they could drink poison without being harmed? Did he let an adulteress off the hook with nothing but a mild warning? Is the doctrine of the Trinity explicitly taught in the New Testament? Is Jesus actually called the "unique God" there? Does the New Testament indicate that even the Son of God himself does not know when the end will come? The questions go on and on, and all of them are related to how one resolves difficulties in the manuscript tradition as it has come down to us.[2]

Depending on which manuscript variant one follows, radically divergent answers to each of these questions may be given. Of course, a person reading the Bible in English may be completely unaware of the fact that what he is reading is a translation from a critical edition made by a team of scholars who decided which particular extant manuscript to follow in a given case.[3]

The fact that we have to rely on these very human decisions to ascertain the original words of Jesus leads some people like Ehrman to view the doctrine of inspiration as "irrelevant to the Bible as we have it." Why? We are not actually in possession of the original words of the Gospels which purport to give us Jesus' words. Even if inspiration is true, argues Ehrman, then "the words God reputedly inspired had been changed and, in some cases, lost."[4]

But that is not all. As Ehrman argues, it is not just in the scribal text that we find crucial differences on questions that bear on the

---

to containing mistakes, contains a great deal of what most people today would call lies. For a book-length treatment of this, see his *Forged: Writing in the Name of God : Why the Bible's Authors Are Not Who We Think They Are* (New York: HarperOne, 2011).

2. Ehrman, *Misquoting Jesus*, 208.

3. For a discussion of what the Christian is to make of these differences in manuscript traditions, see my *Dark Passages of the Bible*, 62–68.

4. Ehrman, *Misquoting Jesus*, 211.

foundations of the Christian faith. The original Gospel texts them-selves are "very human" works, a realization which Ehrman reflects upon anecdotally as he is wont to do in his popular books:

> The more I reflected on these matters, the more I began to see that the au-thors of the New Testament were very much like the scribes who would later transmit those authors' writings. The authors too were human beings with needs, beliefs, worldviews, opinions, loves, hates, longings, desires, situations, problems—and surely all these things affected what they wrote ...
>
> And so I began to see that since each of these authors is different, it was not appropriate to think that any one of them meant the same thing as some other author meant—any more than it is fair to say that what I mean in this book must be the same as what some other author writing about textual criti-cism means in his or her book. We might mean different things. How can you tell? Only by reading each of us carefully and seeing what each of us has to say—not by pretending that we are both saying the same thing. We're often saying very different things.[5]

Ehrman laments that most readers do not take seriously the changes made between one Gospel and another. For example, Mark (whom scholars—including Ratzinger—almost universally recognize to be the first Gospel) reports Jesus crying out "My God, my God, why have you forsaken me?" After this, he utters a loud cry and dies. Luke almost certainly had this version of the story available to him, and he modified it significantly by removing Mark's comment that Jesus was highly distraught. In Ehrman's words, "The point is that Luke changed the tradition he inherited. Readers completely misinterpret Luke if they fail to realize this—as happens, for example, when they assume that Mark and Luke are in fact saying the same thing about Jesus."[6] At the end of the day, a person who pretends that the Gospels are all saying the same thing "is not reading the Gospels themselves— he or she is making up a new Gospel consisting of the four in the New Testament, a new Gospel that is not like any of the ones that have come down to us."[7] With this statement a faithful exegete like Bene-dict XVI need not disagree, as we will see in later chapters. However, Benedict and Ehrman certainly do come down on different sides when

5. Ibid., 212.
6. Ibid., 214.
7. Ibid.

it comes to the question of whether the differences between the four different crucifixion accounts touch the substance of the tradition.

However, there are also more substantial criticisms of Ehrman's project, such as the following: there exist important reasons to think that Benedict is right in seeing the four Gospel accounts as substantially the same—and indeed substantially the same as the disciples' pre-Easter memories. Michael Bird, while certainly aware that the Gospels do not contain verbatim transcripts of Jesus' words and deeds, nevertheless writes:

[W]hat Ehrman says about the New Testament manuscripts makes his inquiry about Jesus methodologically impossible. If the New Testament was so heavily corrupted, then how can you use it as your primary source to reconstruct Jesus' life? Well, to be honest, you can't, but for some reason Ehrman is not perturbed by this. Ehrman likes to play the part of the super-skeptic when it suits him, but on other occasions he seems to move seamlessly from his English Bible all the way back to Jesus of Galilee as if none of these critical issues existed.... Approaches like Ehrman's, which begin by casting doubt on the historical value of the Gospels for reconstructing the life of Jesus, but then proceed to formulate a hypothesis about the historical Jesus anyway, are essentially creating a vacuum and then filling it with scholarly fiction.[8]

Dale Allison likewise writes of the Gospels, "Either they tend to preserve pre-Easter memories or they do not. In the former case, we have some possibility of getting somewhere. But in the latter case, our questing for Jesus is probably pointless and we should consider surrendering to ignorance."[9] Bird and Allison together make the case that the quest of skeptics like Ehrman is to a certain extent self-defeating, for such interpreters are asking their audience to accept arguments based on a text (the New Testament) which they themselves do not view as a reliable historical witness. Among many, this skepticism extends to the Gospel of Mark, which is reckoned the earliest Gospel by most scholars. But once we start claiming that the true words of Jesus have been substantially altered already in Mark's Gospel, our project

---

8. Michael Bird, *How God Became Jesus: The Real Origins of Belief in Jesus' Divine Nature—A Response to Bart Ehrman* (Grand Rapids, Mich.: Zondervan 2014), 48–49.

9. Dale Allison, "The Historians' Jesus and the Church," in *Seeking the Identity of Jesus: A Pilgrimage*, ed. Richard B. Hays and Beverly R. Gaventa (Grand Rapids, Mich.: Eerdmans, 2008), 84–85.

has essentially collapsed in on itself. Thus we can say of Ehrman what N. T. Wright says of John Dominic Crossan: "We may say of Crossan, as he says of Mark, that he is such a gifted script-writer that we are lured into imagining that his scheme is actually historical."[10]

Jesus, Interrupted

The sequel to *Misquoting Jesus*, Ehrman's *Jesus, Interrupted*, rehashes many of his earlier arguments while adding a few others that bolster his case. For example, his rejection of C. S. Lewis famous "trilemma" argument was mentioned in the Introduction. The following is Ehrman's own summary of the results from his inquiry in this book:

♦ I came to see that there were flat-out discrepancies among the books of the New Testament. Sometimes these discrepancies could be reconciled if one worked hard enough at it with pious imagination; other times the discrepancies could not, in my judgment, be reconciled, however fanciful the explanation (Jesus dies on different days in Mark and John).

♦ I further came to see that these differences related not just to small details here and there. Sometimes different authors had completely different understandings of important issues: Was Jesus in doubt and despair on the way to the cross (Mark) or calm and in control (Luke)? Did Jesus' death provide an atonement for sin (Mark and Paul) or not (Luke)? Did Jesus perform signs to prove who he was (John) or did he refuse to do so (Matthew)? Must Jesus' followers keep the law if they are to enter the Kingdom (Matthew) or absolutely not (Paul)?

♦ In addition, I came to see that many of the books of the New Testament were not written by the people to whom they are attributed (Matthew and John) or by the people who claimed to be writing them (2 Peter, 1 Timothy). Most of these books appeared to have been written after the apostles themselves were dead; only eight of the twenty-seven books are almost certain to have been written by the people traditionally thought to be their authors.

♦ The Gospels for the most part do not provide disinterested factual information about Jesus, but contain stories that had been in oral circulation for decades before being written down. This makes it very difficult to know what Jesus actually said, did, and experienced. Scholars have devised ways to get around these problems, but the reality is that the Jesus portrayed in the Gospels (for example, the divine being become human in the Gospel of John) represents a later understanding of who Jesus was, not a historical account of who he really was.

10. N. T. Wright, *Jesus and the Victory of God*, 65.

◆ There were lots of other Gospels available to the early Christians, as well as epistles, Acts, and apocalypses. Many of these claimed to be written by apostles, and on the surface such claims are no more or less plausible than the claims of the books that eventually came to make up the New Testament. This raises the question of who made the decisions about which books to include, and of what grounds they had for making the decisions. Is it possible that nonapostolic books were let into the canon by church leaders who simply didn't know any better? Is it possible that books that should have been included were left out?

◆ The creation of the Christian canon was not the only invention of the early Church. A whole range of theological perspectives came into existence, not during the life of Jesus or even through the teachings of his original apostles but later, as the Christian church grew and came to be transformed into a new religion rather than a sect of Judaism. These include some of the most important Christian doctrines, such as that of a suffering Messiah, the divinity of Christ, the Trinity, and the existence of heaven and hell.[11]

For the most part, Ehrman's claims above are not controversial among biblical scholars. However, important differences will emerge in the next chapter when we contrast how he and Benedict handle the same thorny data.

In the meantime, however, it should be noted that strong arguments have been put forth against the commonplace presupposition that most of the New Testament books were written after the apostles were dead. Says Richard Bauckham:

The assumption that Jesus traditions circulated anonymously in the early church ... was propagated by the form critics as a corollary of their use of the model of folklore, which is passed down anonymously by communities. The Gospels, they thought, were folk literature, similarly anonymous.[12]

Against Ehrman, Bauckham recalls that if one looks at the actual evidence available for the gospel titles, our earliest extant manuscripts reveal that the Gospels were never known by other names and that

---

11. Ehrman, *Jesus, Interrupted*, 273–75.

12. Bauckham, *Jesus and the Eyewitnesses: The Gospels as Eyewitness Testimony* (Grand Rapids, Mich.: Eerdmans, 2006), 300. In like manner, Martin Hengel helpfully observes that, in the ancient world, "[a]nonymous works were relatively rare and must have been given a title in the libraries.... Works without titles easily got double or multiple titles when names were given to them in different libraries." Hengel, *The Four Gospels and the One Gospel of Jesus Christ* (Harrisburg, Pa.: Trinity Press, 2000), 48.

their form was always the same ("Gospel according to" Matthew, Mark, Luke, or John). Bauckham's balanced takeaway:

> Of course, this does not guarantee that the author was named Luke; the attribution to Luke could be later and erroneous. But we are not, at this point, concerned with establishing the real authorship of each Gospel, only with refuting the idea that the Gospels were presented and received as anonymous works whose contents would have been taken as coming from the community rather than from known authors.[13]

We turn next to Ehrman's chapter on orthodoxy and heresy in the early Church. In this important chapter, he characterizes the view of Eusebius that eventually became known as orthodoxy:

> Eusebius maintained that the views he and like-minded Christian leaders of the fourth century held were not only right (orthodox) but also that they were the same views Jesus and his apostles had promoted from day one.... Heresies, then, were seen to be offshoots of orthodoxy that came along as the demons tried to work their nefarious purposes in the church and pervert the truth. Heresy was always secondary (coming after orthodoxy), derivative (altering the views of orthodoxy), and perverted.[14]

This was the standard view of most scholars until Walter Bauer took issue with Eusebius in his 1934 *Orthodoxy and Heresy in Earliest Christianity*. Bauer reconceptualized what had happened in the struggle for theological dominance in the early Church. Ehrman gives an account of what Bauer found through his studies of the earliest evidence for Christianity in a range of geographical regions:

> In many places of early Christianity, forms of Christian belief that were later labeled heretical were the original form of Christianity, and in some parts of the church so-called heretics outnumbered those who agreed with the orthodox form of the faith. In some places Marcionite Christianity was dominant; in other places, one or another of the Gnostic systems prevailed. Moreover, a number of Christian groups saw no sharp divisions between what would later be called heresy and what would be called orthodoxy. The clear theological distinctions of Eusebius's day were not original to the faith, but were created later when the battle lines were drawn up. Some people who were later considered heretics would have been seen, and were seen, as completely orthodox in their own day. The way Bauer saw it, the church of the second and third

---

13. Bauckham, *Jesus and the Eyewitnesses*, 301.
14. Ehrman, *Jesus, Interrupted*, 213.

centuries was not made up of one massive and dominant movement known as orthodoxy, with heretical groups at the fringes. Early on there were all sorts of groups with all sorts of views in lots of different places. Of course, all of these groups believed that their views were right, that their beliefs were orthodox. But in the struggle to win converts, only one group eventually won out; this was the group that was particularly well represented in the city of Rome.[15]

Today the majority opinion among critical scholars is that Bauer was wrong in many of his details and that he overplayed his hand. Ehrman, though, believes that Bauer's portrayal of the early Christian centuries remains correct in its core assertions:

There were lots of early Christian groups. They all claimed to be right. They all had books to back up their claims, books allegedly written by the apostles and therefore representing the views of Jesus and his first disciples. The group that won out did not represent the teachings of Jesus or of his apostles.[16]

I do not think that the emeritus pontiff would disagree with all of these claims. However, the difference is that a Catholic like Benedict holds by faith that the group that "won out" (not Benedict's wording, obviously) was indeed the group that faithfully preserved Jesus' teaching. Bauer and Ehrman, on the other hand, operate on an unprovable first principle, namely that the struggle for orthodoxy in the early Christian centuries was primarily a power play rather than the fruit of divine providence working through the vicissitudes of history.

Ehrman's chapter "Who Invented Christianity?" is an important read for the debate concerning whether Christianity is true and, if so, how one would be able to prove it. The author is right here to argue that Christianity's claim to being divinely inspired is a theological view

15. Ibid., 214.
16. Ibid., 215. On the subject of winners and losers, it is worth remembering that some Christian traditions held to a canon different from the one that came to be accepted as orthodox: "[H]istorically there have always been some churches in some countries (Syria, Armenia, Ethiopia) that have slightly different canons of Scripture from the one we have. Even the twenty-seven book canon with which all of us are familiar did not ever get ratified by a church council of any kind—until the anti-Reformation Catholic Council of Trent in the sixteenth century, which also ratified the Old Testament Apocrypha, in response to the widespread Protestant rejection of these books as noncanonical. In a strange way, the canon, far from being definitively decided upon at some point of time, emerged without anyone taking a vote." Ibid., 190.

that cannot be evaluated on the basis of history alone.[17] It is not as if one can comb through the Old Testament, match up all the prophecies to their fulfillment in Christ, and conclude that he is therefore the long-awaited Messiah. Indeed, Jews living at the time of Christ were not at all expecting the *suffering* savior that Christians claimed Jesus to be. Ehrman forcefully drives home this point:

> When I try to explain to my students how absurd the claim sounded to most Jews, I often resort to an analogy. The gut reaction that many Jews had to the claim that Jesus was the Messiah is comparable to what your reaction would be if I insisted in all earnestness that the Branch Davidian leader David Koresh, who was killed by the FBI at Waco, is the Lord of the universe. David Koresh? Yes, he is the savior of the world and the Lord of all! Oh, sure—what are you, crazy? (I get in trouble for making this analogy every semester; at least one student will say on his or her course evaluation, "I can't believe that Ehrman thinks David Koresh is the Lord of the universe!")[18]

In the next chapter we will address this criticism in light of what Benedict has to say on the subject of Israel's messianic expectations. As ever, the two authors make similar observations but draw radically different conclusions from them.

Ehrman's concluding chapter, "Is Faith Possible?" continues this thread. As with the truth of Christianity in general, so the Resurrection of Christ "was not a historical event that could be proved or disproved, since historians are not able, by the nature of their craft, to demonstrate the occurrence of a miracle. It was a bold mythical statement about God and the world."[19] According to Ehrman, the point of the Resurrection "myth" was to show that this world is not the whole show, that the horrible events of history are not God's last word. Speaking again anecdotally, he recounts:

> I came to think of the Christian message about God, Christ, and the salvation he brings as a kind of religious "myth," or group of myths—a set of stories, views, and perspectives that are both unproven and unprovable, but also undisprovable—that could, and should, inform and guide my life and thinking.[20]

Unlike various other agnostics and atheists, Ehrman does not reject Christianity *in toto*, in the sense of finding its very existence repug-

17. Ibid., 226.
19. Ibid., 276.
18. Ibid., 235.
20. Ibid., 275.

nant. Yet, while continuing to see beauty and inspirations in its moral teachings, he has come to view salvation, the concepts of heaven and hell, and even God himself also as myths. Still, the author claims that it was none of this that made him an agnostic. It was the problem of evil that led him down this path, a problem we will touch upon at the end of this book.

Another major issue Ehrman raises here concerns how to translate the Bible's ancient morality into today's world. In his view, pretty much all of the Bible's norms need to be revised: involved here are the Bible's teachings "about women, about same-sex relations, about extra-marital sex, about capital punishment, about war, about wealth, about slavery, about disease, about ... well, about everything."[21] Not surprisingly, the issue of homosexuality so prominent in public discourse today looms large for Ehrman, who maintains that we are no longer bound by the ancient assumptions undergirding the Church's traditional view:

In thinking about which parts of the Bible have something to say in the modern context, it is important to recall the historical view that the biblical authors were all living in a different world from ours and reflected the assumptions and beliefs of people in their world.... As a result, the very assumptions that lie behind the apostle Paul's denigration of same-sex relations are very different from the assumptions that people in the modern world have about themselves as sexual beings. You cannot very well take Paul's instructions on same-sex relations, remove them from the assumptions that Paul had about sex and gender, and transplant them onto a different set of assumptions.[22]

To be sure, Ehrman is right that assessing the contemporary relevance of the Bible's moral teachings requires us to reflect upon their original context and whether the same norms ought to be reproduced identically today. However, one operating within the classical natural law tradition (and/or the Catholic magisterial tradition) will take issue with the insinuation that Paul's "denigration" of same-sex intercourse is invalid because his assumptions "are very different from the assumptions that people in the modern world have about themselves as sexual beings."[23]

21. Ibid., 281. 22. Ibid., 280.
23. Ibid.

I have heard it argued many times that, given that we no longer execute people for the act of sodomy as prescribed in the Bible (Lv 20:13), then there remains no good argument against sodomy itself. Ehrman makes precisely this sort of argument when he says:

> The same books that condemn same-sex relations, for example, also require people to stone their children to death if they are disobedient, to execute anyone who does any work on Saturday or who eats pork chops, and to condemn anyone who wears a shirt made of two kinds of fabric.[24]

One who maintains the Catholic position that same-sex attraction is intrinsically disordered while denouncing slavery or polygamy is thus accused of picking and choosing from the Bible what he wishes to believe. On this score Ehrman writes, "Some people may think that it is a dangerous attitude to take toward the Bible, to pick and choose what you want to accept and throw everything else out. My view is that everyone already picks and chooses what they want to accept in the Bible."[25]

While Ehrman is on to something here, I believe that Catholicism has a very compelling counterargument to Ehrman's claim that Christianity's moral norms are the haphazard result of picking and choosing. For instance, Benedict XVI certainly recognizes that Christians no longer follow many of the Old Testament prescriptions, but according to Catholicism this is not due to a haphazard process based on personal preferences. Jesus himself said, "Think not that I have come to abolish the law and the prophets. I have come not to abolish them but to fulfil them" (Mt 5:17). In his messianic fulfillment of the law, certain time-bound elements of the tradition were open to change (casuistic law), whereas the fundamental metanorms (apodictic law) of the Old Testament have remained in place. This is what Catholics take to be the meaning of Jesus' saying, "For truly, I say to you, till heaven and earth pass away, not an iota, not a dot, will pass from the law until all is accomplished" (Mt 5:18).[26] Now Ehrman still may well call this

24. Bart Ehrman, *God's Problem: How the Bible Fails to Answer Our Most Important Question—Why We Suffer* (New York: HarperOne, 2008), 17.

25. Ehrman, *Jesus, Interrupted*, 281.

26. See Benedict's discussion of this distinction in *Jesus of Nazareth: From the Baptism in the Jordan to the Transfiguration*, 123–25.

an artificial distinction, but it is far from the haphazard process he describes taking place within the evangelical community to which he formerly belonged.

How Jesus Became God

Of the three Ehrman texts discussed in this chapter, *How Jesus Became God* bears most directly upon my concern in this book, as it sets its sights squarely on the question of Jesus' divinity and Resurrection.

Regarding Jesus' divinity, Ehrman insists that early Christians were not in agreement among themselves as to the meaning behind their claim "Jesus is God." He says that the Gospel of Mark understands Jesus as a human who came to be made divine (exaltation or adoptionist Christology), whereas the Gospel of John understands him as a divine being who became human (incarnation Christology).[27] While Ehrman is convicted that Jesus existed as a historical person, for him Jesus is nevertheless a "legend," in that our earliest source does not clearly have him being divine in the way that Christians subsequently came to believe.[28]

As I discussed in the introduction, Ehrman's position concerning the divinity of Christ can be quickly grasped from his evaluation of C. S. Lewis's famous "trilemma" argument in *Jesus Interrupted*. Accord-

27. Ehrman, *How Jesus Became God*, 230–32.

28. John Dominic Crossan also strongly affirms the existence of Jesus, although he believes that there is considerable distance between the historical Jesus and what most people assume about him from their reading of the Gospels. Describing the four Gospels as four very different mega-parables about Jesus, Crossan writes, "That is my second, internal, and far more definitive reason for accepting Jesus as a historical figure—no matter how creatively he has been portrayed in parable in small ways and large throughout the four gospel versions. Here is the point: If you are inventing a nonhistorical figure, why invent one you cannot live with, but must steadily and terminally change into its opposite? In other words, I find it much more likely that Jesus was an actual historical figure whose radical insistence on nonviolent distributive justice was both accepted and negated by the tradition it engendered. I conclude that Jesus was an actual, factual, historical figure and not a metaphorical, symbolic, or parabolic invention by his first-century Jewish contemporaries." While a traditionally minded exegete like Benedict will rightly question Crossan's reduction of the Gospel narratives to parables about Jesus, there is something to Crossan's point that the Jesus of the Gospels is not the comfortable Jesus we would likely invent for ourselves. Crossan, *The Power of Parable: How Fiction by Jesus Became Fiction about Jesus* (New York: HarperOne, 2013), 251.

ing to Lewis, Jesus' lordship can be shown by reducing to the absurd the possibility that he was either a liar or a lunatic. But Ehrman reveals a problem with Lewis's logic:

> I had come to see that the very premise of Lewis's argument was flawed. The argument based on Jesus as liar, lunatic, or Lord was predicated on the assumption that Jesus had called himself God.... I had come to realize that none of our earliest traditions indicates that Jesus said any such thing about himself ... not three options but four: liar, lunatic, Lord, or legend.[29]

How Jesus Became God endeavors to back up this conclusion that Jesus' divinity is a matter of legend. Ehrman's is not, on its face, an unreasonable position, given the presence of many similar figures in the ancient world: "Even though Jesus may be the only miracle-working Son of God that people know about today, there were lots of people like this in the ancient world."[30]

Divine Humans in the Ancient Mediterranean and in Judaism

In the first chapter of *How Jesus Became God*, Ehrman treats figures in ancient Greece and Rome who were believed to be divine, from the Caesars to the cynic Peregrinus and the Pythagorean philosopher Apollonius.[31] Some divine humans were such because they had been born from the union of a god and a mortal, while some became divine by adoption. Ehrman writes of the moment he realized the deep connection between the emperor cult and the Christian worship of Jesus:

> And it hit me: the time when Christianity arose, with its exalted claims about Jesus, was the same time when the emperor cult had started to move into full swing, with its exalted claims about the emperor. Christians were calling Jesus God directly on the heels of the Romans calling the emperor God. Could this be a historical accident? How could it be an accident? These were not simply parallel developments. This was a competition. Who was the *real* god-

---

29. Ehrman, *How Jesus Became God*, 141.

30. Ibid., 17.

31. Ibid., 25ff. John Dominic Crossan summarizes Jesus' person and message as follows: "The historical Jesus was a peasant Jewish Cynic whose strategy was a combination of free healing and common eating, religious and economic egalitarianism." *Jesus: A Revolutionary Biography* (San Francisco: HarperSanFrancisco, 1994), 198. On the "brokerless kingdom of God," see also Crossan's *The Historical Jesus: The Life of a Mediterranean Jewish Peasant* (San Francisco: HarperSanFrancisco, 1991), 341, 422.

man? The emperor or Jesus? I realized at that moment that the Christians were not elevating Jesus to a level of divinity in a vacuum.[32]

Seeing the parallels between Christian claims about Jesus and the Romans' view of their emperor leads Ehrman and Crossan to conclude that the Christian view was modeled on the latter.[33] Benedict, on the other hand, sees the same evidence and draws a very different conclusion. For him, Christians were indeed calling Jesus God on the heels of the Romans doing the same. But it is not as if the disciples looked at Caesar's divine claims and from there reasoned to Christ's divinity. Rather, a Christian thinks that the disciples already believed Jesus to be divine in some way beforehand, and that the language of Roman emperors was applied to Jesus in order to underscore that this son of God and savior had brought the only Gospel of true peace and the truly everlasting kingdom.[34]

Following this broad discussion of divine humans in the ancient Mediterranean, Ehrman's next chapter hones in on the presence of divine humans in ancient Judaism. He begins by arguing that Judaism was not a uniformly monotheistic religion in Jesus' day. Rather, it still exhibited (at the very least) traces of its earlier henotheism, wherein one God was worshiped while the existence of other, lower-level divinities was not denied.[35] There thus was belief in a spectrum of divinity in ancient Judaism: divine beings who temporarily become human; humans who become angels; divine beings who beget semi-divine beings (Gn 6; Nm 13:3); nonhuman divine figures such the Son of Man, Wisdom, and the Logos; and the king of Israel, who became divine by adoption.[36] Most important for our purposes is the last of these: "Just as within pagan circles the emperor was thought to be both the son of god and, in some sense, himself god, so too in ancient Judaism the king of Israel was considered both Son of God and—astonishingly enough—even God."[37]

32. Ehrman, How Jesus Became God, 49.
33. For Crossan's view, see The Power of Parable, ch. 7.
34. Benedict XVI, Jesus of Nazareth: Holy Week, 54ff.
35. Ehrman, How Jesus Became God, 53. On Israel's henotheism, see my Dark Passages of the Bible, 166ff.
36. Ehrman, How Jesus Became God, 64ff.
37. Ibid., 76.

We know from the promise of 2 Sm 7:12–14 that the son of David would be chosen by God himself and adopted as his own son: "I will raise up your offspring after you, who shall come forth from your body, and I will establish his kingdom. He shall build a house for my name; and I will establish the throne of his kingdom forever. I will be a father to him, and he shall be a son to me." This may not sound very scandalous, but Ehrman's claim gains a lot more traction when one takes a closer look at other texts within the Old Testament on the subject of the king's divine adoption. Psalm 110:1 contains the famous words: "The LORD says to my Lord, 'Sit at my right hand until I make your enemies your footstool.'" What are we to make of this? Who is the "Lord"? Ehrman responds:

What is striking here is that YHWH is speaking to "my Lord" and telling him to "sit at my right hand." Any being enthroned with God is sharing the glory, status, and honor due to God himself. There is not a question of identity or absolute parity here—the king, sitting at God's right hand—is not God Almighty himself. That is clear from what is said next: God will conquer the king's enemies for him and put them under his feet. But he is doing so for one whom he has exalted up to the level of his own throne. The king is being portrayed as a divine being who lives in the presence of God, above all other creatures.[38]

Even more stark in this regard is Psalm 45:6–7. Here the king is addressed in startling terms, as a God: "Your throne, O God, endures forever and ever. Your royal scepter is a scepter of equity; You love righteousness and hate wickedness. Therefore God, your God, has anointed you With the oil of gladness beyond your companions." Ehrman comments:

It is clear that the person addressed as "O God" (Elohim) is not God Almighty but the king, because of what is said later: God Almighty is the king's own God and has "anointed" him with oil—the standard act of the king's coronation ceremony in ancient Israel. And so God has both anointed and exalted the king above all others, even to a level of deity. The king is in some sense God. Not equal with God Almighty, obviously (since the differentiation is made clearly, even here), but God nonetheless.[39]

---

38. Ibid., 78.
39. Ibid., 79.

Finally, Ehrman calls attention to an even more astonishing example, wherein a new king has been given to the people. Christians know this passage very well:

> For a child has been born for us,
> A son given to us;
> Authority rests upon his shoulders;
> And he is named
> Wonderful Counselor, Mighty God [El],
> Everlasting Father, Prince of Peace.
> His authority shall grow continually,
> And there shall be endless peace
> For the throne of David and his kingdom. (Is 9:6–7)

In its original Jewish context, Ehrman notes, the text "appears to be referring not merely to the birth of the king, but to the birth of the king as the son of God—in other words, it is about his coronation. At this coronation, a 'child' has been given to the people —that is, the king has been made the 'son of God.'"[40] This anointed king is clearly not Yahweh himself, yet the epithets bestowed upon him are astounding.

The above considerations are pivotal because they give us an indication of what the earliest Christians may have been thinking when they professed Jesus to be the Messiah, the King of Israel, the Son of God. As Jews, they "believed that divinities could become human and humans could become divine."[41] Now according to Ehrman, if we look at the earliest evidence from the Gospel of Mark, Jesus was not considered to be God in any sense at all. Indeed, he relates:

One of the enduring findings of modern scholarship on the New Testament and early Christianity over the past two centuries is that the followers of Jesus, during his life, understood him to be human through and through, not God. People saw Jesus as a teacher, a rabbi, and even a prophet. Some people thought of him as the (very human) messiah.... As an adult—or possibly even as a child—he became convinced, like many other Jews of his time, that he was living near the end of the age, that God was soon to intervene in history to overthrow the forces of evil and to bring in a good kingdom here on earth. Jesus felt called to proclaim this message of the coming apocalypse, and he spent his entire public ministry doing so.[42]

40. Ibid.   41. Ibid., 46.
42. Ibid. On the expectation that the eschatological kingdom would come about on

Ehrman suggests that soon, perhaps even during his own lifetime, Jesus came to be thought of as divine in the adoptionist sense like the one seen above, wherein he was not equated with God Almighty in an absolute sense. In other words, before Jesus became God in the fourth-century sense, "he had been seen as God before that, by people who did not have this fourth-century understanding of the relationship of the human and divine realms."[43] The point Ehrman wishes to stress here is that the Nicene understanding of Jesus was a "development" with respect to what we find in the earliest strata of Christian belief. Again, I do not think that an orthodox Christian need disagree here, at least not entirely. Taking Bl. John Henry Newman as our guide, the Catholic not only can but should admit the presence of doctrinal development regarding Christology in the early Church. But the difference between Newman and Ehrman is that Newman sees this dynamic as the working of divine providence guiding the Church to a fuller understanding of Christ, whereas skeptics naturally approach the phenomenon in terms of a purely human power struggle.

Before leaving the topic of alleged sources for Jesus' identity in

---

this earth, see Allison, *The Historical Christ and the Theological Jesus*, 95: "[Jesus] envisioned, as did many in his time and place, the advent, after suffering and persecution, of a great judgment, and after that a supernatural utopia, the kingdom of God, inhabited by the dead come back to life, to enjoy a world forever rid of evil and wholly ruled by God. Further, he thought that the night was far gone, the day at hand."

43. Ehrman, *How Jesus Became God*, 44. For a different approach that also contrasts later orthodox Christology with that of the New Testament, Dale Allison writes, "But when one looks at how its advocates have, from ancient times, interpreted certain New Testament texts, one must object, at least if one has been trained to think historically. Again and again Jesus' divinity has all but liquidated his humanity, making him a historically impossible figure." Allison, *The Historical Christ and the Theological Jesus*, 82. Allison continues (84–85): "Our theological tradition is full of tendentious, ahistorical readings of Gospel texts, readings that have served orthodox christological agendas instead of historical truth.... It is impossible, after immersing oneself in the quest for the historical Jesus, with its obligation to set the traditions about Jesus within their first-century contexts, to take any of this seriously as history—and Christians belonging to the more conservative churches should find this disturbing. For the theologians and exegetes I have quoted are not from the margins of ecclesiastical history; they are rather, every one of them, important figures, even ecclesiastical authorities.... What then does it mean that, until relatively recent times, our dominant theologians have put Jesus into a christological straightjacket, that they have, despite their protests otherwise, been docetists of a sort, for whom Jesus' humanity was above all a philosophical problem?"

ancient Rome and Judaism, it is worth stopping to ponder whether Ehrman might have his argument entirely backwards. Agreeing with Richard Bauckham, N. T. Wright contends:

[S]cholars have been looking in the wrong place. The question has been put in the form, Did Judaism have any figures—angels, mediators, messiahs, whatever—who were regarded in an "exalted" fashion prior to the first century, so that there were Jewish categories available when someone came along whose followers wanted to find "exalted" language to use of him? ...

But to raise the question in this way is, I believe, to start at the wrong end. If the phenomenon to be explained is the fact that from extremely early on the followers of Jesus used language for him (and engaged in practices, such as worship, in which he was invoked) which might previously have been thought appropriate only for Israel's God, why should we not begin, not with 'exalted figures' who might as it were be assimilated into the one God, but with the One God himself? Did Judaism have any beliefs, stories, ideas about God himself upon which they might have drawn to say what they now wanted to say about Jesus? The answer is: yes, they did.[44]

But Wright does not stop here. He proposes to build on Bauckham's understanding of "eschatological monotheism":

Central to second-Temple monotheism was the belief ... that Israel's God, having abandoned Jerusalem and the Temple at the time of the Babylonian exile, would one day return. He would return in person. He would return in glory. He would return to judge and save. He would return to bring about the new exodus, overthrowing the enemies that had enslaved his people. He would return to establish his glorious, tabernacling presence in their midst. He would return to rule over the whole world. He would come back to be king. This act, still in the future from the perspective of the pre-Christian Jews, was a vital part of what they believed about "divine identity." And this is the part that best explains not only Paul's view of Jesus but also that of the entire early church. The long-awaited return of YHWH to Zion is, I suggest, the hidden clue to the origin of christology.[45]

44. N. T. Wright, *Paul and the Faithfulness of God* (Minneapolis: Fortress Press, 1992), 653.

45. Ibid., 654. Wright continues, "Whereas in the modern period people have come to the New Testament with the question of Jesus' 'divinity' as one of the uppermost worries in their mind, and have struggled to think of how a human being could come to be thought of as 'divine', for Jesus' first followers the question will have posed itself the other way round. It was not a matter of them pondering this or that human, angelic, perhaps

Did Jesus Think He Was God?

The next chapter of Ehrman's book asks the fascinating follow-up question, "Did Jesus think he was God?" It is difficult to answer this question, the author argues, because our ancient sources "are not as ancient as we would like."[46] The first Christian author was Paul, whose letters date to twenty or thirty years after Jesus' life here on earth. The problem with Paul is that he did not know Jesus personally and does not tell us much about Jesus' teachings or activities. Our next earliest sources for the historical Jesus, then, are the Gospels of the New Testament. Writes Ehrman:

As it turns out, these are our best sources. They are best not because they happen to be in the New Testament, but because they are also the earliest narratives of Jesus's life to survive. But even though they are the best sources available to us, they really are not as good as we might hope.[47]

On the one hand, this is good news for the Christian believer. Even by an agnostic scholar's standards, the canonical Gospels give us a better glimpse into the life of Jesus than later apocryphal texts.[48] However, for Ehrman the problem with the Gospels is that they are not written by eyewitnesses.[49] Who, then, wrote them?

---

quasi-divine figure, and then transferring such categories to Jesus in such a way as to move him up (so to speak) to the level of the one God. It was a matter of them pondering the promises of the one God whose identity, as Bauckham has rightly stressed, was made clear in the scriptures, and wondering what it would look like when he returned to Zion, when he came back to judge the world and rescue his people, when he did again what he had done at the exodus." Ibid. On the further suggestion that Jesus saw himself embodying YHWH's "wisdom" having returned to his people, see ibid., 670ff.

46. Ehrman, How Jesus Became God, 89.

47. Ibid., 90.

48. For an excellent argument in favor of the canonical Gospels' priority over the Gospel of Thomas, see Mark Goodacre, Thomas and the Gospels: The Case for Thomas's Familiarity with the Synoptics (Grand Rapids, Mich.: Eerdmans, 2012).

49. Says Ehrman: "There are good reasons for thinking that none of these attributions is right. For one thing, the followers of Jesus, as we learn from the New Testament itself, were uneducated lower-class Aramaic-speaking Jews from Palestine. These books are not written by people like that. Their authors were highly educated, Greek-speaking Christians of a later generation. They probably wrote after Jesus's disciples had all, or almost all, died. They were writing in different parts of the world, in a different language, and at a later time. There's not much mystery about why later Christians would want to claim that the authors were in fact companions of Jesus, or at least connected with

Just the apostles? It can't have been just the apostles. Just the people whom the apostles authorized? No way. Just people who checked their facts to make sure they didn't change any of the stories but only recounted events that really happened and as they happened? How could they do that? The stories were being told by word of mouth, year after year, decade after decade, among lots of people in different parts of the world, in different languages, and there was no way to control what one person said to the next about Jesus's words and deeds. Everyone knows what happens to stories that circulate this way. Details get changed, episodes get invented, events get exaggerated, impressive accounts get made even more impressive, and so on.[50]

At this juncture Ehrman takes on the claim of those who assert that ancient oral cultures were careful to make certain that their traditions were not changed significantly:

This turns out to be a modern myth, however. Anthropologists who have studied oral cultures show that just the opposite is the case. Only literary cultures have a concern for exact replication of the facts "as they really are." And this is because in literary cultures, it is possible to check the sources to see whether someone has changed a story. In oral cultures, it is widely expected that stories will indeed change—they change anytime a storyteller is telling a story in a new context.[51]

Ehrman contends that our canonical Gospels are no exception to this rule, and that historical criticism confirms it:

Scholars for three hundred years and more have studied them in minute detail, and one of the assured results of this intensive investigation is the certainty that the Gospels have numerous discrepancies, contradictions, and historical problems. Why would that be? It would be better to ask, "How could that not be?" Of course, the Gospels contain nonhistorical information and stories that have been modified and exaggerated and embellished. These books do not contain the words of someone who was sitting at Jesus's feet taking notes.[52]

apostles: that claim provided much needed authority for these accounts for people wanting to know what Jesus was really like." Ehrman, *How Jesus Became God*, 90.

50. Ibid., 92.
51. Ibid., 93.
52. Ibid., 92. While I do not disagree substantially with Ehrman on this point, Dale Allison's criticism of historical criticism from within gives us reason to be "allergic" to any "assured critical result," three words which, as Allison observes, "often function as a simplification for novices and as an excuse for scholars to think less." Allison, *The Historical Christ and the Theological Jesus*, 10–11. As Luke Timothy Johnson has it,

So in Ehrman's opinion, we do not have access to transcripts of what the historical Jesus said or thought. In this he does not differ greatly from Benedict, who also recognizes that the Gospels mediate the words of Jesus through the literary artistry of human authors. The difference, of course, is that Benedict holds it as a first principle that these authors were inspired by the Holy Spirit. Thus, in contrast with Ehrman, he will conclude that the Gospels really do present us with the essential figure of Jesus, even if it is not precisely the same portrait many Christians imagine we have.

Nevertheless, Ehrman does think that we can take a good stab at what Jesus might have said by situating him within his first-century Jewish apocalyptic milieu. He assigns four characteristics to this worldview: dualism (the forces of good engaged in battle with the forces of evil, with the latter ruling the present age and the former the future); pessimism (things are bad in this age and only going to get worse until the end); judgment (when things get as bad as they possibly can, God will intervene to judge not only the living but also the dead); and imminence (all this is going to happen within the current generation).[53] Those who adhered to this apocalyptic perspective were expecting God to act soon and to act definitively. In contrast with early Christian claims about Jesus, Ehrman writes:

[A]s far as we can tell, Jesus did nothing during his life to make anyone think that he was this anointed one. That is to say, he did not come on the clouds of heaven to judge the living and the dead; he was not a priest; and he never raised an army and drove the Romans out of the promised land to set up Israel as a sovereign state ...

"History is a limited mode of human knowing. Historical analysis can yield real knowledge about earliest Christianity and the figure of Jesus. But there are intractable limits to this knowledge.... The New Testament writings yield some historical information, but this is not what they do best." Johnson, *The Real Jesus*, 167. Johnson's is clearly a much more balanced approach in comparison with what we find in some of history's great biblical scholars, for example Rudolf Bultmann: "I do indeed think that we can know almost nothing concerning the life and personality of Jesus, since the early Christian sources show no interest in either, are moreover fragmentary and often legendary; and other sources about Jesus do not exist." Bultmann, *Jesus and the Word* (New York: Scribner's, 1958), 8.

53. Ehrman, *How Jesus Became God*, 99ff.

Ancient Jews had no expectation—zero expectation—that the future messiah would die and rise from the dead. That was not what the messiah was supposed to do. Whatever specific idea any Jew had about the messiah (as cosmic judge, mighty priest, powerful warrior), what they all thought was that he would be a figure of grandeur and power who would be a mighty ruler of Israel.... Jesus, in short, was just the opposite of what Jews expected a messiah to be.[54]

According to Ehrman, arguing that Jesus fulfilled passages like Isaiah 53 and Psalm 22 would have had little to no impact upon a Jewish apocalypticist of the day for one simple reason: these texts were not thought of as messianic prophecies.

How, then, do we account for the earliest Christians proclaiming that Jesus was the messiah? Says Ehrman:

The only plausible explanation is that they called Jesus this after his death because they were calling him this before his death.... Jesus's followers must have considered him to be the messiah in some sense before his death, because nothing about his death or resurrection would have made them come up with the idea afterward. The messiah was not supposed to die or rise again.[55]

John Dominic Crossan writes in a similar vein:

What happened historically is that those who believed in Jesus before his execution *continued* to do so afterward. Easter is not about the start of a new faith but about the continuation of an old one. That is the only miracle and the only mystery, and it is more than enough of both.[56]

We glimpse here quite clearly the philosophical underpinning of Crossan's approach to the Gospels. For him as for Ehrman, the disciples believed in Jesus (whatever precisely the content of that belief might have consisted in) even before his crucifixion. The "only miracle" is that they continued to do so afterwards. Indeed, it is dumbfounding to consider what possibly could have compelled them to continue professing their faith in this crucified rabbi. If one does not believe in the miracle of Jesus' Resurrection, then the Easter faith of the disciples is indeed a "miracle."

Jesus' Messianic Self-Understanding

So Ehrman and Crossan are willing to grant that Jesus claimed the title of messiah for himself, and that the disciples had at least some sort of belief in him during his lifetime. What, then, was Jesus' messianic self-understanding? Ehrman suggests:

[A]s an apocalypticist, Jesus did not think that the future kingdom was going to be won by a political struggle or a military engagement per se. It was going to be brought by the Son of Man, who came in judgment against everyone and everything opposed to God. Then the kingdom would arrive. And I think Jesus believed he himself would be the king in that kingdom.[57]

It may surprise some to learn that, while Ehrman thinks that Jesus viewed himself as the king in the messianic kingdom, Ehrman thinks he did *not* consider himself the Son of Man.

To be sure, Ehrman admits that there are many places in the Gospels where Jesus identifies himself as the Son of Man, but do these texts stand up in a historical-critical analysis? The criterion of dissimilarity is invoked by Ehrman at this point. The gist of this evaluative principle is that a Jesus tradition that differs from what the early Christians would have wanted to say about him is probably historically accurate. So does Jesus' self-identification with the Son of Man pass muster? Ehrman responds: "Obviously not: if you think Jesus is the cosmic judge, you would have no difficulty coming up with sayings in which Jesus is identified as the Son of Man."[58] In contrast, Ehrman argues that the earliest Gospel traditions point to someone other than Jesus being the Son of Man, even though Christians naturally assume that Jesus is talking about himself in these cases. For example, in Mark 8:38 Jesus says, "For whoever is ashamed of me and of my words in this adulterous and sinful generation, of him will the Son of man also be ashamed, when he comes in the glory of his Father with the holy angels." But if Ehrman is right, it is not a matter of Jesus being ashamed of one who has been ashamed of him:

---

57. Ehrman, *How Jesus Became God*, 118.
58. Ibid., 106.

Instead, it says that if anyone is ashamed of Jesus, of that person the Son of Man will be ashamed when *he* comes from heaven. Nothing in this saying makes you think that Jesus is talking about himself. A reader who thinks Jesus is talking about himself as the Son of Man has brought that understanding to the text, not taken it from the text.[59]

This saying also passes the historical-critical method's criterion of embarrassment: Ehrman therefore concludes that it was probably not made up by the early Christian community—which would have been inclined to identify Jesus with the Son of Man. Against Ehrman, however, it should be observed that the earliest Gospel contains a number of texts that both identify the "Son of man" with Jesus and stand up well under historical-critical analysis (for example, Mk 10:33, 45; 14:41, where the Son of man has come to serve and to give his life as a ransom for many).

On the subject of these criteria, it moreover should be observed that respected scholars have questioned their application by the likes of Ehrman and members of the Jesus Seminar.[60] Critiquing the criterion of dissimilarity as applied by Ehrman, Michael Bird writes:

Think about it. A story about Jesus or a saying attributed to Jesus is only historical if it does not sound anything like what the church was saying about Jesus. What historian would say that the historical Plato is different from what the platonic school said about Plato? ... You end up with a Jesus who said, thought, and did nothing that his earliest followers believed that he said, thought, and did.... No wonder, then, that the criterion of dissimilarity has been nearly universally abandoned and replaced with something far more credible, like a criterion of historical plausibility. We can regard a unit in the Gospels as claiming a high degree of historical authenticity when a saying or event attributed to Jesus makes sense within Judaism (i.e., plausible context) and also represents a starting point for the early church (i.e., a plausible consequence).[61]

59. Ibid., 107.

60. For the latter, see Robert Funk, *The Acts of Jesus: The Search for the Authentic Deeds of Jesus* (San Francisco: HarperSanFrancisco, 1998), and Robert Funk and Roy W. Hoover, *The Five Gospels: The Search for the Authentic Words of Jesus: New Translation and Commentary* (New York: Macmillan, 1993). It is worth recalling that Benedict himself employs historical criticism's criteria for ascertaining the authenticity of certain Jesus traditions. For example, in his discussion of Jesus' calling of the disciples he invokes the criteria of multiple attestation, embarrassment, and witness antiquity. *Jesus, the Apostles, and the Early Church* (San Francisco: Ignatius Press, 2007), 9–10.

61. Bird, *How God Became Jesus*, 50–51.

Dale Allison, too, believes these traditional scholarly criteria to be fatally flawed. In addition to the well-known problems with dissimilarity, he argues:

> Multiple attestation overlooks the obvious problem that the more something is attested, the more the early church must have liked it, so the more suspicious we may well be about it.... My question is not Which criteria are good and which are bad? or How should we employ the good ones? but rather Should we be using criteria at all? ... After years of being in the quest business, I have reluctantly concluded that most of the Gospel materials are not subject to historical proof or disproof, or even to accurate estimates of their probability.[62]

We have now seen that Ehrman does not think "the historical Jesus" considered himself the Son of Man. Let us next investigate Ehrman's answer to an additional question: Did Jesus himself ever stake a claim to being divine? After noting that there are indeed sayings in the last Gospel—the Gospel of John—wherein Jesus claims to be divine, Ehrman comments:

> But looked at from a historical perspective, they simply cannot be ascribed to the historical Jesus. They don't pass any of our criteria. They are not multiply attested in our sources; they appear only in John, our latest and most theologically oriented Gospel. They certainly do not pass the criterion of dissimilarity since they express the very view of Jesus that the author of the Gospel of John happens to hold. And they are not at all contextually credible. We have no record of any Palestinian Jew ever saying any such things about himself. These divine self-claims in John are part of John's distinctive theology; they are not part of the historical record of what Jesus actually said.

> Look at the matter in a different light. As I pointed out, we have numerous earlier sources for the historical Jesus: a few comments in Paul (including several quotations from Jesus's teachings), Mark, Q, M, and L, not to mention the finished Gospels of Matthew and Luke. In none of them do we find exalted claims of this sort.[63]

---

62. Allison, *The Historical Christ and the Theological Jesus*, 54–55.

63. Ehrman, *How Jesus Became God*, 125. Note that the assumption of Q as a historical source is not an essential feature of historical criticism. For a powerful argument in favor of Markan priority without Q, see Mark Goodacre's *The Case Against Q* (Harrisburg, Pa.: Trinity Press International, 2002) and his *The Synoptic Problem: A Way through the Maze* (London: Sheffield Academic Press, 2001). My thanks to John Kincaid for putting me onto Goodacre's work.

While Ehrman is surely correct that, among the Gospels, John's has the most developed Christology, I as a reader am left wondering what the skeptic is to make of other portions of the synoptic Gospels that would seem to have Christ claiming divinity for himself. Consider the following instances:

+ In identifying himself as the Bridegroom, Jesus equates himself with Yahweh, Israel's bridegroom in the Old Testament (Mk 2:19–20; cf. Is 61:10–62:5; Ezek 16; Jer 2–3; Hos 1–2; Song). Richard Hays rightly observes, regarding images like that of the Bridegroom, "[I]t is precisely through drawing on OT images that all four Gospels portray the identity of Jesus as mysteriously fused with the identity of God. This is true even of Mark and Luke, the two Synoptic Gospels usually thought to have the 'lower' or most 'primitive' Christologies."[64]

+ In certain places, such as the Beatitudes, Jesus speaks with the authority of God himself, issuing a new, definitive Law (Mt 5).

+ Indeed, he makes it quite plain that following God's law is insufficient and that one must also follow Jesus himself as well (Mk 10:17–31).[65]

+ Jesus forgives sins, which is the prerogative of God alone (Mk 2:7).

+ He calls himself greater than the Temple and Lord of the Sabbath (Mk 2:27–28; Mt 12:8).

+ The natural sense of Jesus' "I have come" statements is that he has come from somewhere beyond this world to accomplish his mission (Mk 2:17; Mt 5:17; 10:35; 20:28; Lk 12:49–51; 19:10).[66]

+ Christ stills the sea in a text whose parallels with Yahweh calming the sea in the Old Testament can hardly be coincidental (Mk 4:35–41; cf. Ps 107).

+ Only a couple of chapters later, Jesus appears walking on the sea

64. Richard Hays, *Reading Backwards: Figural Christology and the Fourfold Gospel Witness* (Waco, Tex.: Baylor University Press, 2014), 108.

65. In recalling Rabbi Jacob Neusner's book *A Rabbi Talks with Jesus* (Montreal: McGill-Queen's University Press, 2000), Benedict XVI points out that this placing of himself at the center of the Law is what caused many of his contemporaries to draw back from him. Benedict XVI, *Jesus of Nazareth: From the Baptism in the Jordan to the Transfiguration*, 103–5.

66. On this subject see also Simon Gathercole, "What Did the First Christians Think about Jesus?" in Michael Bird, *How God Became Jesus*, 94–116.

and telling his disciples, "I am (*egō eimi*); have no fear" (Mk 6:45–52; cf. Ex 3:13–15). Many Bibles translate this text "It is I," but there are more compelling reasons for translating it "I am." Especially important in this connection is the fact that Mark tells us that Jesus had intended to "pass by" the disciples on the sea, a clear reference to Old Testament episodes wherein Yahweh "passed by" Moses and Elijah, who could not see his face (Ex 33:19, 22; 34:6; 1 Kgs 19:11). With Jesus, however, God finally stops and visits his people, who then "worship" him (Mt 14:32–33).[67] Also important is Benedict XVI's treatment of this passage: "At first sight, this instance of the words 'I am he' seems to be a simple identifying formula…. This interpretation does not go far enough, however. For at this point Jesus gets into the boat and the wind ceases…. The remarkable thing is that only now do the disciples really begin to fear…. It is this 'divine terror' that comes over the disciples here. For walking on the waters is a divine prerogative…. The Jesus who walks upon the waters is not simply the familiar Jesus; in this new Jesus they suddenly recognize the presence of God himself…. [T]here is no doubt that the whole event is a theophany, an encounter with the mystery of Jesus' divinity. Hence Matthew quite logically concludes his version of the story with an act of adoration (*proskynesis*) and the exclamation of the disciples, 'Truly, you are the Son of God'" (Mt 14:33).[68]

• Finally and most important, there is the fact that even our earliest Gospel records Jesus being sentenced to death for blasphemy immediately following his claim to be "the Christ, the Son of the Blessed." In response to this question, he replied most unequivocally, "*I am*; and you will see the Son of man seated at the right hand of Power, and coming with the clouds of heaven" (Mk 14:61–64; cf. Dn 7:9–13; Ps 110:1–3).

Given that these examples are drawn for the most part from the earliest Gospel, it seems much more likely than not on historical grounds alone that Jesus did in fact stake some claim to divinity during his lifetime.[69]

Ehrman for his part considers the possibility that Jesus thought of

---

67. My thanks to Brant Pitre for pointing out this connection to me.

68. Benedict, *Baptism*, 351–52; cf. Job 9:8; Ps 76:20 LXX; Is 43:16.

69. In light of these and many other texts that could be adduced, Dale Allison is

himself as divine in the sense of being the messianic king adopted by God. But here too he answers in the negative:

> It is of course possible, but I think it is highly unlikely for the following reason.... [W]e have no known instance of a living Jewish king proclaiming himself to be divine. Could Jesus be the exception? Yes, of course; there are always exceptions to everything. But to think that Jesus is the exception in this case, one would need a good deal of persuasive evidence. And it just doesn't exist. The evidence for Jesus's claims to be divine comes only from the last of the New Testament Gospels, not from any earlier sources.[70]

I think the Christian might respond to Ehrman's point by contesting whether we even need the sort of evidence for which he is looking. Moreover, for a Christian the fact that no other Jewish king ever pro-

---

right to observe that "all the primary sources repeatedly purport that Jesus had astounding things to say about himself. One can dissociate him from an exalted self-conception only through multiple radical surgeries on our texts." Allison, *Constructing Jesus: Memory, Imagination, and History* (Grand Rapids, Mich.: Baker Academic, 2010), 225. Put plainly, Allison concludes (304): "We should hold a funeral for the view that Jesus entertained no exalted thoughts about himself." I think that Michael Bird is on the right track in this regard: "I think it is necessary to explode a popular caricature where Jesus cruises around Galilee announcing, 'Hi, I'm God. I'm going to die on the cross for your sins soon. But first of all I'm going to teach you how to be a good Christian and how to get to heaven. And after that I thought it would be fitting if you all worshiped me as the second member of the Trinity.' This might seem a rather silly way to understand Jesus' identity, but it is a sketch of Jesus that many Bible-believing Christians have. When I contend that Jesus understood himself to be divine, this is definitely not what I am talking about. When I say that Jesus knew himself to be God, I mean that he was conscious that in him the God of Israel was finally returning to Zion (i.e., Jerusalem) to renew the covenant and to fulfill the promises God had made to the nation about a new exodus." Bird, *How God Became Jesus*, 52.

On Jesus embodying Yahweh's return to Zion, see Wright, *Jesus and the Victory of God*, 642–45, 653: "[F]orget the attempts of some well-meaning Christians to make Jesus of Nazareth conscious of being the second person of the Trinity; forget the arid reductionism that some earnest liberal theologians have produced by way of reaction. Focus, instead, on a young Jewish prophet telling a story about YHWH returning to Zion as judge and redeemer, and then embodying it by riding into the city in tears, symbolizing the Temple's destruction and celebrating the final exodus. I propose, as a matter of history, that Jesus of Nazareth was conscious of vocation: a vocation, given him by the one he knew as 'father,' to enact in himself what, in Israel's scriptures, God has promised to accomplish all by himself. He would be the pillar of cloud and fire for the people of the new exodus. He would embody in himself the returning and redeeming action of the covenant God." See also Wright, *The Challenge of Jesus*, 121–23.

70. Ehrman, *How Jesus Became God*, 126.

claimed himself divine adds nothing to the debate. If Jesus is indeed divine, there seems no reason to suppose that others would have made the same claim before him. Moreover, as indicated above, a Christian might object to Ehrman by pointing to other indicators that Jesus saw himself as divine (his miracles, his forgiveness of people's sins, and his reception of adoration from those who bow down before him, etc.). Ehrman, however, dismisses this argument: "There are two points to stress about such things. The first is that all of them are compatible with human, not just divine, authority.... But even more important, these activities may not even go back to the historical Jesus."[71]

How Jesus Became God

Directly related to the question of Christ's divinity is the question of *how* or *why* Jesus came to be considered God. For Ehrman, the short answer is that it flowed from his followers' belief that he had been raised from the dead.

My overarching contention is that belief in the resurrection—based on visionary experiences—is what initially led the followers of Jesus (all of them? some of them?) to believe that Jesus had been exalted to heaven and made to sit at the right hand of God as his unique Son. These beliefs were the first christologies—the first understandings that Jesus was a divine being.[72]

Thus it was only after Jesus had died that his disciples came to believe that he was, at least in some sense, God.

Did Jesus actually rise from the dead or not? Ehrman shows genuine intellectual humility when he acknowledges that history does not disprove Jesus' Resurrection:

71. Ibid., 127.

72. Ibid., 7. In a similar vein Marcus Borg contends, "'Resurrection' does not mean resumption of previous existence but entry into a different kind of existence. To use Paul's phrase, it involves a 'spiritual body' (not a body of flesh and blood); moreover, a resurrected person will not die again. Resurrection could involve something happening to a corpse (transformation of some kind), but it need not. Thus Easter need not involve the claim that God supernaturally intervened to raise the corpse of Jesus from the tomb. Rather, the core meaning of Easter is that Jesus continued to be experienced after his death." Borg, *The God We Never Knew: Beyond Dogmatic Religion to a More Authentic Contemporary Faith* (San Francisco: HarperSanFrancisco, 1997).

I have said that it was the belief in the resurrection that led some of his followers to claim he was God. This is because, as a historian, I do not think we can show—historically—that Jesus was in fact raised from the dead. To be clear, I am not saying the opposite either—that historians can use the historical disciplines in order to demonstrate that Jesus was not raised from the dead. I argue that when it comes to miracles such as the resurrection, historical sciences simply are of no help in establishing exactly what happened. Religious faith and historical knowledge are two different ways of "knowing."[73]

I think that the believer can basically agree with what Ehrman says here. I find especially refreshing Ehrman's recognition that faith and knowledge are two different modes of knowing. Moreover, this is substantially in agreement with Aquinas, according to whom no amount of historical evidence is sufficient for rendering the act of faith warranted. At the most, external evidence may predispose one to the act of faith, but the gift of faith is chiefly from God, who by grace moves us to the act of assent.[74]

According to Ehrman, the reason historians have so much difficulty discussing the Resurrection is that the Gospel accounts of Matthew 28, Mark 16, Luke 24, and John 20–21 "disagree on nearly every detail in their Resurrection narratives."[75] He is right to say that these differences cannot be reconciled without a lot of "interpretive gymnastics," though I would add the caveat that what might simply look like gymnastics from his point of view may from a Christian perspective simply be the rigor required for ascertaining a text's meaning.

Moreover, Ehrman recalls that our earliest "witness" to the Resurrection, Paul, says nothing about the discovery of an empty tomb;

73. Ehrman, *How Jesus Became God*, 132.

74. In the words of Aquinas: "As regards ... man's assent to the things which are of faith, we may observe a twofold cause, one of external inducement, such as seeing a miracle, or being persuaded by someone to embrace the faith: neither of which is a sufficient cause, since of those who see the same miracle, or who hear the same sermon, some believe, and some do not. Hence we must assert another internal cause, which moves man inwardly to assent to matters of faith.... [S]ince man, by assenting to matters of faith, is raised above his nature, this must needs accrue to him from some supernatural principle moving him inwardly; and this is God. Therefore faith, as regards the assent which is the chief act of faith, is from God moving man inwardly by grace." Thomas Aquinas, *Summa theologiae*, II-II, q. 6, a. 1.

75. Ehrman, *How Jesus Became God*, 133; cf. Bart Ehrman, *Jesus: Apocalyptic Prophet of the New Millennium* (Oxford: Oxford University Press, 1999), 228–29.

on the other hand, the earliest Gospel, Mark, narrates the discovery of the empty tomb without discussing any of the appearances (Mk 16:1–8). This has led some scholars to suggest:

> [T]hese two sets of tradition—the empty tomb and the appearances of Jesus after his death—probably originated independently of one another and were put together as a single tradition only later—for example, in the Gospels of Matthew and Luke. If this is the case, then the stories of Jesus's resurrection were indeed being expanded, embellished, modified, and possibly even invented in the long process of their being told and retold over the years.[76]

While a Catholic like Benedict will certainly agree that the stories of Jesus' Resurrection were expanded over the years (as seen, for example, with the multiple endings of Mark), for a Catholic it would be a bridge too far to allege with John Dominic Crossan that these traditions were merely being "invented."[77] Although the Catholic need not affirm that every last detail in the narratives could have been captured on a video camera, a hermeneutic of faith tends to accept each discrete appearance as historical unless there is compelling evidence to suppose it was intended to be taken parabolically.[78]

76. Ehrman, *How Jesus Became God*, 143.

77. John Dominic Crossan articulates this view when he says, "Emmaus never happened. Emmaus always happens." According to Crossan's understanding, a parable is a "story that never happened but always does—or at least should." *The Power of Parable*, 5. Seeing the clear parallels between the Last Supper and the meal at Emmaus (in both, Jesus took bread, blessed, broke, and gave it to the disciples) leads Crossan to conclude that Luke's point was not historical so much as theological and liturgical: "That is parable, not history. The Christian liturgy involves both Scripture and Eucharist with the former as prelude and prologue to the latter.... The story is a parable about loving, that is, feeding the stranger as yourself and finding Jesus still—or only?—fully present in that encounter." Ibid., 4. It is possible that Crossan is onto something here, in that Luke may be embellishing his narrative so as to draw out the liturgical importance of this post-Resurrection eucharistic feast. However, Crossan's view of the story as parable is no more likely than the view that the event has a basis in history. His book makes the fascinating claim that parables *by* Jesus (e.g., the Good Samaritan) were turned into parables *about* Jesus by the evangelists. Here again, though, I see no reason why the causality could not have just as likely operated the other way around. In other words, to me it seems just as likely that the Good Samaritan of Jesus' parable was a veiled allusion by Jesus to himself, as that the supper at Emmaus was a parable masquerading as history.

78. For a helpful articulation of a hermeneutic of faith that views it as reasonable to continue maintaining belief in Scripture's miracles until there is compelling evidence against them, see Paul Williams, *The Unexpected Way: On Converting from Buddhism to Catholicism* (Edinburgh: T and T Clark, 2002), 165–66.

That said, it remains of paramount importance to reflect continually on the question raised by Dale Allison: how much history does theology require? The answer, says Allison, depends on one's presuppositions. Some things once thought essential and immutable have shown themselves to be inessential and mutable, which ought to make one cautious about insisting too strongly that authentic Christian faith requires this or that event to be historical.[79] Like Crossan, Allison suggests that the Gospels would remain intact even if to a certain degree their content were to turn out to be highly parabolic:

> They too are works of literature. Why should we fret much over how much history is in them? Why cannot the Gospels be like the parables that Jesus told? ... Should we not live by the Golden Rule whether Jesus spoke it or not? What difference would it make if we learned that he had been crucified not outside the walls of Jerusalem but outside the walls of Jericho?[80]

Now Allison is not arguing that Jesus never taught us the Golden Rule, but he does want to push us on the question of what we think the validity of this norm depends upon: does it depend upon the saying being traceable to the historical Jesus, or rather is it sufficient that the Golden Rule, no matter what its ultimate provenance, has been included by the Church in the inspired canon of Scripture? I think that Allison is right to press us on this issue, though to be sure the Catholic may disagree with him when it comes to arguing which particular parts of the Gospels need be historical. What I wish to achieve here with the help of Allison is to anticipate a point that Benedict XVI

---

79. Allison, *The Historical Christ and the Theological Jesus*, 39–40. While going farther than many would in applying this principle, Allison candidly asserts, "I am persuaded that, for most theological purposes, we should treat the Gospels the same way that we treat Genesis; we should use them first of all not to reconstruct the past but to construe our world theologically." Ibid., 43. Though the Catholic may rightly contend that Allison overplays his comparison between the Gospels and the opening chapters of Genesis, nevertheless it is evocative to consider the truth in Allison's observation, "[M]any of us within the churches have changed our minds about the importance of history for understanding any number of scriptural books. We no longer, for example, look to Genesis if we are seeking to gather facts about the cosmological or geological past.... This does not mean, however, the Genesis has ceased to function as Scripture. We have learned how to read the text as theology without reading it as history.... Much of what people once took to be history is now known to be, or suspected to be, something else." Ibid., 33–34.

80. Ibid., 33.

will make repeatedly in the next chapter—namely that the faith has an enduring substance that must be distinguished from its accidental features, such as the historicity of certain logia *or events narrated in the Gospels*. But let me be clear: regardless of what individual scholars may happen to think about the historicity of particular episodes in the life of Christ, for Catholics the fundamental components of the Creed (Incarnation, death, Resurrection, etc.) are not negotiable historically. In other words, these cannot be mere parables or else the Christian faith loses its foundation.

Returning to Ehrman, it is unsurprising that he exhibits his usual skepticism regarding Jesus' burial. In his estimation, we cannot know that Jesus received a decent burial or that his tomb was later discovered to be empty:

As the burial tradition came to be told and retold, it possibly became embellished and made more concrete. Storytellers were apt to add details to stories that were vague, or to give names to people otherwise left nameless in a tradition, or to add named individuals to stories that originally mentioned only nameless individuals or undifferentiated groups of people. This is a tradition that lived on long after the New Testament period.[81]

In a brief inquiry into Roman practices of crucifixion, Ehrman cites John Dominic Crossan's infamous suggestion that Jesus's body was eaten by dogs.[82] Ehrman himself does not go this far, but he still remains skeptical of the Christian claim:

My view now is that we do not know, and cannot know, what actually happened to Jesus's body. But it is absolutely true that as far as we can tell from all the surviving evidence, what normally happened to a criminal's body is that it was left to decompose and serve as food for scavenging animals.[83]

It is indeed unlikely that someone innocently moved the body, but Ehrman is right that it is not inconceivable. It is also unlikely that Jesus' followers stole the body and then lied about it, but then again it is by no means impossible that this occurred. Indeed, looking at the matter strictly from a historical point of view, either of these views is less unexpected than the claim that Jesus rose from the dead: "A Resur-

81. Ehrman, *How Jesus Became God*, 150.
82. Crossan, *Jesus: A Revolutionary Biography*, 123ff.
83. Ehrman, *How Jesus Became God*, 157.

rection would be a miracle and as such would defy all 'probability.'"[84] It may disturb some Christians to grapple with this, but I think it is a salutary challenge and also one that I will take up before concluding this volume.

In the meantime, when evaluating Ehrman's and Crossan's claims, it is important to consider the phenomenon of protective anonymity as an alternate explanation for the expansions we find in later Gospels (e.g., why unnamed persons in Mark receive names in the later Gospel of John). As Richard Bauckham observes, "These should not be regarded as instances of some alleged tendency for names to get added in the tradition.... [T]here is little evidence of such a tendency before the fourth century."[85] Regarding Mark's anonymous young man who flees naked (Mk 14:52), Gerd Theissen writes:

It seems to me that the narrative motive for this anonymity is not hard to guess: both of them [the bystander who cut off the ear of the high priest's slave and the young man who ran away from the scene naked] [had] run afoul of the 'police.' ... Their anonymity is for their protection, and the obscurity of their positive relationship with Jesus is a strategy of caution. Both the teller and the hearers know more about these two people.[86]

Concerning the woman who anointed Jesus (Mk 14:3–9), Bauckham argues that this likely would have been perceived in a messianic sense, i.e., as the anointing of the Messiah, the new king of Israel:

What has not been generally recognized is the significance of Mark's placing of this story between his account of the plot by the Jewish authorities to ar-

---

84. Ibid, 165. Ehrman pointedly adds: "And no one should be put off by the claim, 'No one would be willing to die for what he knew to be a lie.' We don't know what happened to most of the disciples in the end. We certainly have no evidence that they were all martyred for their faith. On the contrary, almost certainly most of them were not. So there is no need for talk about anyone dying for a lie. (Moreover, we have lots of instances in history for people dying for lies when they think it will serve a greater good. But that's neither here nor there: we don't know how most of the disciples died.)" I do not think that our evidence for the disciples' martyrdoms is as weak as Ehrman does, but he is right that it is *possible* for someone to "die for a lie" (or because they are delusional). I think that the Christian has to admit this much, but the question remains whether or not this is the best explanation for the apostles' heroic faith.

85. Bauckham, *Jesus and the Eyewitnesses*, 194.

86. Gerd Theissen, *The Gospels in Context: Social and Political History in the Synoptic Tradition* (Minneapolis: Fortress Press, 1991), 186–87.

rest and kill Jesus and his account of Judas' visit to the chief priests in order to hand Jesus over to them. This is a typically Markan 'sandwich' construction, like, for example, the placing of the account of Jesus' demonstration in the Temple between the two parts of the story of the withered fig tree.... We should surely understand that Judas reports the incident of the anointing to the chief priests, for whom it must constitute significant evidence that Jesus and his disciples are planning an imminent messianic uprising.... What would have put these persons in danger in Jerusalem in the period of the earliest Christian community would be their complicity in Jesus' allegedly seditious behavior in the days before his arrest. Furthermore, the whole Christian community was potentially at risk for its allegiance to a man who had been executed for such seditious behavior. We can readily understand that, just as the pre-Markan passion narrative protected certain individuals by leaving them anonymous, so it protected the community by not making too obvious the messianic meaning of the events that had constituted the chief priests' evidence for treating Jesus as a dangerously seditious figure.[87]

Bauckham applies this same logic to the case of Lazarus—whom we are told in Jn 12:10 that the chief priests had sought to kill—and to Peter, who only in John is identified as the one who cut off the ear of the high priest's servant. Thus in the latter case he writes:

Peter is afraid of being identified not just as a disciple of Jesus but as the one who assaulted the servant of the high priest.... [I]n the light of our discussion, we certainly cannot maintain that the connection is historically unlikely simply because it is made only in John's Gospel. It could not have been made in the pre-Markan passion narrative (on which not only Mark, but, by way of Mark, the other Synoptic Evangelists at this point depend), without also identifying Peter as the man who cut off the high priest's servant's ear. The extent of the fear that motivated Peter's denial could not be explained without blowing his cover.[88]

In addition to challenging Ehrman and Crossan on the question of added names in the later Gospels, Craig Evans offers a pointed challenge to these authors on the subject of Jesus' burial. The nonappearance of Joseph of Arimathea in the ancient creed of 1 Cor 15:3–5 leads Ehrman to conclude that his later appearance was a result of the tendency to add names to the tradition over time. However, Evans argues

---

87. Bauckham, *Jesus and the Eyewitnesses*, 192–93.
88. Ibid., 194–95; see also Craig Evans, *Mark 8:27–16:20* (Nashville, Tenn.: Thomas Nelson Publishers, 2001), 359–60.

that Ehrman fails to account either for Jewish custom at the time or for the archaeological evidence. Says Evans:

It is against this legal and cultural backdrop that the story of Joseph of Ari-mathea should be understood.... In short, there is nothing irregular about the gospels' report that a member of the Sanhedrin requested permission to take down the body of Jesus and give it proper burial, in keeping with Jew-ish burial practices as they related to the executed. It is entirely in keeping with all that we know from the literature and from archaeology.... Although archaeology does not prove there was a follower of Jesus named Joseph of Ari-mathea or that Pontius Pilate granted his request for Jesus' body, the gospel accounts describing Jesus' removal from the cross and burial are consistent with archaeological evidence and with Jewish law.[89]

Further, Evans observes on a different note:

But if the gospel stories were filled with as much fiction as Ehrman thinks, one must wonder why the Evangelists did not alter the stories and give more prominence to men.... This in fact happened, as we see in the mocking chal-lenges offered by pagan skeptics like Celsus and Porphyry. The second cen-tury Gospel of Peter, which claims that hostile Jewish leaders and Romans, along with the male disciples themselves, witnessed the resurrection, was composed to answer that criticism.[90]

Finally, as to the commonplace proposition that Jesus' disciples had come to believe that he had "risen" in an immaterial way, Evans concludes:

I find it difficult to explain Paul's proclamation of Jesus as resurrected, had the followers of Jesus spoken only of a spiritual resurrection and had the body of Jesus remained dead and decomposing in a tomb. After all, the Jewish peo-ple had their traditions of ghosts, spirits, and visions, which did not lead to the conviction that people had been resurrected.[91]

Turning from what Ehrman thinks cannot be known about the Resurrection to what we can know about it, I would like to explore in

89. Craig Evans, "Getting the Burial Traditions and Evidences Right," in Bird, *How God Became Jesus*, 94–116.

90. Ibid., 90.

91. Ibid., 92. On this last point see also N. T. Wright, *The Challenge of Jesus*: "For a start, if Peter or Paul had had such experiences [of Christ's "spiritual" rather than bodily resurrection], the category that would have suggested itself would not be 'resurrection'; it would be that of the appearance of Jesus' 'angel' or his 'spirit.'" Wright, 148.

more detail something I mentioned in the introduction: Ehrman affirms that at least some direct followers of Jesus sincerely believed that their master had been raised from the dead. He suggests that "three or four people—though possibly more—had visions of Jesus sometime after he died."[92] Elsewhere he states emphatically, "There can be no doubt, historically, that some of Jesus's followers came to believe he was raised from the dead—no doubt whatsoever."[93] And, unlike some who deny the Resurrection, Ehrman agrees with Christians that the Resurrection being claimed here is not a mere resuscitation, a return to normal earthly human existence as in the case of Lazarus.

Although Ehrman agrees with orthodox Christianity that the alleged Resurrection of Jesus was perceived to be a unique apocalyptic event, he disagrees on the all-important issue of whether the Christian claim is *true*. What was it, then, that caused Jesus' disciples to proclaim that he was resurrected? While ultimately remaining agnostic on the question, he seems to think that the most likely explanation for the claim is that the disciples experienced bereavement visions, a phenomenon that occurs when a person's source monitoring fails to distinguish whether a sensation arises from inside or outside the mind:

Bentall argues that source monitoring judgments are affected by the culture in which a person grows up. If a person's culture subscribes to the existence of ghosts or the reality of dead people appearing, the chance that what one "sees" will be assumed to be a ghost or a dead person is obviously heightened. Moreover, and this is a key point, stress and emotional arousal can have serious effects on a person's source monitoring skills. Someone who is under considerable stress, or experiencing deep grief, trauma, or personal anguish, is more likely to experience a failure of source monitoring. This may be why two of the most frequently reported forms of visions involve the comforting presence of a deceased loved one or of a respected religious figure.[94]

92. Ehrman, *How Jesus Became God*, 192.

93. Ibid., 174.

94. Ibid., 194. Crossan, too, seems to think that the disciples experienced Jesus in trances and visions rather than in the manner described in the Gospels: "Of course there may have been trances and visions. There always are such events in every religion." Crossan, *Jesus: A Revolutionary Biography*, 190; cf. also 168. Crossan thinks that such trances, which continue to occur even today, are not pathological delusions: "Trance and ecstasy, vision and apparition are perfectly normal and natural phenomena. Altered states of consciousness, such as dreams and visions, are something common to our humanity." Crossan, *The Birth of Christianity*, xvii–xviii.

Ehrman thinks that the question of whether these putative experiences were veridical (i.e., whether Jesus was really there or whether they were hallucinatory bereavement visions) is beside his point, but to this reader it seems clear which direction he leans on the issue—a direction that is completely at odds with the requirements of authentic Christian belief in the bodily resurrection of Jesus.

So if their experience of the crucified Jesus was not real, why did the disciples frame it in terms of Resurrection rather than a vision, spirit, or something else? Argues Ehrman:

> [A]nyone who was an apocalyptic Jew like Jesus's closest follower Peter, or Jesus's own brother James, or his later apostle Paul, who thought that Jesus had come back to life, would naturally interpret it in light of his particular apocalyptic worldview—a worldview that informed everything that he thought about God, humans, the world, the future, and the afterlife. In that view, a person who was alive after having died would have been bodily raised from the dead, by God himself, so as to enter into the coming kingdom.[95]

Furthermore:

> If an apocalyptic Jew of this kind were to come to believe that the resurrection of the dead had begun—for example, with the raising of God's specially favored one, his messiah—what would that resurrection involve? It would naturally and automatically involve precisely a bodily resurrection. That's what "resurrection" meant to these people. It did not mean the ongoing life of the spirit without the body. It meant the reanimation and glorification of the body. If the disciples came to believe that Jesus was raised from the dead, they would have on the spot understood that this meant his body was no longer dead but had been brought back to life. They wouldn't need an empty tomb to prove it.[96]

In Ehrman's view, then, it was the disciples' own apocalyptic worldview (informed by Jesus' teachings while he was alive) that led them to think of their visions of the crucified Jesus in terms of Resurrection.

Conclusion

In sum, for Ehrman the disciples' belief in Jesus' Resurrection marked the decisive turning point in the history of Christology. From that point on, Jesus was no longer a mere mortal but was, at least in

95. Ehrman, *How Jesus Became God*, 203.
96. Ibid., 186.

some sense, God. Naturally, this view also had major implications for what the disciples thought would happen next in history. Even before Jesus' Resurrection, the disciples had already believed the following:

> In the very near future, God was going to send a cosmic judge over the earth, the Son of Man, to destroy the wicked powers that were making life so miserable in this world and to set up a good kingdom, a utopian place where good would prevail and God would rule through his messiah. The disciples would sit on thrones as rulers in the coming kingdom, and Jesus would be seated on the greatest throne of all, as the messiah of God.[97]

But with the game-changer of Jesus' bodily Resurrection from the dead, this view clearly required emendation:

> In his own teaching [Jesus] had proclaimed that the Son of Man was to appear as the cosmic judge over the earth. But now it was obviously Jesus himself who was coming from heaven to rule. The disciples very soon—probably right away—concluded that Jesus was the coming Son of Man. So when they told stories about him later, they had him speak of himself as the Son of Man—so much so that it became one of his favorite titles for himself in the Gospels. As we have seen, the Son of Man was sometimes understood to be a divine figure. In that sense also, then, Jesus was God.[98]

Ehrman discusses several key biblical texts in which this change appears to unfold before our very eyes. In Romans 1:3–4, Paul states quite clearly that Jesus "was designated Son of God in power according to the Spirit of holiness by his resurrection from the dead." Similarly, Acts 13:32–33 has Paul identifying the "day" on which the Son of God was begotten (cf. Ps 2) as the day not of his conception or birth but of his *Resurrection*. Peter, too, speaks in similar terms: "Let all the house of Israel therefore know assuredly that God has made him both Lord and Christ, this Jesus whom you crucified" (Acts 2:36; cf. 5:30–31). Ehrman comments:

> During his lifetime Jesus's followers had thought he would be the future messiah who would reign as king in the coming kingdom of God to be brought by the Son of Man, as Jesus himself had taught them. But when they came to believe he was raised from the dead, as Acts 2:36 so clearly indicates, they concluded that he had been made the messiah already. He was already ruling

97. Ibid., 204.
98. Ibid., 209.

as the king, in heaven, elevated to the side of God. As one who sits beside God on a throne in the heavenly realm, Jesus already is the Christ.[99]

Ehrman describes this view of Christ as *exaltation Christology*, for by his Resurrection "the man Jesus is showered with divine favors beyond anyone's wildest dreams, honored by God to an unbelievable extent, elevated to a divine status on a level with God himself, sitting at his right hand."[100] Commonly such a view would be described as low Christology or even as adoptionist Christology, but Ehrman prefers his term for the following reason:

When the earliest Christians talked about Jesus becoming the Son of God at his resurrection, they were saying something truly remarkable about him. He was made the heir of all that was God's. He exchanged his status for the status possessed by the Creator and ruler of all things. He received all of God's power and privileges. He could defy death. He could forgive sins. He could be the future judge of the earth. He could rule with divine authority. He was for all intents and purposes God.[101]

In other words, from our point of view today within orthodox Christianity, Ehrman's view of Christ may be low, but for first-century Jews it would have been an immensely lofty theology.

In the remaining chapters of his book, Ehrman continues to trace the beginnings of Christology from the New Testament through the patristic period. While most of what he argues there exceeds the scope of our volume, it is important to note his conclusion that there were two fundamentally different Christologies at work in the early Church. Writing about the trajectory we find in the Gospels, Ehrman says:

Originally, Jesus was thought to have been exalted only at the resurrection; as Christians thought more about the matter, they came to think that he must have been the Son of God during his entire ministry, so that he became the Son of God at its outset, at baptism; as they thought even more about it, they came to think he must have been the Son of God for his entire life, and so he was born of a virgin and in that sense was the (literal) Son of God; and as they thought about it more again, they came to think that he must have been the Son of God even before he came into the world, and so they said he was a preexistent divine being.[102]

99. Ehrman, *How Jesus Became God*, 228.
100. Ibid., 232.   101. Ibid., 234.
102. Ibid., 237. On this subject I appreciate the following quip, which by no means

In contrast with this trajectory, Ehrman contends that Paul had an incarnation Christology in which Jesus was an angel who came to earth from above.[103] Given the widely divergent views of Paul and the Gospels, it is no wonder that an ecumenical council was required to determine the precise nature of Jesus Christ, and that even afterwards—contrary to the popular imagination—"nothing could be farther from the truth" than to think that there was universal agreement on the question.[104]

Ehrman concludes his book with an appeal to Martin Hengel, who famously claimed that the early Church's Christology developed more in the first twenty years than in all the centuries of dogmatic development that have followed. Here is Ehrman's assessment:

> There is a certain truth to this claim. Of course, a lot did indeed happen after the first twenty years—an enormous amount. But the major leap was made in those twenty years: from seeing Jesus as his own disciples did during his ministry, as a Jewish man with an apocalyptic message of coming destruction, to seeing him as something far greater, a preexistent divine being who became human only temporarily before being made the Lord of the universe.[105]

Perhaps a Catholic need not dispute Ehrman's claim entirely. Perhaps more did happen in the first twenty years in terms of Christology than in the remaining two thousand years of Church history. But the question is whether the Christology developed during this period was the fruit of truthful and providential reflection upon the mystery of Jesus, or whether it was a misguided, delusional, desperate, or even conniving power play.[106] Similarly, was the hope that Christ would return

---

refutes Ehrman but does raise a meaningful objection: "At the transfiguration, God says of Jesus: 'This is my Son, whom I love. Listen to him!' (Mk 9:1). Presumably God is not adopting Jesus again. But it is hard to see how the voice at the baptism could refer to God's adoption of Jesus and the similar-sounding voice at the transfiguration could mean something different." Gathercole, "What Did the First Christians Think about Jesus?" 99.

103. Ehrman, *How Jesus Became God*, 252ff.

104. Ibid., 356.

105. Ibid., 371; cf. Martin Hengel, *The Son of God: The Origin of Christology and the History of Jewish-Hellenistic Religion* (London: SCM, 1975), 4.

106. Unlike Ehrman, those who belong to the so-called "Early High Christology Club" contend that this development discussed by Hengel was faithful to Jesus' own self-conception and can be described as a "big bang" origin to the Church's Christology. The antiquity of this explosion can be seen in Paul's letters, which were written mostly

in judgment as Lord of the universe founded in Jesus' own teaching and faithful reflection upon it, or was it merely wishful thinking? It is to this subject, the question of Christ's imminent return, that we will turn further in chapter 6. But first we will look at how Benedict XVI handles the same sort of (and indeed, in many cases, the very same) issues addressed by Ehrman. The point here has been to clarify what precisely it is that a faithful exegete like Benedict is up against, to let ourselves be challenged by the plausibility of Ehrman's approach, given his first principles, and to highlight certain areas in which Ehrman's approach can be seen to be flawed.

A final note on that score: A clear example of an unwarranted scholarly assumption can be glimpsed in how Ehrman dealt above with Rom 1:3–4 (Jesus "was designated Son of God *in power* according to the Spirit of holiness by his resurrection from the dead"). Ehrman considers the small phrase "in power" is insignificant, for he asserts that Paul "probably added" it to an early creed he had inherited.[107] However, some Christian interpreters have come to a different interpretation by accentuating the "in power" portion of this verse. Benedict XVI, for instance, insists, "The novelty of the Resurrection consists in the fact that Jesus, raised from the lowliness of his earthly existence, is constituted Son of God 'in power.'"[108] Simon Gathercole likewise writes, "This is what it means that Jesus at the resurrection

---

in the 50s yet use what appear to be traditional, stereotyped formulations for talking about Jesus' identity and divine status (e.g. Rom 1:3–4; 1 Cor 8:6; Gal 4:4; Phil 2:5–11). Writes Michael Bird: "When the early Christians mentioned God, they had to mention Jesus as well, and whenever they mentioned Jesus, they felt constrained to mention God in the same breath. It's like God was Jesified and Jesus was Godified.... [I]t seems that what happened was that among Jesus' earliest followers there was an immediate move to reconfigure Jewish monotheism, whereby the one God of Israel was now known and experienced as the Lord Jesus Christ and God the Father." Bird, *How God Became Jesus,* 13–14, 28, 40. Development in the case of the Holy Spirit did not follow these precise lines; some described the early Church's theology in terms of binitarianism or Christological monotheism. Ibid., 28. See 1 Thes 1:1; Gal 1:3–5; Larry Hurtado, *Lord Jesus Christ: Devotion to Jesus in Earliest Christianity* (Grand Rapids, Mich.: Eerdmans, 2003), 151–52. For a recent treatment of Hengel, Hurtado, Bauckham, and others in the "Early High Christology Club," see N. T. Wright, *Paul and the Faithfulness of God.* 647–56.

107. Ehrman, *How Jesus Became God,* 224.

108. Benedict XVI, *St. Paul* (San Francisco: Ignatius Press, 2009), 69.

becomes Son of God *in power,* and Lord and Christ in a new sense. He is 'Son of God in power,' in stark contrast to his physical condition in his earthly ministry, which culminated in his death."[109] In this same text Gathercole unmasks the "unwarranted prejudice" of Ehrman's assumption by showing that it reflects more the skeptic's presupposition that the early Church considered Jesus adopted by God than the relevant ancient evidence itself, which is precisely what we have in Romans. In other words, we know that historical-critical exegesis has overplayed its hand when it starts claiming that the truth of what happened must lie before or behind the earliest historical texts we have at our disposal. At this point one can only ask: which is more made visible by this sort of exegesis—the face of the historical Jesus or the face of the interpreter?

109. Gathercole, "What Did the First Christians Think about Jesus?" 115.

5

THE LIFE, DEATH, AND RESURRECTION OF CHRIST: BENEDICT XVI

In the previous chapter, we examined Bart Ehrman's approach to the life of Christ and saw that his and the believer's respective conclusions follow from mutually incommensurable presuppositions about the Bible in relation to history and truth. For a Catholic, the question is whether the Christology that developed in the earliest days of the Church was the fruit of truthful and providential reflection upon the mystery of Jesus, or whether it was a misguided, delusional, desperate, or even conniving power play. In this chapter, we will explore how Benedict XVI and the Pontifical Biblical Commission handle the same sort of—and indeed in many cases the very same—issues addressed by Ehrman.

General Principles from the PBC and Benedict's *Jesus* Forewords

In its 2014 work *The Inspiration and Truth of Sacred Scripture*, the Pontifical Biblical Commission provides an indispensable key to countering Ehrman's assertion that the early Church invented Christ's divinity and resurrection. First, it is of paramount importance that the document in fact acknowledges rather than avoids the sound conclusions drawn by modern scholars. For example, Ehrman thinks it bla-tantly obvious that the words of Jesus presented in the Gospels are often not his actual words. So too the PBC admits, "In many cases, in fact, we do not have the *ipsissima verba* of the prophet (inspired by God), unless in the words of his disciples. This is typically the case in the gospels, whose inspiration is not in question."[1] In the Old Testa-ment and New Testament alike, we are not talking about transcrip-tions or video camera recordings. On this point modern scholars are in agreement regardless of their faith persuasions.[2]

So if we are not in possession of Jesus' precise words, then of what

1. PBC, *The Inspiration and Truth of Sacred Scripture*, 161. See also the PBC's 1964 instruction *The Historicity of the Gospels*: "The truth of the Gospel account is not com-promised because the Evangelists report the Lord's words and deeds in different order. Nor is it hurt because they report His words (*verba*), not literally, but in a variety of ways, while retaining the same meaning (*sensus*)." A point worth pondering in this regard is that the quotation marks in our modern bibles (which are not in the original Greek and Hebrew) give us the unfounded impression that speech reported in the Bible represents verbatim locutions from God, Jesus, etc. This is not to say that the biblical languages have no way of conveying direct discourse, but it does challenge the naïve impression of many Christians and skeptics alike: namely, that we are able to retrieve with certainty the precise words of Jesus such as they came out of his mouth. Here it is critical to pon-der the full ramifications of the christological analogy formulated in Vatican II's *Dei Verbum*, 13: "The words of God, expressed in human language, have been made like hu-man discourse, just as the Word of the eternal Father, when He took to Himself the flesh of human weakness, was in every way made like men." If God's word is truly both a divine *and a human* word, and human words are not immune from being transmitted im-perfectly, then why should we expect God's word to be immune from these realities? In other words, why would it not be the case that the Bible truthfully conveys the substance of God's word even in the presence of the imperfections inherent to human verbal and written communication?

2. "[T]here is real reason to wonder whether the Gospel tradition and the evange-lists were all that concerned about the precise wording of what Jesus said.... For example, we have four reports of what Jesus said over the bread and wine at the Last Supper ... and all four versions differ among themselves.... Obviously, Jesus was able to say these words only once before his life abruptly ended; hence ... importance to the early Church guar-anteed agreement in *substance*, not in exact wording. If this is true for these vital "words of institution" at the Last Supper, do we have any reason to think that other words of Jesus were preserved with greater zeal for word-for-word accuracy?" John Meier, *A Mar-ginal Jew: Rethinking the Historical Jesus*, 4 vols. (New Haven, Conn.: Yale University Press, 1991, 1994, 2001, 2009), 1.43 (emphasis added). My thanks to Brant Pitre for put-ting me onto Meier's formulation whereby it is understood that we possess not the exact words of Christ but rather the *substance* of his words.

use are the Gospels, and what do they actually provide us? The PBC answers, "We must, therefore, bear in mind that the gospels are not merely chronicles of the events in the life of Jesus, since the evangelists also intend to express in narrative form the theological significance of these events."[3] The Gospels certainly convey history, but not exactly in the way many moderns think of history. Explains the PBC:

> In other words, the intention of announcing Jesus, the Son of God and Savior of all—an intention which can be called "theological"—is widespread and fundamental in the gospels. The reference to concrete facts which we encounter in the gospels falls within the framework of this theological announcement. This means that while the theological affirmations about Jesus have a direct and normative import, the purely historical elements have a subordinate function.[4]

The primary aim of the Gospels, then, is to proclaim Jesus. They are not purely historical documents, but neither are they anti-historical. An authentic Christian appropriation of the Gospels recognizes that they have a historical nucleus, yet one which is intimately bound up with the various authors' unique attempts to draw us into the mystery of Christ. In a particularly helpful formulation, Erasmo Leiva-Merikakis writes that the Gospels communicate "the objective reality of history, but offered *as kerygma*."[5]

The above understanding of the Gospels was not invented but rather inherited by the PBC, and in no small part through a reception of Benedict XVI's exegesis of the Gospels. As Benedict will say below in the context of the infancy narratives, the Gospels are histories, to be sure, but they are *interpreted* histories that present us with the life of Jesus Christ through the lens of the early Church's faith. In saying this, Benedict demonstrates that he is just as aware as Ehrman that the Gospels do not contain transcripts of the *ipsissima verba* of

3. PBC, *The Inspiration and Truth of Sacred Scripture*, 142.
4. Ibid.
5. Erasmo Leiva-Merikakis, *Fire of Mercy, Heart of the Word: Meditations on the Gospel According to Saint Matthew*, vol. 2 (San Francisco: Ignatius Press, 2004), 45; cf. ibid., 44. While differing significantly on the extent to which the gospels preserve the historical nucleus of Christ's life, Crossan formulates this idea well when he says, "The gospels are written for faith, to faith, and from faith." *The Birth of Christianity*, 21.

Jesus.[6] Yet at the same time Benedict rejects the common scholarly dichotomy between the "Jesus of history" and the "Christ of faith."[7] In the foreword to his first volume of the *Jesus* series, he observes that the common result of historical-critical scholarship operating on this assumed rupture is that many now think we have very little certain knowledge about the man Christians profess to be God incarnate.[8]

Benedict took up this same theme in his 2006 Regensburg Address. Identifying nineteenth- and twentieth-century liberal exegesis as the precursor to the widespread cultural pluralism of today, the pontiff observed that its goal "was to bring Christianity back into harmony with modern reason, liberating it, that is to say, from seemingly philosophical and theological elements, such as faith in Christ's divinity and the triune God."[9] The central idea of Adolf von Harnack, liberal theology's "outstanding representative," was to get back to the man Jesus and his simple message that have been covered over through centuries of theological accretions.[10] In order to achieve this end, liberal

6. Benedict is by no means the first Catholic to acknowledge this. A century ago Marie-Joseph Lagrange could write, "We must be ready to give up the untenable. Since Jesus did not fix his teaching in writing, it was impossible that the terms of that teaching should have always been preserved for us with mathematical accuracy. Those of the evangelists are in part borrowed from the Church and given back to the Church; she provides them and she accepts them." Lagrange, *Historical Criticism and the Old Testament* (London: Catholic Truth Society, 1905), 44.

7. It should be noted that even some of the most archetypal modern scholars now reject this dichotomy. John Dominic Crossan, for instance, writes of his most recent project: "This, by the way, is emphatically not the old challenge of the 'Jesus of history' versus the 'Christ of faith.' The new challenge is whether we consider the 'Jesus of history' and/or 'the Christ of faith' to have been nonviolent or violent. This is a new and different challenge, not just another dreary repetition of an outdated one." Crossan, *How to Read the Bible and Still Be a Christian: Struggling with Violence from Genesis Through Revelation* (New York: HarperOne, 2015), 37. Nevertheless, it is the case that Crossan identifies the historical Jesus with the biblical Christ in the way that Benedict does. We see this when Crossan says, "If, for Christians, the biblical Christ is the criterion of the biblical God, then, for Christians, the historical Jesus is the criterion of the biblical Christ." Ibid., 5.

8. Benedict XVI, *Jesus of Nazareth: From the Baptism in the Jordan to the Transfiguration*, xi–xii.

9. Benedict XVI, "Faith, Reason, and the University: Memories and Reflections," Address at the University of Regensburg (September 12, 2006).

10. Benedict XVI, *Jesus of Nazareth: From the Baptism in the Jordan to the Transfiguration*, xii. Benedict also brings up Harnack in this connection in his introduction to the first volume of *Jesus*. Harnack claimed that Jesus' message was only about the Father, and

exegesis committed methodologically to accept only mathematical or empirical certainties, relegating the question of God to the realm of the unscientific or pre-scientific. As a result, Benedict writes that interpreters of the Bible today find ourselves "faced with a reduction of the radius of science and reason, one which needs to be questioned."[11]

Anticipating a point that will emerge again at the end of this book, Benedict "critiques the critique" by taking issue with the modern dehellenizing tendency to bracket the philosophical question involving God. The irony of deciding to exclude the God question is that this decision is itself philosophical in nature, a first principle assumed rather proved empirically. In response, Benedict argues that we need to overcome "the self-imposed limitation of reason to the empirically falsifiable" while at the same time taking care not to lose sight of the goods that have been achieved through modern biblical criticism:

This attempt, painted with broad strokes, at a critique of modern reason from within has nothing to do with putting the clock back to the time before the Enlightenment and rejecting the insights of the modern age. The positive aspects of modernity are to be acknowledged unreservedly: we are all grateful for the marvelous possibilities that it has opened up for mankind and for the progress in humanity that has been granted to us.... While we rejoice in the new possibilities open to humanity, we also see the dangers arising from these possibilities and we must ask ourselves how we can overcome them. [12]

As mentioned above, one important danger of excluding philosophical or religious elements within exegesis is that we lose sight of the true figure of Jesus presented in the Gospels. But another is that when the whole of science is reduced to the empirical, "it is man himself who ends up being reduced, for the specifically human questions about our origin and destiny, the questions raised by religion and ethics, then have no place within the purview of collective reason as defined by 'science,' so understood."

---

therefore Christology had no place in it. Benedict argues that this is a fallacy: Jesus is able to speak the way he does only because he is in full communion with the Father, and this mystery of the Son as revealer of the Father is present in everything he says and does. Ibid., 7. Benedict believes that we have to start here if we wish to understand the figure of Jesus, for it is "the central point" that anchors all that the New Testament tells us about the words, deeds, suffering, and glory of Christ. Ibid., 5.

11. Benedict XVI, "Faith, Reason, and the University."

12. Ibid. (also quote below).

Returning to the foreword of *Jesus*, Benedict writes that this reduction leads to a "dramatic situation for faith, because its point of
reference is being placed in doubt; intimate friendship with Jesus, on
which everything depends, is in danger of clutching at thin air."[13] This,
then, is why Benedict dedicated so many years late in his career to
penning the *Jesus* trilogy. The emeritus pontiff's chief concern and the
"main implication" of his method is that the Jesus of the Gospels *is* the
historical Jesus. Benedict is adamant that we can trust the Gospels—
and find in them the path to a personal encounter with Jesus Christ.[14]
In what follows, we will examine more concretely just how Benedict
goes about defending the truth of specific Gospel texts through a serious and judicial appropriation of modern exegesis.

Jesus of Nazareth: From the Baptism in the Jordan to the Transfiguration

Baptism and Temptations

While it would be reasonable to begin at the infancy of Christ, for
our present engagement with the mysteries of Christ's life I have decided to follow the order Benedict himself adopted in authoring the
Jesus trilogy. After the foreword and introduction to his first volume
discussed above, Benedict begins by considering the baptism and
temptations of Jesus (Mt 3–4; Lk 3–4). Anchoring the story of Jesus in
such historical persons as Tiberius Caesar, Pontius Pilate, and Herod,
Luke wishes his audience to understand Jesus's activity not as taking
place in a mythical "anytime" (which can mean always or never) but
rather as something that happens only once within human history itself.[15] Unlike many other religious traditions, the Gospels purport to
convey real history, albeit presented through the lens of faith.

To be sure, even the Gospels contain elements which might retain something of a mythic character, but that does not mean we are
justified in dismissing their core claims. For example, Benedict urges

---

13. Benedict XVI, *Jesus of Nazareth: From the Baptism to the Transfiguration*, xii.

14. Ibid., xxi. Benedict repeats this conviction in the foreword to the final volume of
the trilogy, *Jesus of Nazareth: The Infancy Narratives*, xii.

15. Benedict XVI, *Jesus of Nazareth: From the Baptism to the Transfiguration*, 11.

that the second temptation of Christ "has to be interpreted as a sort of vision."[16] The event, in other words, is not something that we would have been able to capture on a video camera, but this is not to say that it has no historical basis or that Satan is not real. Quite contrary to such a supposition, Benedict is emphatic that the figure of Satan is indispensable for understanding the mission of Jesus and, in turn, the Church.[17] But regardless of which aspects of the temptation narrative would pass as history according to our modern preconceptions, Benedict insists that "the point at issue" is revealed in Jesus' answer, "You shall not put the Lord your God to the test" (Dt 6:16).[18]

One of the most fascinating insights of Benedict's book lies in his excursus on the dialogue between Jesus and Satan in the temptation scene. Benedict describes this exchange as a theological debate among scholars over the correct interpretation of Scripture. Satan cites Scripture and twists it to his own purposes; Christ cites it right back at him according to the spirit in which it was written.[19] The point is that,

16. Ibid., 34.

17. Ratzinger, "Farewell to the Devil?" 202. See also my article by the same title at http://www.thegregorian.org/blog/farewell-to-the-devil.

18. Benedict XVI, *Jesus of Nazareth: From the Baptism in the Jordan to the Transfiguration*, 37. Dale Allison concurs in viewing the temptation narratives as something other then mere history: "Although I may be wrong about this, the temptation narratives ... do not strike me as sober history. For one thing, and as Origen already observed, there is no high place from which one can see the whole world. For another, doubting the historicity of the similar dialogues between rabbis and Satan strikes me as sensible, and turnabout is fair play. Why should I evaluate the Synoptic encounter differently? In any event, I concur with many that our story is the product of a sophisticated Christian scribe who spun a delightful haggadic tale out of Deuteronomy and the Psalms." Allison, *The Historical Christ and the Theological Jesus*, 25. At the same time, Allison adds that the narratives are not myth pure and simple: "The Temptation narrative may not be history as it really was, yet it is full of memory. My judgment is that, taken as a whole, its artistic originator has managed to leave us with a pretty fair impression of Jesus, even if the episode does not contain one word that Jesus spoke or narrate one thing that he did. Memory and legend are not easily disentangled, so when we try to weed out the fictions, will we not be uprooting much else besides?" Ibid., 25–26.

19. The pope bases his comments on Vladimir Solovyov's short story "The Antichrist," a work that, since he also refers to it in his Erasmus Lecture and his book *Eschatology*, we may surmise he finds important. In Solovyov's work, the figure of the Antichrist tries to seduce Christians by touting the honorary doctorate in theology he has been awarded by the University of Tübingen. Tübingen has historically been a mecca for historical-critical biblical research. Solovyov, then, is unabashedly connecting the

while Benedict does not reject scholarly biblical interpretation as such, he wishes to caution us against its possible aberrations. Thus he writes (pp. 35–36):

> The fact is that scholarly exegesis can become a tool of the Antichrist.... The alleged findings of scholarly exegesis have been used to put together the most dreadful books that destroy the figure of Jesus and dismantle the faith. The common practice today is to measure the Bible against the so-called modern worldview, whose fundamental dogma is that God cannot act in history.... And so the Bible no longer speaks of God, the living God; no, now *we* alone speak and decide what God can do and what we will and should do. And the Antichrist, with an air of scholarly excellence, tells us that any exegesis that reads the Bible from the perspective of faith in the living God, in order to listen to what God has to say, is fundamentalism; he wants to convince us that only his kind of exegesis, the supposedly purely scientific kind, in which God says nothing and has nothing to say, is able to keep abreast of the times. The theological dispute between Jesus and the devil is a dispute over the correct interpretation of Scripture.

One would be hard-pressed to find a harsher criticism of modern biblical scholarship at such a high level within the Catholic Church, and yet all this from the pen of a pope who engages such criticism not merely to critique but also to harvest the great good found within it.

The Kingdom of God

The third temptation of Christ discussed above concerns the same question Benedict addresses in his next chapter on the nature of the kingdom. Satan offers Jesus all the kingdoms of the world in exchange for a little worship. According to the emeritus pontiff, this is the "fundamental temptation because it concerns the question as to what sort of action is expected of a Savior of the world."[20] As Ehrman noted in the previous chapter, Jews living at the time of Christ were not at all expecting the suffering savior that Christians claimed Jesus to be, but rather a political figure who would usher in an everlasting kingdom here on earth. Benedict in his own turn echoes this concern:

---

hermeneutic of suspicion practiced at Tübingen with the work of the Antichrist, and ultimately the devil.

20. Benedict XVI, *Jesus of Nazareth: From the Baptism in the Jordan to the Transfiguration*, 42.

It is our Jewish interlocutors who, quite rightly, ask again and again: So what has your "Messiah" Jesus actually brought? He has not brought world peace, and he has not conquered the world's misery. So he can hardly be the true Messiah who, after all, was supposed to do just that.[21]

Is there anything more tragic, is there anything more opposed to belief in the existence of a good God and a Redeemer of mankind, than world hunger? Shouldn't it be the first test of the Redeemer, before the world's gaze and on the world's behalf, to give it bread and end all hunger?[22]

So what does Benedict think Jesus' kingdom is? What has Christ brought if not world peace, universal prosperity, and bread for the world? This is a most important question, for according to Benedict the proclamation of the kingdom constitutes "the core content of the Gospels" upon whose proper understanding "everything depends."[23] Ehrman for his part thinks that Jesus brought nothing new because, quite frankly, his promised kingdom failed to materialize. Or, as the Catholic modernist Alfred Loisy has it in a passage referenced by Benedict: Jesus preached the kingdom, but what came was the Church.[24] Are Ehrman and Loisy right? Did Jesus' kingdom fail, and we Christians end up with a disappointing Church as our compensation? Benedict acknowledges that the message of the Church shifted from the kingdom to Christ at a very early stage. But was this shift warranted?

As ever, Benedict observes some of the same phenomena as Ehrman (for example, the very obvious reality that world hunger has not been eliminated and that the Church began to focus more on Christ than on the kingdom in its earlier Jewish sense). The emeritus pon-

21. Ibid., 116. It is striking that Benedict formulates this question critical of Christianity in much the same way he cites Byzantine emperor Manuel II Paleologus against Islam in the Regensburg Address: "Show me just what Mohammed brought that was new, and there you will find things only evil and inhuman, such as his command to spread by the sword the faith he preached."

22. Ibid., 31.

23. Ibid., 47–48.

24. Ibid., 48. On this score Michael Bird argues, "Jesus may have spoken of himself in far more elevated ways than Ehrman imagines. It is certainly not the case that Jesus proclaimed God's kingdom and later on the church proclaimed Jesus. For even within Jesus' kingdom message there was always an implicit self-reference." Bird, *How God Became Jesus*, 52.

tift, however, draws a completely different conclusion from his observations, insisting that the primary question is not about the Church
but rather about the relationship between the kingdom and Christ.
So what is the *novum* in the kingdom? What has Christ brought that
is new?

The answer is very simple: God.... He has brought God, and now we know
his face, now we can call upon him. Now we know the path that we human
beings have to take in this world. Jesus has brought God and with God the
truth about our origin and destiny: faith, hope, and love.[25]

As both the Hebrew *malkut* and the Greek *basileia* indicate, the kingdom of God is not a static thing but rather a dynamic event: "God's
being Lord" in history.[26] Above all, Benedict points to Jesus as the
autobasileia, the kingdom in person. Within the New Testament perspective, the kingdom being at hand means that God is acting now in
the person of Jesus; it is through him that God is being Lord among
us. In other words, in this kingdom the messenger himself is the message.[27]

According to Benedict, this radical perspective on the kingdom
was perhaps an even more formidable motivation for many Jews' rejection of Jesus. Instead of exhorting his people to follow God, Jesus
places himself at the center of the Law when he says, "Come and follow me" (Mt 19:21). It thus is not what Jesus subtracts from the Law
(e.g. dietary regulations, circumcision, etc.) but what he *adds* it that
the Jews found problematic.[28] Contrary to certain modern interpretations, Benedict is adamant that Jesus was not merely a "liberal reform

25. Benedict XVI, *Jesus of Nazareth: From the Baptism in the Jordan to the Transfiguration*, 44.

26. For all the differences between his and Benedict's views of the kingdom, it is
noteworthy that John Dominic Crossan also thinks of it in terms of power, rule, and
"process" rather than as a static place. Crossan, *Jesus: A Revolutionary Biography*, 55. See
also N. T. Wright, *The Challenge of Jesus*, 36. Wright's work is especially penetrating
when it comes to showing how everything Jesus did in his ministry was aimed at enacting
and embodying the coming kingdom of Yahweh in his own person.

27. As Benedict relates, the kingdom of God is a dynamic reality that admits of ecclesiastical, mystical, eschatological, and christological interpretations. For these and for
his understanding of the kingdom as an event, see *Jesus of Nazareth: From the Baptism in
the Jordan to the Transfiguration*, 49ff.

28. Ibid., 99ff.

rabbi," but rather a man claiming to be God himself.[29] Indeed, this is shown in Benedict's observation that "[n]o one would crucify a teacher who told pleasant stories to enforce prudential morality."[30] Jesus was not a moralist. Rather, as we find in his parables—which according to Benedict constitute the heart of his teaching—the deepest theme of Jesus' message was nothing other than himself.[31]

Benedict is well aware that, to someone who thinks that the Messiah should have put an end to all wars and solved the problem of world hunger, his own understanding of the kingdom may come across as a cheap response. But according to Benedict, it is only our hardness of heart that makes us think of this as too little. The truth of the matter is that, while poverty and hunger continue to plague humanity unto this day, man does not live by bread alone. To be sure, Jesus is not indifferent to human hunger and to our bodily needs, "but he places these things in the proper context and the proper order."[32] The issue, then, is the primacy of God as the reality without which nothing else can be good.

Of course, we always wish that God's presence were as evident as the more tangible things of our everyday experience, but the mysterious divine plan has ordered things in such a way that God "can be

---

29. Ibid., 119.

30. Ibid., 186. Interestingly, Ehrman agrees to some extent here: "[If] Jesus had simply been a great moral teacher, a gentle rabbi who did nothing more than urge his devoted followers to love God and one another, or an itinerant philosopher ... then he would scarcely have been seen as a threat to the Romans and nailed to a cross. Great moral teachers were not crucified—unless their teachings were considered subversive." Bart Ehrman, *The New Testament: A Historical Introduction to the Early Christian Writings* (New York: Oxford University Press, 2012), 275–76.

31. *Jesus of Nazareth: From the Baptism in the Jordan to the Transfiguration*, 183, 188. As noted in the previous chapter, this view is in contrast with that of Crossan, who believes that the gospel histories themselves are parables. Says Crossan: "My general proposal is that parables by Jesus during his life begot parables about Jesus after his death; and, furthermore, that the four gospels not only contain parables about Jesus, but are best understood as four discrete megaparables about Jesus." *The Power of Parable*, 154. Even though his and Benedict's views are clearly incompatible on this important point, it is worth reflecting on Crossan's description of parables (*The Power of Parable*, 243) as participatory pedagogy wherein the narrative lures one into its plotted micro-world to participate as an outsider-insider in its ongoing adventure.

32. *Jesus of Nazareth: From the Baptism in the Jordan to the Transfiguration*, 32.

sought and found only when the heart sets out on the 'exodus' from 'Egypt,'" a process that occurs "first and foremost by obedience to God's word."[33] Christ conforms his faithful to himself, making us "sons in the Son" and members of his Mystical Body who are called to be his hands and feet in the world. The key here is that Christ wishes to heal the world not through a snap of his fingers but rather through that obedience by which we become cooperators in his own saving work: "Only when this obedience is put into practice does the attitude develop that is also capable of providing bread for all."[34] But of course, this whole picture of becoming sharers in God's own nature and work is itself dependent on the Church's faith. The issue here as ever ends up being philosophical in nature. If we are committed to reading the Gospels without this faith, then Benedict's answer will hardly appeal. If on the other hand we approach the Gospels with a hermeneutic of trust, then we can admit that Jesus did not fulfill Jewish messianic expectations in the way most anticipated. Indeed, it does not follow from the incarnation being a surprise that God's plan was not fulfilled through it.

Jesus of Nazareth: Holy Week: From the Entrance into Jerusalem to the Resurrection
The Last Supper

The second volume of Benedict's *Jesus* trilogy begins on Palm Sunday with the triumphal entry into Jerusalem and takes us through Holy Week, finishing with an epilogue on the Ascension. However, in the effort to be concise, I will focus on just a few key events that are particularly relevant to the theme of our book. In this regard there is no better place to begin than with the methodological foreword embedded in Benedict's chapter on the Last Supper. Considering the fact that many modern scholars doubt that the Last Supper happened in any way resembling how it is depicted in the Gospels, it is significant that Benedict states point blank that "the text in question concerns the very heart of Christianity."[35] The problem, however, is that the events

33. Ibid., 34.   34. Ibid.
35. Benedict XVI, *Jesus of Nazareth: Holy Week*, 103.

of the Last Supper and the institution of the Eucharist have been "caught up in a dense undergrowth of mutually contradictory hypotheses, which seem to make access to the real event nearly impossible."[36] In this connection it is imperative to understand that, for Benedict, the historical method can at best produce high probability but not absolute certainty over every detail of our inquiry. This is why he focuses on the task of getting to know the figure of Jesus through the Gospel narratives, while leaving "the details to the experts."[37]

All the same, the emeritus pontiff insists that Christians cannot ignore the historicity question concerning the events that unfolded during Holy Week. For him it is "essential that these events actually occurred in the history of this world."[38] These are not myths or symbolic stories of timeless meta-historical truths. Indeed, Benedict is so convicted of this as to avow that if the historicity of such events were disproved, then the Church's faith would lose its foundation.[39] Our task then, is "to ascertain whether the basic convictions of the faith are plausible and credible when today's exegetical knowledge is taken in all seriousness."[40] This is not the same as proving that the events happened. Accepting that a given historical event happened inevitably involves an act of trusting the witness reporting it. According to Benedict, all the believer needs to do at this point is to defend the plausibility of the Christian claim and to answer objections to the effect that our Church's teachings are incompatible with reason.

Benedict begins his response to this question by drawing the distinction he frequently makes between the substantial and the accidental, the essential and the details. While many details of the Gospels remain open to multiple interpretations, for Benedict the fundamental historicity of basic Christian truths such as the Incarnation, Last Supper, cross, Resurrection remains essential. As was indicated above, however, absolute certainty for these claims is unattainable by means of the historical method alone. Where, then, does the Christian get his certitude?

---

36. Ibid.
38. Ibid., 103–4.
40. Ibid., 105.

37. Ibid.
39. Ibid., 104–5.

It is faith that gives us the ultimate certainty upon which we base our whole lives—a humble commonality of belief in company with the Church of every age under the guidance of the Holy Spirit. On this basis, moreover, we can serenely examine exegetical hypotheses that all too often make exaggerated claims to certainty.[41]

At the end of the day, it is the gift of faith that gives us certainty. This point, introduced briefly above, is something to which we will return in our conclusion. For now, the point is that no amount of historical evidence is sufficient to give us certainty when it comes to the mysteries of Christ's life, and if we are waiting for infallible certainty before accepting them, then we will probably never get there.

Turning from these methodological points to the text of the Gospel itself, a significant portion of Benedict's chapter focuses on the dating of the Last Supper. Here in particular the emeritus pontiff demonstrates his exegetical prowess and his interest in a sincere engagement with modern hypotheses. To begin, it is striking to see Benedict say that "[t]he problem of dating Jesus' Last Supper arises from the *contradiction* on this point between the Synoptic Gospels, on the one hand, and Saint John's Gospel, on the other."[42] While it might catch some Christians off guard to hear Benedict speak of the Gospels as mutually contradictory in some way, the fact of the matter is that the respective chronologies of the Triduum differ by one day. The synoptic Gospels situate the Last Supper contemporaneously with that year's evening Passover vigil meal:

And on the first day of Unleavened Bread, when they sacrificed the passover lamb, his disciples said to him, "Where will you have us go and prepare for you to eat the passover?" (Mk 14:12)

After the Last Supper–Passover meal, Jesus goes to pray in Gethsemane, where he is arrested and led away; he is then tried, denied by Peter, and held overnight in Caiaphas's prison. Early the next morning, he is condemned to death by Pilate, taken outside of the city and crucified around the third hour, and breathes his last at the ninth hour (Mk 15:34). Mark makes it abundantly clear that his body was then taken down in the evening before sunset:

41. Ibid. (emphasis added).
42. Ibid., 106 (emphasis added).

And when evening had come, since it was the day of Preparation, that is, the day before the sabbath, Joseph of Arimathea, a respected member of the council, who was also himself looking for the kingdom of God, took courage and went to Pilate, and asked for the body of Jesus. (Mk 15:42; cf. Lk 23:54)

Jesus' body fittingly rests in the tomb the following day, the day of the weekly Sabbath. Then, "very early on the first day of the week" (Mk 16:12), Jesus rises from the dead and the empty tomb is discovered by the holy women (whose names differ somewhat depending on which Gospel one is reading).[43]

The Gospel of John agrees with the synoptic Gospels in placing the resurrection on the first day of the week (Jn 20:1). However, the Johannine chronology clearly differs when it comes to the placement of the Last Supper and crucifixion. Whereas the synoptic Gospels portray Jesus as celebrating the Last Supper as a Passover vigil meal, John goes to great lengths to show that the Last Supper was *not* a Passover meal. Introducing the events of that fateful night, the evangelist writes:

Now before the feast of the Passover, when Jesus knew that his hour had come to depart out of this world to the Father, having loved his own who were in the world, he loved them to the end. (Jn 13:1–2)

As in the synoptic tradition, Jesus is arrested and put on trial afterwards. The apparent disagreement between the Gospel accounts is that the evening Passover vigil described in the first three Gospels had not yet taken place at the time of Jesus' morning trial in John:

Then they led Jesus from the house of Caiaphas to the praetorium. It was early. They themselves did not enter the praetorium, so that they might not be defiled, but might eat the Passover. (Jn 18:28)

John thus has Jesus being crucified at the sixth hour, earlier on the same day that the synoptics say that he celebrated the Last Supper, the "day of Preparation for the Passover" (Jn 19:14). But then John gives us this puzzling piece of information:

Since it was the day of Preparation, in order to prevent the bodies from remaining on the cross on the sabbath (for that sabbath was a high day), the Jews asked Pilate that their legs might be broken, and that they might be taken away. (Jn 19:31)

43. Note that this chronology is from our earliest Gospel, thus undermining Crossan's claim that Jesus' body was eaten by dogs.

What was this "day of Preparation" of which the Gospels speak? For the synoptics, it is clearly the day in which the people prepared for the weekly Sabbath. But for John as noted above, it was the day of preparation for the Passover (Jn 19:14). Now here in John it emerges that the preparation was for both the Passover *and* the Sabbath, which happened to fall on the same day that year.

The question thus naturally arises: which of the two traditions is more historical? In favor of the synoptic tradition, all three of these Gospels were composed before John and thus were closer to the event of the Last Supper itself. Moreover, according to Benedict, the Last Supper seems so closely tied to Passover "that to deny its Passover character is problematic."[44] Finally, there is the argument from tradition: the long tradition assigning the Last Supper to Holy Thursday was established as early as the second century.[45]

Benedict, however, seems to favor the Johannine chronology. Following John Meier, whose solution is "astonishingly simple and in many respects convincing," he suggests that the Last Supper was not the traditional Passover meal but rather Jesus' own Passover. Knowing that he was about to die and would not be able to eat the Passover with his disciples, according to this hypothesis Jesus invited his disciples to a Passover of a very different kind in which he himself was the Lamb slain for the sins of the world. In contrast with the longstanding tendency to see John's Gospel as more theological (e.g., John has Jesus killed at the same hour the paschal lambs were slaughtered), Benedict believes that John's chronology is "more probable historically than the Synoptic chronology."[46] The main factor driving him to this conclu-

44. Ibid., 109.
45. Ibid., 111.
46. Ibid., 109. Benedict does not cite Meier in the first installment of *Jesus*, but his work is referenced several times in the second volume of the trilogy. One wonders whether the pontiff in the meantime had read and taken to heart Richard Hays's incisive observation that "[Benedict's] dialogue partners in New Testament exegesis are, for the most part, the great scholars of earlier generations." Hays adds, *"Jesus of Nazareth* does not seem to be informed at all by the more recent, and now much more influential, work of even such great Catholic scholars as Raymond Brown and John Meier. It is perhaps not surprising that an eighty-year-old scholar would continue to focus on the categories and questions that were current in the German academy during the era of his own training and more active scholarly career. But it is regrettable that Benedict did not bring his

sion is his supposition that the Jews would not have tried and executed someone on such a feast day as the Passover; to him it seems "questionable" and indeed "scarcely conceivable."[47]

Even so, to my mind Benedict's argument here does not convincingly undermine the traditional position. If the Jewish authorities saw Jesus' presence in Jerusalem that week as an imminent threat, might not they have been willing to break from protocol? But regardless of what side of the debate one ends up on, the larger point here is that the debate showcases Benedict's method, casting into relief how he appropriates modern criticism with fidelity to the Church. While many Christians may feel uncomfortable with Benedict finding it "questionable" that the Last Supper took place on the Passover, the pontiff is not afraid of the problems posed by modern scholarship. It is clear that even when calling certain things questionable or contradictory he

---

discussion up to date. His dismissive discussion of Jesus as an apocalyptic teacher would profit greatly from engagement with the work of scholars such as E. P. Sanders and Dale Allison. And it would be fascinating to know what the pope thinks of the work of N. T. Wright, whose books on Jesus are widely influential in the English-speaking world." Richard Hays, "Benedict and the Biblical Jesus," *First Things* (August, 2007). In this regard it should be observed, first, that Benedict's work does in fact evince deep acquaintance with the scholarly literature from the 1960s to 80s and, to a lesser exent, the 90s and later. Moreover, it ought to be recalled that *Jesus of Nazareth* was conceived to be an account of his own personal search for the face of the Lord, not an exhautive monograph. All the same, Hays's criticism has its merits, and in this volume I have attempted a partial rectification of this situation by incorporating some of the most recent scholarship available that bears upon the topics addressed by Benedict and Ehrman. Much of this can be found in the footnotes of this chapter.

47. *Jesus of Nazareth: Holy Week*, 107, 109. In this connection it is worth recalling the argument recorded in Mark, "Not during the feast, lest there be a tumult of the people" (Mk 14:1–2). In this section Benedict also dismisses Annie Jaubert's attempt to harmonize the Johannine and Synoptic chronologies as "fascinating ... but too weak to be convincing." Jaubert's interpretation proceeds from the observation that there were two different Jewish calendars used in Jesus' day, and it then hypothesizes that Jesus celebrated the Last Supper following the calendar not sanctioned by the authorities in Jerusalem. Such a solution would enable one to hold that Jesus really celebrated a Passover meal (as in the Synoptics), while maintaining that it was not the Passover meal of the Jewish authorities (as in John). Yet Benedict remains cautious, avowing that we can reconstruct the world at the time of Christ only to a limited degree. Ibid., 109–11. On the question of whether John or the Synoptic dating tradition is more probable, I am open to, but remain unconvinced by, Benedict's argument in favor of the Johannine chronology. See also Dale Allison's critique in *The Historical Christ and the Theological Jesus*, 86.

remains firmly convinced that these contradictions are only apparent and that they can be explained if only we work *through* them rather than ignoring them. For Benedict, the various Gospel accounts of the Last Supper certainly exhibit "differences in detail," but they remain "very similar in essentials."[48]

An important example: the New Testament contains four distinct Eucharistic institution narratives following two principal lines of tradition (Mark 14/Matthew 26 on the one hand, and Luke 22/1 Corinthians 11 on the other). In a telling moment in which he discusses the relative antiquity of these two models, Benedict acknowledges that Paul's text is older in literary terms, even though both Paul's and Mark's texts ultimately have roots in the 30s.[49] It really does not matter which of the two is older, for Benedict rightly states that these accounts have taken on "an essential meaning for the Church's reception of this whole tradition." In other words, given the degree to which these accounts have been received in the Church's life over the past two millennia, a Catholic cannot assume that they were invented, as many modern scholars do. The presence of two strands of tradition within the canon demonstrates that the Church permitted "a degree of nuanced redaction." At the same time, the nascent Church "was conscious of a strict obligation to faithfulness in essentials."[50]

As a final word on the subject of the Last Supper, it is fascinating to read Benedict's thoughts on why its historicity is so commonly called into question. Says Benedict:

Given the uniquely powerful event described in the Last Supper, in terms of its theological significance and its place in the history of religions, it could hardly fail to be called into question in modern theology; something so utterly extraordinary was scarcely compatible with the picture of the friendly rabbi that many exegetes draw of Jesus.... As this concerns the very heart of Christianity and the essence of the figure of Jesus, we must take a somewhat closer look.[51]

48. Benedict XVI, *Jesus of Nazareth: Holy Week*, 115ff.

49. Ibid., 117. Note that Benedict, following the majority of modern scholars and thus distancing himself from the majority opinion throughout Church history, assumes Markan priority here as he does throughout his corpus.

50. Ibid., 127.

51. Ibid., 117–18.

As Benedict tells us, the principal argument levied against the historicity of the institution narratives concerns their seeming incompatibility with Jesus' image of God and his message of the kingdom. Wherein lies this tension? Jesus taught that the Father is unconditionally ready to pardon all people, and yet at the Last Supper the Gospel authors would have him say that his blood was shed "for you—for many," not for all. This leads to a striking and incisive moment within Benedict's criticism of the criticism. He explains:

This is the real reason why a good number of modern theologians (not only exegetes) reject the idea that the words of the Last Supper go back to Jesus himself. It is not on the basis of historical evidence: as we have seen, the eucharistic texts belong to the earliest strand of tradition. From the point of view of historical evidence, nothing could be more authentic than this Last Supper tradition. But the idea of expiation is incomprehensible to the modern mind. Jesus, with his proclamation of the kingdom of God, must surely be diametrically opposed to such a notion [so think many moderns]. At issue here is our image of God and our image of man. To this extent, the whole discussion only *appears* to be concerned with history.[52]

This sort of dynamic is what underlies Benedict's conviction that the modern exegetical debate is at bottom philosophical in nature. Following historical-critical methodology as faithfully as possible, Benedict sees no reason to doubt the essential veracity of the Last Supper traditions (granting that each differs in matters of detail). According to Benedict, the real problem moderns have with the Last Supper is not historical in nature, but rather that we find the idea of expiation repugnant.

In conclusion, Benedict describes the claim that the Eucharist was invented by the Apostles as "absurd, even from a historical point of view." While deeming this suggestion "absurd" may be more than some historians would be willing to grant, Benedict rightfully calls attention to the inconsistency of those who base their reconstruction of the historical Jesus largely on the Synoptic tradition but then proceed to reject a tradition that is found not only in all three Synoptic Gospels but also in St. Paul. Moreover, to my mind Benedict's following

52. Ibid., 119.

question is spot-on: "How could the first generation of Christians—as early as the 30s—have accepted such an invention without anyone calling it into question?"[53] Of course, to be fair to skeptics one must concede that it is always possible that someone did call it into question, but that their complaint was either not registered in writing or later disposed of by the proto-orthodox. But the skeptic just stating that this is possible does not constitute an argument. I think that exegetes like Ehrman are asking a lot more than they appear to be asking when they allege that key traditions such as the Last Supper and the Resurrection were invented during the first decade after Jesus' crucifixion. The best historical evidence we actually have on this matter is the New Testament itself, whose earliest strands affirm the historicity of these mysteries. Moreover, these Gospel witnesses themselves may be older than scholars generally assume.[54]

Trial(s), Crucifixion, and Resurrection

One who reads Benedict's account of Holy Week in its entirety will find that he makes the same sort of moves in the effort to uphold the historicity of later events that he made in the case of the Last Supper. For example, the various accounts of Jesus' dialogue with Caiaphas "differ in detail" in light of the overall context of each Gospel and by the audiences being addressed. At the same time, Benedict makes it clear that these differences occur only in accidental matters and that "[t]he essential content of the exchange nevertheless emerges quite unequivocally from the three different accounts.... In all essentials, the four Gospels harmonize with one another in their accounts of the progress of the trial."[55] That said, Benedict follows the standard line of historical criticism in concluding that Mark presents us with

53. Ibid., 125.
54. The primary foundation for a late-first-century dating of the synoptic gospels rests squarely on the unfounded assumption that Jesus' foretelling of the Temple's demise must have been invented by the evangelists. This is an entirely unsurprising assumption, given that many modern biblical scholars assume the impossibility of miracles in general, including prophecy. But even granting this unfounded assumption, would it really have required the gift of prophecy for Jesus to read the signs of the times and figure out that the end of the Temple was near?
55. *Jesus of Nazareth: Holy Week*, 179, 184.

"the most authentic" form of the dramatic dialogue between Jesus and Caiaphas.[56] And when it comes to the dialogue between Jesus and Pilate, he notes that this is "of course" contested by exegetes who inevitably become wary when a tradition is recorded only in John.[57] To this challenge Benedict responds by acknowledging, "Certainly no one would claim that John set out to provide anything resembling a transcript of the trial." With this all modern scholars would agree. But Benedict veers from the norm when he professes, "Yet we may assume that [John] was able to explain with great precision the core question at issue and that he presents us with a true account of the trial."[58] As in the case of the Last Supper, the pontiff insists that there is a core or essence to the event that each of the various Gospels captures faithfully, even as each account differs in matters of detail which cannot be harmonized according to the standards of modern historiography.[59]

56. Ibid., 179.   57. Ibid., 184.
58. Ibid.
59. A valuable approach to this reality can be found in Dale Allison's *Constructing Jesus: Memory, Imagination, and History* (Grand Rapids, Mich.: Baker Academic, 2010) and his shorter *The Historical Christ and the Theological Jesus*, which I cite here. Employing different language to capture the same dynamic, Allison, in the latter of these two works, begins by distinguishing the "general" from the "particular," arguing (61): "Even when human memory fails to retain the particulars, it can still get general impressions right." Regarding gospel texts that testify to Jesus' self-conception, he writes (65): "I do not contend (or deny) that Jesus formulated any of the sayings just cited.... I am rather displaying a pattern. Jesus' starring role in the eschatological drama is all over the tradition.... So my inference is that, whatever titles he may or may not have used, Jesus probably believed himself to be not just an eschatological prophet, but the personal locus of the end-time scenario, the central figure of the last judgment." In another place (95) he writes: "I do not contend, because I do not believe, that all this material comes from Jesus, directly or indirectly. Nor do I insist that any of it is word-perfect memory ... the Synoptics are not primarily records of what Jesus actually said and did but collections of impressions. They recount, or rather often recount, the sorts of things that he said and did, or that he could have said and done." Allison's account of memory is balanced and realistic; he admits (61): "We mix memories with imagination.... [W]e impose narrative connections on events in order to make them intelligible ... projecting our current circumstances and beliefs backward in time.... We need not be bottomless skeptics to see that our sources have not been miraculously immune to all the usual failures and biases of memory. All one has to do is peruse a synopsis, which will reveal variations in order, contradictions in description, and discrepancies in wording." Accordingly, he says (62): "Given that we typically remember the outlines of an event or the general purport of a conversation rather than the particulars ... [w]e should rather be looking for

The same logic applies in the case of the crucifixion accounts that appear in the Gospels. No two of these accounts come even close to matching up perfectly, and indeed one gets the sense that there is a good deal of theology injected into the protagonists' speeches. Benedict carefully demonstrates how Jesus' Passion is painted as a fulfillment of the Old Testament texts such as Isaiah 53, Psalm 22, Psalm 69, and Wisdom 2. But when one sits down and compares these Old Testament texts with their New Testament counterparts, the whole thing might come across as too neat to be true. In other words, the natural objection from Ehrman and others in his camp is to assert that the Gospel authors invented their narratives based on these Old Testament texts, and it is this—rather than their being prophecies—that accounts for the resemblance between the two. On Ehrman's account, these connections were made only after the Resurrection, when the disciples began to think that Jesus was, in some sense, God. Or, as John Dominic Crossan has it, "What we have now in those detailed passion accounts is not history remembered but prophecy historicized.... Prophecy, in this sense, is known after rather than before the fact."[60]

Actually, Benedict agrees to a certain extent on this last point but differs in his evaluation of whether the Gospels' post-resurrection exegetical moves were warranted. Here is how he describes the dynamic:

Underpinning this particular way of recounting events is the learning process that the infant Church had to undergo as she came into being. At first, Jesus' death on the Cross had simply been an inexplicable fact that placed his entire message and his whole figure in question.... In the light of the Resurrection,

repeating patterns and contemplating the big picture." By approaching the Gospels in this way, Allison departs from the standard scholarly practice of applying criteria to ascertain whether a particular saying or deed is attributable to the historical Jesus. While his approach may not appear very significant at first glance, it allows us to conclude many things about Jesus that contradict the conclusions of Ehrman or the Jesus Seminar (63–64): "Working through the tradition in the way I suggest leads to a large number of conclusions. Jesus must have been an exorcist who interpreted his ministry in terms of Satan's downfall. He must have thought highly of John the Baptist. He must have repeatedly spoken of God as Father. He must have composed parables. He must have come into conflict with religious authorities."

60. Crossan, *Jesus: A Revolutionary Biography*, 145.

in the light of this new gift of journeying alongside the Lord, Christ's followers had to learn to read the Old Testament afresh.[61]

At this point Benedict affirms what just above we saw Ehrman declaring, namely, that the Jews did not anticipate a crucified Messiah. But then he parts paths with the agnostic:

It was not the words of Scripture that prompted the narration of facts; rather, it was the facts themselves, at first unintelligible, that paved the way toward a fresh understanding of Scripture.[62]

Whether one is going to accept Benedict's or Ehrman's take on this matter boils down to the question of whether we are committed to seeing the early Church's theological developments as a human work guided by divine providence, or whether we are going to see the process as a purely human effort to rationalize the crucifixion of Jesus. As I have said above and I will repeat again below, at bottom the decision one makes here is ultimately driven by prior philosophical and religious commitments.

Benedict deepens this same point in his ensuing discussion of the resurrection. Demonstrating how important the question is, he writes that the Christian faith "stands or falls with the truth of the testimony that Christ is risen from the dead," and that in the quest to know the figure of Jesus revealed in Scripture, "the Resurrection is the crucial

---

61. Benedict XVI, *Jesus of Nazareth: Holy Week*, 202–3. The apostles also had to rethink other events of Christ's life in light of the crucifixion. Thus the Transfiguration scene (Mt 17:1–8) is painted by the evangelist in parallelism with his account of the crucifixion (Mt 27:31–50). For a concise summary of these parallels, see Allison, *The Luminous Dusk*, 58–59.

62. Benedict XVI, *Jesus of Nazareth: Holy Week*, 203. For a serious challenge to the standard assumption (shared by Benedict and Ehrman) that no one before Christ had expected a crucified Messiah, see Brant Pitre, *Jesus, the Tribulation, and the End of the Exile: Restoration Eschatology and the Origin of the Atonement* (Tübingen: Mohr Siebeck, 2005), especially pp. 56–57. Although Pitre acknowledges that the Suffering Servant prophecy of Isaiah 52–53 is not explicitly identified with the Messiah, there is one text—Dan 9:25–27—in which an "anointed one" would rise up before "the end" and be "cut off." Considering Jesus' clear self-identification with the Son of Man figure found just two chapters earlier in Daniel, Pitre's argument that Jesus understood his mission in these terms is entirely reasonable within a first-century Jewish context and merits serious consideration. On Jesus treating the figures of Daniel 7 and Daniel 9 as the same person, see Pitre, 393–99.

point."[63] As he did with the crucifixion, Benedict proceeds to examine texts such as Psalm 16:27–28 and Hosea 6:1–2, which prophesy or at least appear to foreshadow Christ's resurrection. It is important that Benedict agrees with the mainstream scholarly consensus, which holds that these two texts were not originally written as prophecies of the Messiah's cross and resurrection. Indeed, the Hebrew version of Psalm 16 has its sights set on deliverance from dying in the first place rather than rising again after having died.[64] And as for the "third day" discussed in Hosea 6, Benedict maintains that this was not originally a prophecy but rather "could become an anticipatory pointer toward resurrection on the third day only once the event that took place on the Sunday after the Lord's crucifixion had given this day a special meaning."[65]

So what are we to make of the divergences in the Gospels' resurrection accounts, inasmuch as they differ from one another every bit as much as those of the crucifixion? And what are we to make of the many Old Testament foreshadowings of Christ's resurrection which appear almost too good to be true? Benedict elaborates:

The process of coming to Resurrection faith is analogous to what we saw in the case of the Cross. Nobody had thought of a crucified Messiah. Now the "fact" was there, and it was necessary, on the basis of that fact, to take a fresh look at Scripture.... Admittedly, this new reading of Scripture could begin

---

63. Benedict XVI, *Jesus of Nazareth: Holy Week*, 241–42. See also 1 Cor 15:14–15.

64. Ibid., 255. For more on Psalm 16, especially the differences between the original Hebrew and the Greek cited by Peter in Acts 2, see Ramage, *Dark Passages of the Bible*, 270–71.

65. Benedict XVI, *Jesus of Nazareth: Holy Week*, 257–58. As Peter Enns writes on another passage that originally did not point to resurrection, "No one reading and coming across [Exodus] 3:6 would think that resurrection was suddenly the topic of conversation." Enns, *Inspiration and Incarnation* (Grand Rapids, Mich.: Baker Academic, 2005), 114; cf. Lk 20:27–40; Mt 22:23–33; Mk 12:18–27. Enns elaborates, "The New Testament authors were not engaging the Old Testament in an effort to remain consistent with the original context and intention of the Old Testament author.... To put it succinctly, the New Testament authors were explaining what the Old Testament means in light of Christ's coming." Ibid., 115–16. In other words, "It is not that the Old Testament words are taken out of context and tossed into the air to fall where they may. Rather, the New Testament authors take the Old Testament out of *one* context, that of the original human author, and place it into *another* context, the one that represents the final goal to which Israel's story has been moving." Ibid., 153.

only after the Resurrection, because it was only through the Resurrection that Jesus was accredited as the one sent by God. Now people had to search Scripture for both Cross and Resurrection, so as to understand them in a new way and thereby come to believe in Jesus as the Son of God.[66]

An important contemporary Evangelical scholar, Peter Enns, speaks similarly in the context of Jesus' appearance along to the road to Emmaus:

For any Jew who saw him or herself as one of the Chosen People, hearing a claim like this [that Jesus had risen] would have been hard to take in—frankly, it would have sounded ridiculous, as if God was turning his back on their unique tradition, their rich heritage, their story—the story God himself had written. What we've got here is more than just a slight adjustment to Israel's story.

You can read the Old Testament as carefully and as often as you want—standing on your head, backward, with special decoder glasses, or in Klingon—and you won't find anything about a future messiah dying and rising from the dead on the third day , the very thing Jesus says you will find there [Lk 9:22]. Not a word. Don't even bother looking. So what's Luke's angle? Why does Jesus say something is in the Bible when it clearly isn't? That makes no sense. No, it doesn't—until we are clear on what Jesus is actually telling his disciples. Jesus didn't mean for the disciples to root through their Bibles to find the places where a dying-and-rising-from-the-dead messiah was hid-

66. Benedict XVI, *Jesus of Nazareth: Holy Week*, 245. Benedict notes that this deepened understanding of Christ's mystery is seen in the two endings of Mark: "The ending of Mark poses a particular problem.... The authentic text of the Gospel as it has come down to us ends with the fear and trembling of the women." Ibid., 261. To this a second-century redactor later added a concluding summary which brings together the most important resurrection traditions and the mission of the disciples to proclaim the Gospel to the whole world (Mk 16:9–20). Also worthwhile reading in this connection is Richard Hays's comment, "A Gospel-shaped hermeneutic necessarily entails reading backwards reinterpreting Israel's Scripture in light of the story of Jesus." In addition to the texts Benedict discusses, Hays mentions such examples as Jn 2:22, wherein the disciples realized the meaning of Jesus' Temple prophecy only after his resurrection. Hays, *Reading Backwards*, 104. Concerning the Emmaus narrative in Lk 24:13–35, Hays further elaborates on how the gospels teach us how to read the Old Testament aright: "Jesus' teaching does not produce that result immediately. The moment of recognition comes only as they sit at the table and Jesus breaks bread with them (vv. 30–32). This point, too, is significant for understanding how the Gospels teach us to read the OT. We come to understand Scripture only as we participate in the shared life of the community, enacted in meals shared at table." Ibid., 15.

ing.... Jesus isn't "in" Israel's story that way. You'll never read Israel's story on its own terms and "find Jesus" on the surface. To see Jesus, you won't get there by sticking to the script. You will only see Jesus there in hindsight and under the surface, where your reading of the Old Testament is driven by faith in Christ, where Jesus has become the starting point for re-understanding Israel's story, not the logical conclusion of Israel's story. Here in Luke's Gospel Jesus is not telling his disciples to stick literally to the script. He is telling them to reread the script in light of his death and resurrection.[67]

Unlike Ehrman, who views the early Church's handling of the Old Testament as a work of creative fiction, Benedict and Enns consciously decide not to approach the Gospels with a hermeneutic of suspicion. From this standpoint of faith, they admit that Jesus' forebears never expected the messiah to die and rise, and yet they also insist that the Old Testament connections to Christ's resurrection were planned providentially by God.

Finally on the subject of the resurrection, Benedict is quite honest about the apparent contradictions within the four Gospels' accounts of Easter Sunday:

The dialectic [between recognition and nonrecognition of Jesus], which pertains to the nature of the Risen Christ, is presented quite clumsily in the narratives, and it is this that manifests their veracity. Had it been necessary to invent the Resurrection, all the emphasis would have been placed on full physicality, on immediate recognizability, and perhaps, too, some special power would have been thought up as a distinguishing feature of the risen Lord. But in the internal contradictions characteristic of all the accounts of

67. Enns, *The Bible Tells Me So*, 201–2. Enns speaks similarly of understanding Jesus' infancy narratives: "The real Jesus can only be truly understood from a later vantage point—interpreted after the resurrection when the broader implications of who Jesus was and what he did could be better grasped. That is the Jesus the Gospel writers give us, each in his own way. That's where I land, but I'm just riffing, and if it's not convincing to you, leave it to the side and work it out some other way. We're all free to put the pieces together as we think best. The bigger point here is that the stories of Jesus's birth behave the way stories do, and we can't wish that away." Ibid., 86. These words remind me of a quote from William James, "It is true that we instinctively recoil from seeing an object to which our emotions and affections are committed handled by the intellect as any other object is handled." James, *The Varieties of Religious Experience* (Cambridge, Mass.: Harvard University Press, 1985), 17. It is difficult for many Christians to come to terms with the reality that the biblical stories are truly human stories and are susceptible to the methods of investigation that we apply to texts within other areas of enquiry.

what the disciples experienced, in the mysterious combination of otherness and identity, we see reflected a new form of encounter.[68]

For the evangelists, Jesus' resurrected presence is entirely physical, and yet the Lord is not bound by physical laws. Jesus did not simply return to normal biological life in his resurrection, nor is he a ghost or simply alive in the hearts and minds of the disciples. And yet, for all this, the four Gospels still are not perfectly clear as to the nature of Jesus' resurrected body. As Benedict says, the question is addressed "quite clumsily" and with "internal contradictions."

With the above admission, Benedict aligns himself with the vast majority of modern biblical scholars. As before, however, he does not take these admitted tensions as an indication that the Gospels have lost the essential figure of the historical Jesus. On the contrary, the tensions only serve to highlight what the International Theological Commission observed: "The Easter accounts, precisely because of their divergences, show that they are not simple chronicles."[69] The evangelists were not trying to capture Jesus on video camera. Not only did they not have cameras, but even if they had this technology it would not have yielded the kind of history that interested them. Just to take one example, the ITC considers the earthquake of Matthew 27:51–54 and its attendant phenomena (in particular the bodies of the saints rising, entering the holy city, and appearing to many) to be part of Matthew's theological style: "It is likely, therefore, that Matthew uses this 'literary motif.' By mentioning the earthquake, he wishes to underline that the death and resurrection of Jesus are not ordinary events but 'traumatic' events in which God acts and achieves the salvation of the human race ... The evangelists, then, do not speak of an earthquake whose force could be measured according to the grades of a specific scale but seeks to awaken and direct the attention of his readers toward God."[70] What magnitude would this earthquake have registered on the Richter scale? There will never be a definitive answer to this question on this side of eternity, but the ITC seems to think that the

68. Benedict XVI, *Jesus of Nazareth: Holy Week*, 266–67.
69. ITC, *The Inspiration and Truth of Sacred Scripture*, 155.
70. Ibid., 139–40.

answer is zero.[71] Regardless of how one answers this question, the essential point that Jesus was raised from the dead remains at the heart of the Christian faith and cannot be set aside as part of a particular evangelist's theological style.

Jesus of Nazareth: The Infancy Narratives
Why Are These Narratives Not in Mark's Gospel?

Clocking in at just 132 pages, the short "antechamber" to Benedict's *Jesus* trilogy reveals the emeritus pontiff's exegetical approach just as candidly as its lengthier prequels.[72] The author begins by discussing the overarching concern of the four canonical Gospels: "Who is Jesus? Where is he from? The two questions are inseparably linked. The four Gospels set out to answer these questions."[73] The purpose of the Gospels, in other words, is to put us in touch with the figure of Jesus. Yet in our journey through the infancy narratives we encounter cer-

71. Dale Allison similarly concludes, "Surely, then, if anything in the New Testament is haggadic fiction, this is it." Allison, *The Historical Christ and the Theological Jesus*, 21. The wonders that, according to Matthew, accompanied Christ's death left no trace in the other gospels, Acts, Paul, or Josephus; Allison is led to observe that "if such marvels really had some basis in fact, they would instantly have become the bedrock of Christian apologetics." For another take on this "strange passage," see N. T. Wright, *The Challenge of Jesus*, 136, and Wright, *The New Testament and the People of God* (Minneapolis: Fortress Press,1992), 329–34. Ultimately, whether we take this or other pericopes as historical depends on the philosophical presuppositions we bring to the text. Moreover, as Allison does well to observe, even if we may think a particular event legendary, there is no way determine whether Matthew, Mark, Luke, or John was of the same mind. In a text that evinces great wisdom but perhaps also some tension with the Catholic approach to Scripture, Allison states, "More importantly, the intention of the texts cannot be our sole or even chief guide. Contemporary Christians who read Genesis as theological saga instead of historical record do so not because of what a close reading of the book has taught them but because of what science and archaeology have demanded. That is, convictions acquired independently of the text have moved us to construe it in a certain fashion. And this is the rule for all our reading: presuppositions extrinsic to the texts govern how we interpret them.... Determining whether Matthew, Mark, Luke, or John believed something is not necessarily the same as determining whether we can or should believe it." Allison, *The Historical Christ and the Theological Jesus*, 38–39.

72. Benedict XVI, *Jesus of Nazareth: The Infancy Narratives*, xi. Though it was the third installment of the *Jesus* trilogy to be published, Benedict explicitly wrote that he viewed it less as a third volume than an "antechamber" to the other two works.

73. Ibid., xvi.

tain peculiarities which pose potential stumbling blocks for our quest to meet Jesus.

The first of these consists in the simple fact that the birth of Jesus is found only in later Gospels, prompting one to ask quite naturally: where did these stories come from, then? And why does Mark, our first Gospel, not mention them? Referencing Joachim Gnilka, Benedict concludes that the infancy stories are clearly derived from Jesus' own "family traditions" for the obvious fact that Mary alone could have reported the event of the Annunciation to the disciples.[74] He acknowledges that modern exegetes will naturally tend to dismiss such connections as naïve. Yet the emeritus pontiff responds:

> But why should there not have been a tradition of this kind, preserved in the most intimate circle and theologically elaborated at the same time? Why should Luke have invented the statement about Mary keeping the words and events in her heart, if there were no concrete grounds for saying so? Why should he have spoken of her "pondering" over the words (*Lk* 2:19; cf. 1:29) if nothing was known of this?[75]

In other words, the modern assumption that the infancy narratives were invented after the fact may be reasonable and even plausible, but it remains just that: an assumption. It is also possible that Mark himself simply did not know the stories or that he chose not to include them for some other reason.

In order to determine which of the above possibilities is more likely, it is always important to remember that people on both sides bring presuppositions to the debate. On the one hand, skeptics assume that the later genealogies and birth narratives were invented—otherwise Mark would have mentioned them. On the other hand, people approaching the Bible with a hermeneutic of faith believe that the infancy narratives are essentially true and for two thousand years have operated on the assumption that such is the case. Nevertheless, from a purely historical point of view, it would appear that the skeptic's position squares quite well with what we know about how Israelite historiography worked at the time of Christ. Over time, stories were con-

74. Ibid., 16.
75. Ibid.

stantly being expanded, so it stands to reason that the later infancy narratives of Matthew and Luke themselves could represent literary embellishments rather than history as such.

What, then, are we to say positively about the fact that Mark omitted the infancy narratives? Early in his book Benedict replies: "I would add that the late emergence, particularly of the Marian traditions, can be similarly explained by the discretion of the Lord's mother and of those around her: the sacred events of her early life could not be made public while she was still alive."[76] The emeritus pontiff later returns to this issue and suggests that the infancy stories were not made known earlier lest the mystery surrounding Christ's birth be reduced to an event like any other. Only at the proper time could this mystery be made public:

> It seems natural to me that only after Mary's death could the mystery be made public and pass into the shared patrimony of early Christianity. At that point it could find its way into the evolving complex of Christological doctrine and be linked to the confession of Jesus as the Christ, the Son of God—yet not in the manner of a story crafted from an idea, an idea reformulated as a fact, but vice versa: the event itself, a fact that was now in the public domain, became the object of reflection—understanding was sought.[77]

Here, as we saw above in the cases of the crucifixion and the resurrection, Benedict remains firm that the stories of Jesus' birth were not crafted from the evangelists' prior ideas but rather represent the fruit of reflection upon an event that really happened in history. Clearly this approach to the infancy narratives differs from that of many modern exegetes, but it is certainly plausible and cannot be disproved by the historical-critical method. At the same time, even after pondering Benedict's book for a few years, I still do not find his argument surrounding Mary's death compelling. To me it is understandable that she did not make these events known during Jesus' lifetime lest others besides Herod would seek to kill him before it was his time. But why this revelation had to wait until *Mary's* death escapes me.[78]

---

76. Ibid.   77. Ibid., 53.

78. It is interesting that Benedict speaks of Mary's "death" here rather than her assumption or dormition, words which preserve the mystery of whether she died or not. Contrary to what many Catholics assume, the belief that Mary died has a long pedigree

The Genealogies

At any rate, the question of origins is only one issue we face when dealing with the infancy narratives: another is the fact that the Matthean and Lukan genealogies we have do not readily line up with one another. For one thing, the genealogies occur at different places within their respective texts. This, however, is not an issue, since it is clear that Matthew and Luke have strategically placed their genealogies for theological motives. Matthew's version comes at the very beginning of his work so as to introduce his readers to Jesus Christ as "the son of David, the son of Abraham" (Mt 1:1). For Matthew, Jesus is indeed the New David, the true King of Israel come to fulfill God's promise of an everlasting worldwide dominion which the old David had failed to establish. Matthew also makes it clear that Jesus descended from the line of Abraham, the patriarch through whom God had promised that all the nations of the earth would bless themselves (Gn 18:18). In this way, Matthew ties the beginning of his Gospel to its end, wherein the risen Jesus commissions his disciples to go and "make disciples of all nations" (Mt 28:19). As the pontiff says, "[T]he universality of Jesus' mission is already contained within his origin."[79]

In contrast with Matthew, Luke chose to place his genealogy not at the beginning of the book but at the outset of Jesus' public ministry. However, this difference in placement is not much of an obstacle when it comes to reconciling the evangelists' respective genealogies. Neither is it particularly problematic that Matthew's genealogy runs from the past to the present, while Luke's traces back from the present to the past. It is more thought-provoking to observe that Luke's genealogy is much broader than Matthew's, tracing Jesus' lineage not merely to Abraham but to "Adam, the son of God"—that is to say, the very first human being. Here once again, this is explicable by the fact that the two evangelists had different theological motives in penning these genealogies. There is no reason Matthew should have been compelled to

in Western Christianity and can be seen in the Church's art through the Middle Ages (e.g., in the stained glass at Chartres) and the baroque era (e.g., Caravaggio's *Death of the Virgin*).

79. Benedict XVI, *Jesus of Nazareth: The Infancy Narratives*, 5.

go all the way back to Adam if it did not help him convey his primary message. Luke's concern, however, is precisely to illumine Jesus' role as the New Adam. Like Adam, Jesus is the son of God, and in him all of humanity starts anew. In the emeritus pontiff's words, "the underlying intention" of Luke is to show us that "Jesus takes upon himself the whole of humanity, the whole history of man, and he gives it a decisive re-orientation toward a new manner of human existence."[80]

A thornier difficulty noted by Benedict concerns the likelihood that Matthew and Luke based their genealogies on distinct preexistent sources, and thus "agree on only a handful of names; not even the name of Joseph's father is common to the two."[81] Thus far, we have seen some clear differences in emphasis between the two Gospel genealogies, but how can it be that the Gospels seem to get it wrong on the basic historical question of who belongs to Jesus' family lineage? Does this mean that the Gospels contradict one another and that one or both of them is in error?

To address this sort of challenge, below we will discuss a principle laid out by Benedict early in his book: the Gospels do record "real history that had actually happened," but they are also "interpreted history."[82] As for the present case, let us just say that, in contrast with what we might expect and wish for as moderns, Matthew and Luke are not trying to give us a video report of Jesus' family life or a precise transcript of his family history. Those simply were not the concerns of Jews living in Jesus' day, and to hold them to our standards of historiography is anachronistic. This modern mindset misses out on what is really most important in the Gospel genealogies. Each has a unique emphasis that reveals its "essential purpose," to use the words of the emeritus pontiff.[83] This phrase is a technical expression that we have seen Benedict use time and again. Although the infancy narratives are inspired and inerrant, we must carefully discern the precise nature (the substance) of what is being formally asserted or taught if we wish to avoid falling into the fundamentalist position of thinking that every last word within them constitutes a categorical truth claim. With this

---

80. Ibid., 11.   81. Ibid., 8.
82. Ibid., 17; cf. 119.   83. Ibid., 4.

principle in mind, Benedict draws the following conclusion regarding the purpose of these genealogies:

Neither evangelist is concerned so much with the individual names as with the symbolic structure within which Jesus' place in history is set before us: the intricacy with which he is woven into the historical strands of the promise, as well as the *new beginning* which paradoxically characterizes his origin side by side with the *continuity* of God's action in history.[84]

In Benedict's view, if the Gospel genealogies stand in some degree of tension with one another, this should not to be an obstacle to our belief. Their real concern lies in the symbolic structure, that is to say, the typological theology conveyed through the literary artistry of the evangelists' interpretive histories. It is important to keep this precise concept of historiography present before us when we consider Benedict's use of the word "symbolic," for by no means is he saying that the Gospel accounts are *mere* symbols devoid of historical content.

Benedict finishes his treatment of the Gospel genealogies with a discussion of John's prologue. He observes that, though John does not present us with a genealogy in the strict sense of the word, the evangelist repeatedly raises the question of Jesus' provenance in his own way: "In the beginning was the Word, and the Word was with God, and the Word was God" (Jn 1:1). For John, the "genealogy" of Jesus is to be traced not merely back to Abraham or even to Adam, but to God himself. Jesus' origin lies within God; he is "the only Son, who is in the bosom of the Father" (Jn 1:18). Not only that, John further writes that "to all who received him, who believed in his name, he gave power to become children of God; who were born, not of blood nor of the will of the flesh nor of the will of man, but of God" (Jn 1:12). John's astounding purpose here is to reveal that those who believe in Jesus share in his own divine sonship, becoming "sons in the Son" as the Church Fathers would have it. The emeritus pontiff's conclusion is that "John has recapitulated the deepest meaning of the genealogies," namely, that "those who believe in Jesus enter through faith into Jesus' unique new origin, and they receive this origin as their own.... so it can now be said of us that our true 'genealogy' is faith in Jesus."[85] The Gospel genealogies thus present Jesus' family history as well as our own family history as adopted sons of God.

84. Ibid., 8–9 (emphasis in original).   85. Ibid., 12.

Interpreted History

After his introductory discussion of the genealogies of Jesus, Benedict pauses for an important word concerning method before considering the infancy narratives proper. Rigorous thinker that he is, the emeritus pontiff tells us that we need to step back for a moment before we delve into study of the events surrounding Jesus' birth: "Before we consider the content of the texts, a brief word about their particular literary character is necessary."[86]

The statement that the Gospels have a "particular" literary character is something many believers find hard to appreciate. As has been said multiple times above, it is critical to emphasize that the Gospels are not simply video-camera representations of the life of Christ. However, as Christians we profess that they are not legends or myths, either. How, then, are we supposed to discern what historical claims the evangelists are actually making? How are we supposed to know what would have appeared if the apostles had happened to have a video camera on hand? How are we supposed to know what we should really be taking away from the Gospel narratives? On what grounds are we to trust their historical trustworthiness? In his characteristically blunt manner, Benedict ties these questions together and applies them to the subject at hand:

Finally we must ask in all seriousness: when the evangelists Matthew and Luke tell us, in their different ways and following different traditions, about Jesus' conception from the Virgin Mary by the power of the Holy Spirit, is this a historical reality, a real historical event, or is it a pious legend?[87]

A clue to answering this challenge emerges right at the outset of Benedict's treatment of the Annunciation. He tells us that "attempts have been made" to explain the Gospel genre in terms of haggadic midrash, an interpretative method used by the rabbis consisting in an exegesis of Scripture by means of narratives.[88] In midrash, the rabbis sought to tell a pre-existing story in a new way to a new audience in light of their circumstances. An author might condense a text, expand

---

86. Ibid., 14.   87. Ibid., 51.
88. Ibid., 15.

it, fill in gaps, or clarify potentially misleading verses. Famous examples abound.[89]

In the case of Matthew's Gospel, it is often supposed that the slaughter of the innocents and flight into Egypt were not historical events. Not only is there no extra-biblical evidence to confirm these events, but we have good reason to consider the possibility that Matthew's narrative is operating more as midrash than history on this point. Benedict thus considers the widespread motif of the persecuted child-king, which could have served as the story's model. He also refers to the rabbinic work *Moses Haggadah*, which has been handed on to us by Josephus.[90] In this text, God appears to Moses's father, promising to save his child, much in the same way an angel of the Lord appears to Joseph in a dream telling him to take the holy family to Egypt to escape Herod's persecution.

Approaching the Gospels from a very different point of view, John Dominic Crossan likewise refers to this work as well as to the later *Book of Remembrances*. Crossan declares quite unabashedly, "That story, with its four successive scenes, is the model for Matthew's account of Jesus' birth.... It is not the bare biblical account but the expanded popular versions of Moses' birth that served Matthew as the model for the birth of Jesus."[91] This aligns with Crossan's more recent thesis that the Gospels as whole are more parabolic than historical in nature: "[I]n this parabolic rather than historical overture, Matthew is creating a parallel between the evil Pharaoh, who slaughters the infant males in Exodus 1–2, and the evil Herod, who does the same in Matthew 1–2."[92] Crossan obviously recognizes that there are important differences between Matthew's account and these texts, but for him these discrepancies are to be expected, given Matthew's concern to channel the tradition in the direction of Jesus.

89. Outside the Bible, one of my favorite examples of this sort of move is when the Book of Jubilees retells the command to sacrifice Isaac in a way that resolves the tension of having a good God command someone to do an evil deed. In this account, God is not responsible for commanding Abraham to sacrifice Isaac, but rather the demon Mastema instigates it. Within the Old Testament, the Book of Wisdom is likewise illuminating. Wisdom 10 puts a new spin on the Fall of Adam and the cause of the Flood.

90. Ibid., 109–10.

91. Crossan, *Jesus: A Revolutionary Biography*, 12, 15.

92. Crossan, *The Power of Parable*, 178.

In addressing these parallels, Benedict makes the characteristic moves that appear elsewhere in his exegesis of Jesus' life and of the infancy narratives in particular. First, he differs from Crossan in maintaining that the differences between the rabbinic Moses traditions and Matthew's Gospel are too great to constitute a true parallel. Second and more importantly, he points out that the *Antiquitates* of Flavius Josephus—even if based upon earlier traditions—are almost certainly later in date than Matthew.[93] Finally, even though there is no external evidence supporting the slaughter of the innocents or Jesus' flight into Egypt, we must ask whether it is right to expect this evidence in the first place. Why would we expect the Romans to have preserved a record of this, and why would we expect the Egyptians to have maintained records of a small family spending a short time in their land? On the other hand, from what we know of Herod, it is perfectly in keeping with his character to kill hundreds of Jewish infants.[94] The emeritus pontiff's conclusion is that Matthew's narrative was not mere midrash, though he does admit that, in the case of Luke at least, "literary resemblance is beyond dispute."[95]

According to this author, Benedict's argument above is fundamentally sound on the whole but could have been more nuanced. For one thing, his dismissal of the parallels between Matthew and the rabbinic Moses traditions seems hasty. Unlike Benedict, I find that Crossan and others make a strong case for Matthew's awareness of these rabbinic traditions. However, like Benedict and on the basis of his very principles, I argue that a certain amount of literary license on the part of Matthew is compatible with holding his account to be fundamentally historical in nature. Also worth considering is the following view articulated recently by Peter Enns:

Scholars disagree on a good many things, but most think Matthew probably created at least some of these scenes to shape his story. A star—millions of light-years away—can't actually move and then stop over one specific house

93. Benedict XVI, *Jesus of Nazareth: The Infancy Narratives*, 110. Crossan himself dates Josephus' work wherein this tradition appears to 93 or 94 A.D., which places it well after when most scholars think Matthew was composed.

94. Ibid., 108. Having known that Herod killed three of his own sons, the emperor Augustus once quipped that it was safer to be Herod's pig (*hus*) than his son (*huios*).

95. Ibid., 15.

on earth, nor do stars even appear to do so from our earthly vantage point. Herod's massacre of children isn't hinted at in any other ancient source of the day, which also rouses some suspicion over whether it happened.

So is Matthew a liar? Is that what we're supposed to think? Only if you grade Matthew along with the other Gospel writers by a standard they clearly weren't operating under.

Matthew's portrait of Jesus serves his purpose: he drops into his Gospel images of Jesus that remind you of Moses and the exodus story. So a guiding star is like the pillar of fire that guided the Israelites to safety across the Red Sea. Herod's edict to kill the children and Jesus's escape is like Pharaoh's edict to throw the male infants into the Nile with baby Moses escaping. Jesus's trek down into Egypt as an infant and then back home again echoes Moses's and later Israel's journeys to and from Egypt.

Is Matthew reporting history as we understand the word? Did all these things happen? I am committed to keeping an open mind, but, along with most scholars, I think not in this case.[96]

Unlike Crossan, and in concert with Benedict, Enns affirms the fundamental historicity of Jesus' Incarnation; yet, unlike Benedict, Enns agrees with the mainstream scholarly consensus in seeing Matthew's narrative more as midrash than history through and through. Nevertheless, Enns's approach to this question aligns remarkably well with Benedict's own exegetical inclinations, even if the two do differ regarding the extent to which Matthew's infancy narrative is historical.[97]

96. Enns, *The Bible Tells Me So*, 82–83. Also worth pondering are Enns's comments elsewhere on the flight of the Holy Family into Egypt: "Matthew is not reading Hosea 'objectively.' He did not arrive at his conclusion from reading Hosea. Rather, he began with the event by which all else is now to be understood. It is the reality of the risen Christ that drove him to read Hosea in a new way: 'Now that I see how it all ends, I can see how this part of the OT, too, drives us forward'.... If Matthew were to be transported back into Hosea's time and had the opportunity to tell Hosea that his words would be fulfilled in the boy Jesus, and that, furthermore, this Jesus would be crucified and rise again for God's people, I am not sure if Hosea would have known what to make of it. But if Hosea were to go forward to Matthew's day, it would be very different for him. There Hosea would be forced, in light of recent events, to see his words—precisely because they are inspired by God, the divine author—in the final eschatological context. In a stunning reversal, it is now Matthew who would show Hosea how his words fit into God's ultimate redemptive goal: the death and resurrection of Christ. And so Hosea's words, which in their original historical context did not speak of Jesus of Nazareth, now do." Peter Enns, "Fuller Meaning, Single Goal: A Christotelic Approach to the New Testament Use of the Old in Its First-Century Interpretive Environment," in *Three Views on the New Testament Use of the Old Testament* (Grand Rapids, Mich.: Zondervan, 2008), 201–2.

97. It is also important to remember that the Mosaic theme runs throughout

Whether one finds Benedict's approach or Enns's more convincing, the key takeaway is that, for a Christian, the Gospels constitute a form of interpreted history that differs significantly from our modern expectations. As Benedict puts it:

[W]hat Matthew and Luke set out to do, each in his own way, was not to tell "stories" but to write history, real history that had actually happened, admittedly interpreted and understood in the context of the word of God. Hence the aim was not to produce an exhaustive account, but a record of what seemed important for the nascent faith community in the light of the word. The infancy narratives are interpreted history, condensed and written down in accordance with the interpretation.[98]

Matthew's gospel. For a concise listing of parallels from the birth of Moses to his reception of the Ten Commandments, see Allison, *The Luminous Dusk*, 110–11. For a concise summary of the Transfiguration as a rewriting of the story of Moses on Sinai, see Allison, *The Historical Christ and the Theological Jesus*. Rather than considering the Transfiguration narrative to be a video camera account, Allison suggests, "We need also to keep firmly before our minds that it was a habit of the early Christians to score theological points by inventing fantastic, picturesque stories." Ibid., 69. On the fantastical apocryphal work *The Acts of Peter and Andrew*, Allison writes in this connection, "The author of this vivid and outlandish fantasy had to know, while he was making it all up, that he was making it all up. Further, his far-fetched tale so sacrifices all probability for the sake of delight in storytelling that later readers or hearers must have known this too.... Is it not, then, natural to suppose that some or even many of the miracle stories about Jesus were likewise composed to teach theological lessons, not record historical facts? ... Excellent candidates for this last category include Matthew's infancy narrative, Peter walking on the water, and the many corpses coming to life at Jesus' crucifixion. Is not the sensible verdict that the transfiguration is likewise not a report but a myth, whose meaning can have nothing to do with what really happened?" Ibid., 71–72. Despite his skepticism with regard to the historicity of the transfiguration, Allison makes the philosophically balanced admission that the miracles associated with Jesus need not be late inventions: "And yet, having said all this, the judgment that the transfiguration is nothing but mythology may turn out to be premature. For the inference implicitly assumes that people are never transfigured into light." Allison then proceeds to discuss Gregory of Nyssa on a similar miracle involving his brother Basil: "Some might feel free to dismiss these words as ancient credulity, or maybe as a rhetorical flight of fancy. I hesitate, however. Not only was Gregory an extraordinarily intelligent man, but I have, over the years, formed an opinion of his character, and it is hard for me to discount his apparently earnest witness. It is easier for me to believe that he saw a light he could not explain, whatever its origin may have been." Ibid., 72. In other words, given the trust he has in the person of Gregory, it is easier for Allison to believe in the highly improbable miracle to which he testifies than to believe that his teacher has been deceived or deceiving.

98. Benedict XVI, *Jesus of Nazareth: The Infancy Narratives*, 17. On the subject of the gospels as interpreted history, it is instructive to situate them within the contemporary

There is a lot of meat to digest within this paragraph, but I wish to make just a few observations. First, Benedict is adamant that the Gospels describe real events that actually happened. For us today, it means that on principle they could have been captured on video camera. Second, this history nevertheless does not contain precisely what would have been recorded on video, since it is "admittedly interpreted" and "understood in the context of the word of God." This means that the Gospel histories reflect a history prior to themselves—that of the Old Testament. Because they seek to retell that history in light of Christ, the Gospel accounts might vary from what otherwise would have appeared on a video camera. Third, the Gospels' aim is not to produce an exhaustive account; rather, each evangelist crafted his narrative with an eye to what was important for his flock to know in the concrete circumstances of their lives.

The pontiff is careful to maintain a careful hermeneutical balance here. In contrast with how Ehrman, Crossan, and others would have it, he says that the account of Jesus' conception is not "a story crafted from an idea, an idea reformulated as a fact."[99] This is precisely the same move he made in discussing the crucifixion and resurrection above. For Benedict, that an author writes an interpretive history does not mean that he invents facts to support his own preconceived ideas. According to Christians, the reality is the other way around: "[T]he

---

genre of Graeco-Roman *bioi*. Richard Burridge argues, "The four canonical gospels exhibit a clear family resemblance with other Graeco-Roman *bioi* and have at least as much in common with them as these other *bioi* have with one another." Burridge, *What Are the Gospels? A Comparison with Graeco-Roman Biography* (Cambridge: Cambridge University Press, 1992), 258. Indeed, he goes so far as to affirm that "any idea of the gospels as unique, *sui generis* works is a nonsense." Ibid., 255. But this does not mean that the gospels were biographies in the sense of attempts to be completely objective: "Just as many other ancient *bioi* were used by philosophical groups in order to teach their beliefs and attack other groups, so we should approach the gospels with the expectation that they too will include didactic, apologetic, and polemical dimensions." Ibid., 256. Craig Keener writes in this vein, "Public lives tended to be encomiastic, magnifying heroes, but such an emphasis does not make them fictions." Keener, *The Historical Jesus of the Gospels* (Grand Rapids, Mich.: Eerdmans, 2009), 80n91. To be sure, the evangelists had their theological agendas; thus the gospels have an "essentially historical as well as propagandistic function." Ibid., 80n96.

99. Benedict XVI, *Jesus of Nazareth: The Infancy Narratives*, 53.

event itself, a fact that was now in the public domain, became the object of reflection—understanding was sought. The overall picture of Jesus Christ shed light upon the event, and conversely, through that event, the divine logic was more deeply grasped."[100] As a result, it is Christ's Incarnation alone that gives Old Testament texts their full meaning, "which hitherto could not be recognized."[101]

Indeed, Benedict writes that in Jesus' day some passages of the Hebrew Bible were still "stray," as it were, until the early Christian narrative provided these "waiting" words with their "owner."[102] In this connection Benedict highlights Isaiah 53 (the Messiah as suffering servant) and Isaiah 7:14 (the virgin who would conceive and bear a son who would be "God with us") as texts which ultimately attained clarity only with the coming of Christ. When it comes to the latter, he writes, "Exegesis has therefore searched meticulously, using all the resources of historical scholarship, for a contemporary interpretation—and it has failed." Thus, it is "rightly objected" that there must have been a meaning to this conception at the time of King Ahaz, yet Benedict concurs with Rudolf Kilian that "[n]o single attempt at interpretation is entirely convincing."[103] The passage about the virgin, like that of the Suffering Servant song, was a "word in waiting," or, as Marius Reiser has it, "a miraculously formed keyhole" into which the key of Christ fits perfectly. These texts, incomprehensible for so long, came true at the moment Christ was conceived in the womb of the virgin Mary.[104]

Wrapping up his discussion of the virgin birth in relation to Old Testament prophecy, Benedict characteristically poses the modern question point blank:

Finally we must ask in all seriousness: when the evangelists Matthew and Luke tell us, in their different ways and following different traditions, about Jesus' conception from the Virgin Mary by the power of the Holy Spirit, is this a historical reality, a real historical event, or is it a pious legend?[105]

100. Ibid., 53–54.

101. Ibid., 15.

102. Ibid., 17.

103. Ibid., 48–49. Benedict considers four possibilities for the child prophesied in this passage: the Messiah; a son of King Ahaz; a son of Isaiah; the New Israel.

104. Ibid., 50–51.

105. Ibid., 51.

Is it true? Or is it possible that archetypal concepts have been transferred onto the figures of Jesus and his mother?[106]

With these "archetypal concepts," Benedict has in mind the attempts to provide a natural explanation for the virgin birth. Since the time of Martin Dibelius, interpreters have looked to the history of religions for evidence likening Jesus' birth to that of the heroes from the Greco-Roman world and the pharaohs of Egypt. Within the more germane Egyptian context, the divine generation of the pharaohs (resulting from the divinity approaching a human woman) was a political theology crafted in order to legitimize the cult of the ruler.[107]

While not ignoring these pagan parallels to Christ's birth—for which many more could be adduced than Benedict takes the time to discuss—the emeritus pontiff rejects them out of hand: "The difference between the concepts involved is so profound that one really cannot speak of true parallels."[108] Whereas these other traditions envision a miraculously conceived demi-god as part of a cosmic allegory, the Gospel accounts are realist in that they staunchly preserve the oneness of God and the infinite distance between him and the creature. This leads Benedict to conclude: "The accounts of Matthew and Luke are not myths taken a stage further. They are firmly rooted, in terms of their basic conception, in the biblical tradition of God the Creator and Redeemer."[109] The ITC's most recent publication on the inspiration and

106. Ibid., 55.
107. Ibid., 51–52.
108. Ibid., 52.
109. Ibid., 53. On this subject I find C. S. Lewis's reflections very helpful. According to Lewis, the resemblance between pagan myths and the Christian faith is not surprising for those who think that divine, diabolical, and human elements are all involved in mythology: "The resemblance between these myths and the Christian faith is no more accidental than the resemblance between the sun and the sun's reflection in a pond, or that between a historical fact and the somewhat garbled version of it which lives in popular report, or between the trees and hills of the real world and the trees and hills in our dreams. One can, without any absurdity, imagine Plato or the myth-makers if they learned the truth, saying, 'I see ... so that was what I was really talking about. Of course. That is what my words really meant, and I never knew it.'" Lewis, *Reflections on the Psalms*, 107–8. In other words, while the skeptic's reading of Christ as just another myth is possible, it is also possible that the world's religions have these parallels with Christ precisely because God wished to plant the *semina verbi* among them as prepara-

truth of Scripture aligns well with Benedict and to my mind captures concisely the view that ought to be affirmed by the Christian on this matter: "In the infancy narratives, not all details of the accounts can be verified historically, while the virginal conception of Jesus is clearly affirmed."[110] In other words, Benedict, Enns, and the ITC agree that it is unlikely every last detail recorded in the infancy narratives would have been captured on a video camera had one been available at the time. However, the virginal conception of Jesus is clearly affirmed by the evangelist as essential to the figure of Jesus, a belief that has remained foundational to Christianity for two millennia.

Why, ultimately, do many people today find it difficult to accept the core content of the infancy narratives? As mentioned above, certainly one obstacle is the understandable allurement of seeing Jesus' miraculous birth as just one among many myths with similar characteristics. But, according to Benedict, at the end of the day this is often not why the historicity of these narratives is rejected. Just as many reject the historicity of the Last Supper on the ground that it does not corroborate their image of Jesus as a liberal reform rabbi, so the birth and resurrection of Jesus shatter the figure of Jesus as a good teacher and resident of this world alone. In short, for Benedict the underlying motivation for rejecting the miraculous birth and resurrection of Jesus is often philosophical in nature. As we saw earlier in this volume, it ultimately boils down to whether or not we believe the premise that God can enter meaningfully into human history:

These two moments [the virgin birth and the resurrection of Jesus] are a scandal to the modern spirit. God is "allowed" to act in ideas and thoughts, in the spiritual domain—but not in the material. That is shocking. He does not belong there. But that is precisely the point: God is God and he does not operate merely on the level of ideas. In that sense, what is at stake in both of these moments is God's very godhead. The question that they raise is: does matter also belong to him? … [H]ere we are not dealing with the irrational

---

tion for the gospel. From a purely rational point of view, this conclusion may be no more likely to be true than that of skeptic, but that is precisely the point. In line with the overall aim of this chapter, all the Christian needs to do is to show that his view is a plausible alternative to the popular view afforded by Ehrman.

110. ITC, *The Inspiration and Truth of Sacred Scripture*, 154.

or contradictory, but precisely with the positive—with God's creative power, embracing the whole of being. In that sense these two moments—the virgin birth and the real resurrection from the tomb—are the cornerstones of faith. If God does not also have power over matter, then he simply is not God.[111]

In this rich paragraph we return to the pivotal discussion with which this volume opened. The debate in modern exegesis is at bottom a philosophical debate, a matter of competing worldviews and their competing presuppositions and methods. One who approaches the Bible from an agnostic or atheist point of view will of course deny Jesus' miraculous birth, because no God exists to work such miracles in the first place. On the other hand, one who becomes convicted that God exists cannot preclude his entering into human history through miracles, for if the divinity lacks dominion over matter, he is not really God.

The Census and the Date of Jesus' Birth

While there are many other aspects of the infancy narratives that could be considered, the question of the census in particular is an issue that typically raises red flags in the eyes of modern exegetes. The reason is that, while Luke's Gospel tells us that the Romans were in the process of taking a census at the time of Jesus' birth, there remains much debate regarding whether Luke faithfully reported the details of this census. Benedict responds by pointing out that the census would have taken several years to complete, regardless of when it started. According to Josephus, to whom we owe most of our knowledge of Jewish history for this period, it took place in A.D. 6 under the governor Quirinius. Luke, however, explicitly states that the census took place during the reign of Herod the Great, who died in 4 B.C. According to Benedict, this ten-year discrepancy is explicable on the supposition that Luke was writing during the initial phase of the census when all the persons and property were registered with the state, whereas Josephus was writing during the final stage of the census, when payments were determined. It was this final, more injurious moment that led to the uprising of Judas the Galilean (Acts 5:37).[112]

---

111. Benedict XVI, *Jesus of Nazareth: The Infancy Narratives*, 56–57.
112. Ibid., 62.

The dating of Herod's death to 4 B.C. also means that the traditional date of Jesus' birth on which we base our calendars is incorrect and "is therefore to be placed a few years earlier."[113] While it may disturb some Christians to learn that Jesus was not born in the year A.D. 0, Benedict's willingness to accept the best of modern historical scholarship shines through here. Moreover—and this should come as no surprise—he invokes his standard hermeneutical line to account for this tension between what Christians thought for centuries and what turns out really to be the case in light of our present knowledge: "Regarding the details, the discussion could continue indefinitely.... Yet the essential content of Luke's narrative remains historically credible all the same"[114] The precise date of Jesus' birth is thus a detail, accident, or secondary feature, whereas the birth of Jesus in human history is the true content or essence of the matter.[115] Here Benedict repeats the central point: "It is not with the timelessness of myth that Jesus came to be born among us."[116] The birth of Jesus is a real historical event, even as it bursts open the categories of time and space.

Regardless of the precise date to which we fix the census of Judea, Benedict issues a salutary reminder: "In any case, [Luke] was situated much closer to the sources and events than we could ever claim to be, despite all our historical scholarship."[117] Sure, Luke was not the first Gospel written, but even from a purely historical point of view his attempt to produce "an orderly account" (Lk 1:3) of Jesus' life ought to be taken seriously. The same goes for Matthew, although it is fascinating that Benedict does not shy away from critiquing certain features of Matthew's infancy narrative. Noting that Luke and Matthew "evidently belong to quite distinct narrative traditions," Benedict proceeds to observe that "Matthew apparently did not know that Joseph and

113. Ibid., 61–62. The traditional date of Jesus' birth goes back to the monk Dionysius Exiguus around the year A.D. 550 Benedict writes that he "evidently miscalculated by a few years."

114. Ibid., 63.

115. Thus the ITC comments on the infancy narratives: "The differences, which can be harmonized in part, refer to secondary aspects common to the two evangelists that relate to the central figure of Jesus." *The Inspiration and Truth of Sacred Scripture*, 134.

116. Benedict XVI, *Jesus of Nazareth: The Infancy Narratives*, 64.

117. Ibid., 63.

Mary were both originally from Nazareth."[118] Upon returning from Egypt, Matthew has Joseph wanting to go to Bethlehem, and it is only the news that a son of Herod is reigning in Judea that causes him to travel to Galilee instead. Luke, on the other hand, makes it clear from the outset that the holy family returned directly to Nazareth.

Because of this and other differences, Benedict describes "significant exponents of modern exegesis" as thinking that the birth of Jesus in Bethlehem was a theological rather than historical affirmation on the part of the evangelists. Contrary to what the Gospels say, these exegetes believe that Jesus was born in Nazareth where he grew up. According to this view, the evangelists reshaped history theologically "to designate Jesus ... as the long-awaited shepherd of Israel," the New David who would restore the kingdom of God (cf. Mi 5:1–3; Mt 2:6), just as they had reshaped history to portray Jesus as the new Moses. In Benedict's response to this suggestion, we find an outstanding critique of the historical-critical method on its own terms:

I do not see how a basis for this theory can be gleaned from the actual sources, As far as the birth of Jesus is concerned, the only sources we have are the infancy narratives of Matthew and Luke.... If we abide by the sources, it is clear that Jesus was born in Bethlehem and grew up in Nazareth.[119]

According to Benedict, if we abide by historical criticism's own criterion of multiple attestation, it is highly significant that Bethlehem as the birthplace of Jesus is attested equally by the two "quite distinct" traditions of Matthew and Luke.[120] Benedict finds the fact that these two Gospels, despite their differences, share this tradition gives good reason to believe that Bethlehem was indeed Jesus' birthplace. Of

118. Ibid., 65.
119. Ibid., 66.
120. Another fascinating move Benedict makes is to invoke the ancient local traditions that place Jesus' birth in Bethlehem. The tradition that Jesus was born in a cave that Christians in Palestine could point to dates back at least to Justin Martyr and Origen in the second century. After the Jews were expelled from the Holy Land, Rome turned the cave into a shrine of Tammuz-Adonis in the effort to suppress the cult of Jesus on the site. As Benedict puts it, "Local traditions are frequently a more reliable source than written records. So a considerable measure of credibility may be assigned to the tradition that Bethlehem was Jesus' birthplace, a tradition to which the Church of the Nativity also bears witness." Ibid., 67–68.

course it is always possible that both Gospels were making the same theological move, but Benedict is keen to point out that these are the only two sources we have on the subject. Thus it may be a matter of belief to hold that Jesus was born in the city of David, but it is equally an act of belief to hold that he was *not* born there. In fact, in a very real sense the former belief would appear more warranted on historical grounds alone.

Conclusion: The Magi and Other Nonessential Matters

Not surprisingly, modern scholars frequently dismiss the story of the magi as part of Matthew's distinctive theology rather than an attempt to report history. Benedict asks the question in his characteristically candid manner: "[H]ow are we to understand all this? Are we dealing with history that actually took place, or is it merely a theological meditation, presented under the guise of stories?" It is highly instructive to observe that Benedict treats the story of the magi differently than he does that of the Annunciation to Mary, even though they both come from the infancy narratives. Specifically, whereas he insists that the Annunciation narrative touches upon the core of the Christian faith, Benedict is open to the possibility that the story of the magi was Matthew's own theological invention:

In this regard, Jean Daniélou rightly observes: "The adoration of the Magi, unlike the story of the annunciation [to Mary], does not touch upon any essential aspect of our faith. No foundations would be shaken if it were simply an invention of Matthew's based on a theological idea.".... Daniélou himself, though, comes to the conclusion that we are dealing here with historical events, whose theological significance was worked out by the Jewish Christian community and by Matthew. To put it simply, I share this view. [121]

Despite his inclination to view the magi story as historical, Benedict is aware that many ecclesially minded exegetes reject its historicity, and he confirms that these individuals remain within the bounds of orthodoxy notwithstanding their position on this matter.[122] So why

---

121. Ibid., 118.
122. Ibid., 119. In contrast with the virginal conception, crucifixion, resurrection, etc. affirmed in creeds throughout Christian history, not all events recorded in the gospels

does Benedict gravitate toward viewing the magi as historical? Here he provides a principle from Klaus Berger which can serve as a guide for theologians on any number of questions that arise concerning the Gospels' historicity: *"Even when there is only a single attestation [of a given Gospel text] ... one must suppose, until the contrary is proven, that the evangelists did not intend to deceive their readers, but rather to inform them concerning historical events."*[123] Benedict argues that contesting the historicity of a Gospel account on mere suspicion exceeds the competence of the historian. His application of this principle leads Benedict to conclude, "The two chapters of Matthew's Gospel devoted to the infancy narratives are not a meditation presented under the guise of stories, but the converse: Matthew is recounting real history, theologically thought through and interpreted, and thus he helps us to understand the mystery of Jesus more deeply."[124]

At the end of the day, then, some events recorded in the Gospels must be affirmed as historical by the orthodox Christian, whereas on other matters one may gravitate to one or another interpretation. But even for those events that belong to the core of Christian faith (e.g., the virginal conception of Jesus, the resurrection, other elements of the creed, etc.), we must remember that the biblical authors were not the kind of historians we might mistakenly take them to be or wish they had been. As faithful Jews, their historiography operated on the assumption that to embellish the past and bring it into contemporary relevance was *more*, not less true to reality than a video of Jesus' life could

---

have equal claims to historicity. To my knowledge no infallible statement has ever been issued by a pope or council requiring Catholics to maintain that belief in the historical visit of the magi or flight into Egypt is *de fide*. Though this point may be disconcerting to some Christians, for me it only reinforces the pivotal importance of the Magisterium in safeguarding the deposit of faith. That said, within the Church there are different levels of magisterial teaching including many "irreformable" doctrines that require "irrevocable assent." For a discussion of these levels along with examples of doctrines that fall within each, see Congregation for the Doctrine of the Faith, "Doctrinal Commentary on the Concluding Formula of the *Professio Fidei*" (1998). Thinking about how much flexibility there is within Catholic exegesis reminds me of Chesterton's line that the Catholic Church may have high doctrinal walls, but inside one finds a great playground.

123. Berger, *Kommentar zum Neuen Testament*, p. 20; quoted by Benedict XVI in *Jesus of Nazareth: The Infancy Narratives*, 119.

124. Benedict XVI, *Jesus of Nazareth: The Infancy Narratives*, 119.

ever be. Speaking of storytellers in general and the Gospel authors in particular, Peter Enns is right on the mark:

They are not objective observers and don't pretend to be. They are artists bringing past and present together to leave the audience with something to ponder, to persuade—to inspire.... To do their thing, storytellers "shape" the past. They decide what to include, what order to put things in, how to compress or combine scenes to save time and get to the money shot, and so on. They also invent dialogue and scenes to knit the narrative together. They have to, since much of the past is inaccessible to storytellers—they themselves weren't there to see and hear what happened.[125]

It would have never dawned on the evangelists that just sticking to the objective facts (which is impossible at any rate) would have been better than what they set out to do. For what drove the Bible's storytellers to recount the life of Christ the way they did was the quest to make it possible for others to experience him in the present. This is perhaps best formulated in a short comment from Benedict on the discourses in John's Gospel: "What the Gospel is really claiming is that it has correctly rendered the substance of the discourses ... so that the readers really do encounter the decisive content of this message and, therein, the authentic figure of Jesus."[126] That certain facts recorded in the Gospels do not always readily square with one another was not a game changer for the early Church. In fact, it is perhaps the surest sign that the way our forefathers thought of history differs considerably from the standards to which we misguidedly seek to hold them accountable. Benedict does well to remind us that the early Church's concern was to present the "decisive content" of Jesus' message always with an eye to fostering a genuine encounter with him.

In sum, my main concern throughout this chapter has been to show that Benedict XVI's exegesis offers a reasonable and even compelling explanation for the discrepancies we find among the Gospels. But in concluding, I also wish to echo Peter Enns's point that Christians often devalue the Bible that we have by wanting it to be something that it is not. The Bible as seen by Benedict XVI is not one that

---

125. Enns, *The Bible Tells Me So*, 75.
126. Benedict, *Jesus of Nazareth: From the Baptism in the Jordan to the Transfiguration*, 229.

conforms strictly to modern canons of history; the problem is not the Bible but rather the ill-considered expectations we impose upon it. If there is one thing I hope the reader will take away from this chapter, it is that the rigorous hermeneutic of faith espoused here offers a plausible and attractive alternative to Ehrman's agnostic approach to the Gospels, one that is every bit as scholarly and no more reliant on unprovable assumptions.

6

THE PROBLEM OF AN IMMINENT
PAROUSIA

Building on Benedict XVI's approach to the life, death, and Resurrection of Christ discussed in the previous chapter, this chapter will
show how the theology of the emeritus pontiff offers a robust hermeneutic for New Testament texts dealing with the end times, specifically the early Church's ostensibly failed expectation that Christ's
second coming (*parousia*) would occur within the apostolic period.
The question that arises from a reading of these texts is quite simple:
Why has Christ not come back yet, as he seemed to say he would? By
searching out the intention of Scripture's sacred authors in relation to
their expectation of an imminent *parousia*, Benedict offers a compelling alternative to the agnostic approach of Ehrman and others who
look upon the early Church's eschatology as wishful thinking that
never panned out. As above, I will begin with a survey of the difficulty
at hand through a frank engagement with the opposing view that calls
into question Christian doctrine at its core. Then I will examine problematic biblical and magisterial texts to further establish the parameters of the problem at hand, after which a solution will be advanced in
light of magisterial texts and the corpus of Benedict XVI.

Ehrman on Christian Eschatology
The Origins of Apocalypticism

In *Jesus, Interrupted*, Ehrman pointedly contrasts present-day Christian discourse on heaven and hell with the view of Jesus and the first apostles, arguing that the two are radically different. He begins his discussion with a personal reflection on oddities he perceives within Christian beliefs concerning the afterlife, at the end of which his major claim emerges:

In some corners of Christendom today, especially the ones that I was at one time associated with, the religion is all about the afterlife. On the very personal level, people are eager to experience the joys of heaven and to avoid the fires of hell. Most Christians I meet today believe that when you die, your soul goes to one place or the other. I've never quite figured out all the inconsistencies of this view. On the one hand, the afterlife of the soul sounds like some kind of disembodied existence, since your body stays in the grave; on the other hand, people think that there will be physical pleasure or pain in the afterlife, and that you'll be able to recognize your grandparents. That would require having a body. The earliest Christians, starting with Jesus, did not believe in that sort of heaven and hell, as a place that your soul goes when you die. This, too, is a later Christian invention.[1]

This claim touches the heart of the Christian faith and has everything to do with the doctrine of the *parousia* under consideration in this chapter. Looking at the same evidence as Benedict XVI and other Christian believers, Ehrman concludes that our expectation of the second coming represents a serious departure from the vision of Jesus and his apostles, a departure brought about because their apocalyptic predictions failed.

The Jewish apocalyptic worldview first started to take shape in the centuries immediately preceding the birth of Jesus as a way to deal with the problem of theodicy. While this term was not coined until the seventeenth century by Leibniz, it appropriately reflects the concern of Jewish apocalypticism after the Babylonian exile and the persecutions of the Maccabean period. The question posed in apocalypticism concerns how to reconcile faith in a just and loving God with the

1. Ehrman, *Jesus, Interrupted*, 261.

untold misery that his people were experiencing at the time. Ehrman observes that the apocalyptic response to this question is first found in the Hebrew Bible within the book of Daniel from the second century B.C. In brief, the answer runs along these lines:

For apocalypticists there would be justice. Not in this life or this age, but in the resurrection, in the age to come. God would raise all people from the dead, bodily, to give them an eternal reward or an eternal punishment. No one would escape. Evil would not have the last word; God would have the last word. And death would not be the end of the story.[2]

It is no coincidence that this is the first (and last, if one does not accept the deuterocanon) book of the Hebrew Bible to exhibit belief in the resurrection of the body. For the author of Daniel, resurrection was the answer to the problem of theodicy. The resurrection of the righteous to life and the resurrection of the unrighteous to contempt (Dn 12:1–3; cf. 2 Mc 6–7, 12; Wis 3) explains how a just God could allow good people to be tortured and murdered while the wicked get away with remaining powerful and rich.[3]

Later Christians Transformed Jesus' Apocalyptic Worldview

Ehrman's account above may not come across as very controversial, but what he does next understandably raises eyebrows. To begin, he summarizes in more detail the events that were expected to unfold at the consummation of history:

So taught the early Jewish apocalypticists, and so taught Jesus. The Kingdom of God was soon to appear with the coming of the Son of Man. People needed to prepare for it by mending their ways and siding with God, even though it meant suffering in this age. But a new age was coming in which God and his

---

2. Ibid., 263.

3. Ehrman explains elsewhere, "Apocalypticism is nothing so much as an ancient kind of theodicy, an explanation of why there can be so much pain and suffering in this world if a good and powerful God is in charge of it. The apocalyptic answer is that God is indeed completely sovereign, and that he will reassert his sovereignty in the future when he overthrows the forces of evil and vindicates everyone who has sided with him (and therefore suffered) in this age." Ehrman, *God's Problem*, 256. For more on the development of Old Testament doctrine concerning the afterlife, see Ramage, *Dark Passages of the Bible*, ch. 6.

ways would rule supreme, in the Kingdom of God to come, here on this earth. All would eventually be made right with this world, and everyone would be brought back to life, bodily, to see and experience it.... *They would then live eternally, here on earth.* Thus, for Jesus, Paul, and the earliest Christians, eternal life was a life lived in the body, *not above in heaven but down here where we are now.*[4]

There is clearly a significant difference between orthodox Christian belief and what Ehrman attributes to Jesus here. According to this view, the earliest Christians hoped neither to live forever in heaven nor to live spiritually in some other manner; rather, the hope was to reign with Christ eternally *on this earth* in the re-established kingdom of God.

It is interesting that Ehrman emphasizes the physicality of this longed-for resurrection. In 1 Cor 15, Paul stresses this point against his opponents who thought that they had already experienced a spiritual resurrection: "The resurrection was physical, and since it was physical, it obviously had not happened yet. This world is still carrying on under the forces of evil, and only at the end will all be resolved and the followers of Jesus be vindicated, transformed, and given an eternal reward."[5] In saying this, Ehrman might seem closer to orthodox Christianity than those who claim Jesus' resurrection was merely spiritual. However, it must be recalled that he envisions Paul locating the fulfillment of this hope here on earth. According to Ehrman, this is also the view presented in the book of Revelation. At the end of days, "a new heavens and a new earth" will appear as the new, heavenly Jerusalem that will come down from above to replace the old, corrupt, and now destroyed Jerusalem. And it is here on earth, in this new City of God, that the saints will live forever (Rv 21:1–2).

What Happened When the Expected End Did Not Materialize

So what did Christians do when the apocalyptic scenario that Jesus expected to occur in "this generation" (Mt 24:34; Mk 13:30; Lk 21:32) never came about? Or when Paul's expectation that he would be alive

---

4. Ehrman, *Jesus, Interrupted,* 263 (emphasis added).
5. Ibid., 264.

at the second coming of Christ was disconfirmed by his own death? Faced with these facts, people who wanted to remain faithful to the original vision of Jesus had to explain how a seemingly essential element of that vision could have been so wrong. Ehrman expounds:

One thing that happens, of course, is that some people begin to mock. That is the problem addressed in the last book of the New Testament, 2 Peter, whose author insists that when God says that it will all happen very soon, he means by the divine calendar, not the human. And one needs always to remember that "with the Lord, a day is as a thousand years and a thousand years as one day" (2 Pt 3: 8).[6]

When the end never came, Christians simply reconceptualized the anticipated timeline for the *parousia*. As Ehrman describes it, the apocalyptic duality of two ages—this one and the world to come— was transposed spatially into two spheres—this world and the world above. This duality, Ehrman claims, worked itself out in the doctrine of heaven and hell that Christians know today. In short, this is what he thinks happened:

[W]ith the passing of time, the apocalyptic notion of the resurrection of the body becomes transformed into the doctrine of the immortality of the soul. What emerges is the belief in heaven and hell, a belief not found in the teach-ings of Jesus or Paul, but one invented in later times by Christians who real-ized that the kingdom of God never would come to this earth. This belief became a standard Christian teaching, world without end.[7]

I find a couple of things problematic in the paragraph above. First, I do not appreciate the "world without end" statement at the end that—at least to me—comes across as snarky. More substantially, I am not sure it is fair to characterize the Christian belief that eventually emerged as "immortality of the soul" as contrasted with resurrection. That said, these observations of mine do not touch Ehrman's central point, that later Christians altered the views they had inherited in accordance with the events of Christ's life. Nor do they mitigate what he argues elsewhere at greater length:

When the author of Revelation expected that the Lord Jesus "was coming soon" (Rv 22:20), he really meant "soon"—not two thousand years later. It was

6. Ibid., 265.
7. Ibid., 266.

only a later bit of sophistry that devised the idea that "soon" with God meant "the distant future"—that "with the Lord a day is as a thousand years and a thousand years as a day," as the author of 2 Peter put it (2 Pt. 3:8). This redefinition of what "soon" might mean makes sense, of course. If the author of Revelation, and other ancient Christian prophets like Paul, thought the end was to come right away, and it never did come, what else could one do but say that "right away" meant by God's calendar, not by earthly calendars?[8]

When the end did not come as expected, some of Jesus's followers transformed this temporal dualism (this age versus the age to come) into a spatial dualism, between the world below and the world above. Or put differently, they shifted the horizontal dualism of apocalyptic expectation of life in this age versus life in the age to come (horizontal dualism because it all takes place on this plane, here on earth) into a vertical dualism that spoke instead of life in the lower world versus life in the world above (with an up and down). In other words, out of the ashes of failed apocalyptic expectation there arose the Christian doctrine of heaven and hell.[9]

To address Ehrman's arguments meaningfully, we will need the help of Benedict XVI's exegesis. But first it is necessary to spend some time with the Scriptures themselves so as to drive home more forcefully Ehrman's pointed criticisms.

Biblical Texts Seemingly Incompatible with the Events of History

In its 1989 work *The Interpretation of Dogma*, the International Theological Commission affirmed that "the *Paradosis* [tradition] of the Church is universally valid and unchangeable in substance."[10] Based on the authority of the First Vatican Council, this document makes it clear that Catholic dogmas are "irreversible" and that in their regard "there can be no departure from the meaning once and for all defined by the Church."[11] The dogma of the *parousia* is no exception to this

8. Ehrman, *God's Problem*, 247.
9. Ibid., 256.
10. International Theological Commission, *The Interpretation of Dogma*, A.II.1.
11. International Theological Commission, *The Interpretation of Dogma*, B.II.1; cf. First Vatican Council, *Dei Filius*, ch. 4. Warning against relativism in the field of dogma and insisting upon the importance of maintaining the Church's precise dogmatic language, the document also draws from Paul VI, *Mysterium Fidei*, 24, and Pius XII, *Humani Generis*, 14–17. The latter is particularly harsh on those who "want to reduce to a minimum the meaning of dogmas" and thus "cherish the hope that when dogma

rule. There is abundant evidence of hope for the Second Coming of Christ within the New Testament and apostolic tradition, a teaching enshrined in the creed promulgated already at the First Council of Nicea and still affirmed today.[12] Difficulties arise, however, when one compares the content of the New Testament's hope to the actual events of history that ensued. In what follows, I will introduce just a few thorny biblical texts that illustrate this problem. Then I will bring the problem into even greater relief by highlighting certain magisterial statements which appear to conflict with these texts and with the events of history.

1 Thessalonians 4:13–18

One of the earliest New Testament works, dating to around A.D. 50, 1 Thessalonians offers a privileged vantage point from which to catch a glimpse of the nascent Church's mind concerning the *parousia* of Christ:

> But we would not have you ignorant, brethren, concerning those who are asleep, that you may not grieve as others do who have no hope. For since we believe that Jesus died and rose again, even so, through Jesus, God will bring with him those who have fallen asleep. For this we declare to you by the word of the Lord, that *we who are alive, who are left until the coming of the Lord*, shall not precede those who have fallen asleep. For the Lord himself will descend from heaven with a cry of command, with the archangel's call, and with the sound of the trumpet of God. And the dead in Christ will rise first; then *we who are alive, who are left*, shall be caught up together with them in the clouds to meet the Lord in the air; and so we shall always be with the Lord. Therefore comfort one another with these words.

Here we are presented with one of the clearest indications that the apostles expected Christ to return within their lifetimes. To be sure,

---

is stripped of the elements which they hold to be extrinsic to divine revelation, it will compare advantageously with the dogmatic opinions of those who are separated from the unity of the Church." Ibid., 14.

12. Though this chapter generally refers to the Second Coming of Christ with the Greek term *parousia* (cf. 1 Cor 15:23; 2 Thes 2:1), the New Testament employs several other terms and expressions to denote the same expectation: *epiphaneia* (2 Thes 2: 8); *apokalypsis* (1 Pet 4:13); "that Day" (2 Tm 1:12); "the day of the Lord" (1 Thes 5:2); "the day when the Son of man is revealed" (Lk 17:30); and "the last day" (Jn 6:39–40). The Second Coming is likewise graphically portrayed in the words of Jesus and throughout the New Testament without using these precise terms.

one may raise the question of whether Paul intended his words to be taken literally or rather to be read in light of a broader apocalyptic genre, yet it is difficult to ignore the discrepancy between his words and the events of history.

1 Corinthians 7:29, 10:11, and 15:51–52

Another very early text, composed around A.D. 54/57, 1 Cor seems to reflect an outlook and circumstances similar to those we find in 1 Thessalonians. In 1 Corinthians 7, Paul offers practical instructions to guide the behavior of the young community, his assumption being that these Christians were living in an interim state awaiting Christ's imminent return: "I mean, brethren, *the appointed time has grown very short*; from now on, let those who have wives live as though they had none" (7:29). A few chapters later he adds an admonition, "Now these things happened to them as a warning, but they were written down for our instruction, upon whom the end of the ages has come" (10:11).

Paul's extensive discourse on the resurrection in 1 Cor 15 reveals this same outlook: "Lo! I tell you a mystery. *We shall not all sleep*, but we shall all be changed, in a moment, in the twinkling of an eye, at the last trumpet. For the trumpet will sound, and the dead will be raised imperishable, and we shall be changed" (15:51–52). The allusion to the trumpet also resonates with the discourse mentioned above in 1 Thessalonians (4:16). It is difficult to ignore the ostensible fact that Paul expected some people alive in his day still to be alive when Christ returned in glory.[13]

13. It is also worth mentioning what the Gospel of John has to say concerning Christ's return: "When Peter saw him, he said to Jesus, 'Lord, what about this man?' Jesus said to him, 'If it is my will that he remain until I come, what is that to you? Follow me!' The saying spread abroad among the brethren that this disciple was not to die; yet Jesus did not say to him that he was not to die, but, 'If it is my will that he remain until I come, what is that to you?'" (Jn 21:21–23). As John reports Jesus raising a question rather than making a positive assertion, this text is relatively easy to reconcile with the events of history in comparison with the above texts from Paul. Nevertheless, Dale Allison does well to observe, "Obviously behind these verses is Christian anxiety: the Beloved Disciple had died but Jesus had not yet returned." Within the context of this anxiety and uncertainty, the fundamental message here, as in other texts broaching the imminent return of Christ, is the necessity of watchfulness and steadfastness ("Follow me!") no matter what might be the timing of the *parousia*. Allison, *The Historical Christ and the Theological Jesus*, 100.

Mark 13 with Its Parallels in Matthew 24 and Luke 21

Jesus' discourse in Mark 13 is narrated also in the other synoptic Gospels. In Mark it follows Jesus' saying to the disciples, "Truly, I say to you, there are some standing here who will not taste death before they see that the kingdom of God has come with power" (Mk 9:1). This is a text Ehrman explicitly cites in arguing that Jesus "thought the apocalyptic end would arrive very soon, before his disciples had all died."[14] Couched in the imagery of an apocalyptic genre not meant to be interpreted in an overly literal fashion, these passages abound with wars, earthquakes, famines, trials, false christs, stars falling, and the like. Some of what Jesus says here, however, is difficult not to take as a literal prediction of the future:

And then they will see the Son of man coming in clouds with great power and glory. And then he will send out the angels, and gather his elect from the four winds, from the ends of the earth to the ends of heaven.... So also, when you see these things taking place, you know that he is near, at the very gates. *Truly, I say to you, this generation will not pass away before all these things take place.* Heaven and earth will pass away, but my words will not pass away. But of that day or that hour no one knows, not even the angels in heaven, nor the Son, but only the Father. Take heed, watch; for you do not know when the time will come. (Mk 13:26–33; cf. Mt 24:34; Lk 21:32)

What precisely Jesus is predicting here has been the subject of debate for some time, but whether he intended it as a literal prediction of the end of time, the fall of the Temple, or something else, two things are clear: On the one hand, Jesus affirms that no one knows the precise day or hour of his return; on the other hand, he seems clearly to affirm that "this generation will not pass away before all these things take place."[15] When read only in light of the gospel itself, a figurative reading of this

14. Ehrman, *How Jesus Became God*, 102.

15. For an interesting read on Jesus himself not knowing the day or hour of his own return, see Allison, *The Historical Christ and the Theological Jesus*. Allison asks, "How could the judge of the last day not know when his own court would be in session?" He then rightly dismisses a number of patristic explanations for this as "far-fetched," going so far as to allege that this exegesis "must be regarded as defensive exegesis, as special pleading. The church fathers read the logion with presuppositions foreign to it, presuppositions that indeed contradict it. They found only what they wanted to find, reading their own Christology into the Gospels so that Jesus might hand it right back to them." Ibid, 82–83.

text might seem compelling. However, when approached in light of the unity of Scripture—in particular the texts from Paul described above dating from roughly the same period—a strong case could be made that Jesus intended to describe something more vast and definitive than the end of the Jewish world, namely, the end of the world itself.

Magisterial Texts Seemingly Incompatible with the Scriptures and History

Another set of difficulties concerning the *parousia* arises within a 1915 document of the Pontifical Biblical Commission.[16] While the problems presented by this text may at first appear trivial in comparison with those found in Scripture and are not on Ehrman's radar, it must be remembered that at this time the PBC served as an organ of the Magisterium. This makes the discrepancy between its teachings and modern approaches (including that of Benedict XVI discussed below) much more significant.[17] Like the other *responsa* issued by the PBC at the time, this document follows a question-and-answer format, the answers representing the Magisterium's teaching on the matter in question.

Question 1: Whether it is permissible for a Catholic exegete, in solving difficulties that occur in the Letters of St. Paul and the other apostles, where the so-called "Parousia" or Second Coming of our Lord Jesus is mentioned, to

16. Pontifical Biblical Commission, *On the Parousia or Second Coming of Our Lord in the Letters of St. Paul the Apostle* (June 18, 1915). The English translation reproduced here is taken from Béchard, *The Scripture Documents*, 207–8. Italics have been added for emphasis. Several years earlier, Pius X had weighed in on a closely related topic, condemning the following proposition: "Everyone who is not led by preconceived opinions can readily see that either Jesus professed an error concerning the immediate Messianic coming or the greater part of His doctrine as contained in the Gospels is destitute of authenticity." Pius X, *Lamentabili Sane*, 33. Like the PBC, the pontiff was careful not to issue a blanket condemnation but rather a condemnation of those who claimed that one could "readily see" that Jesus or the gospels erred in the matter of expecting an imminent *parousia*. For a contemporary critical appraisal of this condemnation, see Allison, *The Historical Christ and the Theological Jesus*, 96–97. Speaking more bluntly than Ratzinger on the subject, Allison characterizes the Church's anti-modernist statements as examples of "the cognitive dissonance of people who, preferring their theological inclinations to the historical facts, mistreat our sources, thereby obtaining a Jesus more to their liking."

17. The commission was restructured by Paul VI in 1971 so that it acts no longer as an official organ of the Magisterium but rather as an advisory forum in which the Magisterium and expert exegetes work together in the quest to illumine matters concerning Sacred Scripture.

assert that the apostles, although they teach no error under the inspiration of the Holy Spirit, nevertheless do express their own human views, into which error or deception can enter.

Response 1: Negative.

This answer combats the notion that Scripture contains certain statements which issue from the pen of human authors who are liable to err when they are not writing under the inspiration of the Holy Spirit. In other words, what is condemned here is the attempt to preserve biblical inerrancy by saying that problematic parts of Scripture are not inspired but rather constitute merely the expression of the human author's point of view. In line with the PBC's statement, Vatican II precluded this approach by affirming that "the books of both the Old and New Testaments in their entirety, with all their parts, are sacred and canonical because written under the inspiration of the Holy Spirit, they have God as their author."[18]

In the same section of *Dei Verbum* cited above and reprised by the PBC, the council further teaches that "everything asserted by the inspired authors or sacred writers must be held to be asserted by the Holy Spirit."[19] It is therefore not possible to admit that only certain parts of Scripture are inspired or that certain parts affirm erroneous human views. How, then, are we to account for the presence of the biblical texts mentioned above if not by admitting that they merely expressed the erroneous views of their respective human authors? To give a hint of the argument that will be made further below, the key to addressing discrepancies between magisterial texts like this and the manifest sense of biblical texts like those described above lies in determining just what the sacred authors are asserting in a given instance. For Benedict XVI, the exegete's endeavor must be to ascertain the "fundamental message" and "essential points" being made in texts which appear to contradict the facts of history.[20]

18. Second Vatican Council, *Dei Verbum*, 11.
19. Ibid. See International Theological Commission, *Theology Today*, 22, as well as the PBC's earlier *The Interpretation of Dogma*, C.I.3.
20. For a thorough treatment of Benedict's method of searching out the essence or kernel of key problematic biblical texts, see Ramage, *Dark Passages of the Bible*, especially chapter 4.

Turning now to the second question of the PBC decree in question, we are presented with a question which raises the stakes in our conversation about the relationship between history, dogma, and exegesis. I have abbreviated the question due to its length and convoluted grammatical structure:

Question 2: Whether ... it is fitting to affirm that the apostle Paul certainly declared in his writings nothing that is not in perfect harmony with that ignorance of the time of the Parousia, which Christ himself proclaimed to obtain among human beings.

Response 2: Affirmative.

This text contains a double negative that makes it grammatically challenging, but taking it out one finds that the PBC teaches it is "fitting" to affirm that what Paul taught concerning the *parousia* was "in perfect harmony" with what Jesus said on the topic—namely that we know neither the day nor the hour when he will come again. The underlying reference is to Mark 13:32 discussed above.

The expression "whether ... it is fitting" (*utrum ... oporteat*) is perhaps significant. While the English translation I have reproduced employs the relatively mild term "fitting," this verb frequently takes on the stronger meaning of "demanded," "proper," "right," "requisite," "inevitable," "reasonably expected," or "required."[21] Is the PBC *requiring* Catholics to affirm that Paul's teaching concerning the time of the *parousia* is perfectly consonant with that of Jesus? When one takes into account the overall tenor of the PBC documents from this period it seems unlikely that the commission would have been open to acknowledging a discrepancy between the thought of Paul and that of Jesus. In summary, in this question we observe the PBC teaching that both Paul and Jesus affirmed the impossibility of knowing when the time of the Second Coming would be. However, the fact remains that

21. The following meanings are taken from the entry *oportet* in the *Oxford Latin Dictionary*, ed. P. G. W. Glare (Oxford: Clarendon Press, 1982), 1254–55: 1: "It is demanded by some principle or standard, it is proper, right, requisite, etc. (often represented by Eng. 'ought,' 'should')"; 2: "(in a confident precision) It is bound to happen, it is inevitable"; 3: "(expr. The presumed certainty of a fact) It must surely be the case, it may be reasonably expected"; 4: "To require (to be done, etc.)" I offer gratitude to my erudite colleague Edward Macierowski for his assistance with navigating the nuances of the Latin in this text.

this reply has yet to offer a sufficient *argument* that confronts the problem of the early Church apparently erring in its expectations concerning the Second Coming. Does it in any way leave room for the possibility that Paul thought Christ would return in his lifetime even while Jesus himself did not claim to know the precise hour? Once again to anticipate our answer below, it should be noted that this PBC document primarily served a practical purpose. It was not concerned with providing sophisticated arguments but rather with giving concise, concrete guidance to Catholic exegetes in the early twentieth century.

Finally, I would like to turn our attention briefly to the third question of the PBC's document on the *parousia*:

Question 3: Whether, after considering [the phrase "we who are alive, who are left until the coming of the Lord" of 1 Thes 4:15] ... we may reject as farfetched and unfounded the explanation traditional in Catholic schools ... which explains the words of St. Paul in 1 Thes 4:15–17 without in any way implying the affirmation of a Parousia so imminent that the apostle added himself and his readers to those of the faithful who would survive to meet Christ.

Response 3: Negative.

This question makes a particularly helpful contribution to our discussion because it explicitly addresses a biblical text that has proved to be a stumbling block for exegetes, a text that is numbered among the texts already mentioned above when introducing the problem of the *parousia*. If I am reading the document correctly, here the PBC is not demanding that Catholic exegetes reject the possibility that Paul thought the *parousia* would occur in his lifetime. Rather, the question is phrased so as to teach that the traditional explanation (i.e., the view that Paul did *not* expect the Second Coming in his day) is not to be rejected as far-fetched and unfounded. There is quite a difference between these two statements, and the commission members would certainly have been aware of the difference between the two. If the approach here is the same as what we find in the PBC's other decrees from this period, such language was probably devised deliberately in order to avoid an imprudent blanket condemnation of the view that Paul expected Christ to return in his lifetime.

Toward a Solution: Principles and Illustrations from Benedict XVI's Exegesis

The aim of the previous section was to cast in relief key biblical and magisterial texts that illustrate the discrepancy between the events of history and the early Church's apparently mistaken expectation of the *parousia* within the first century. Now we are in a position to turn to the more positive side of things with a view to finding a solution to the aforementioned problems. The principles below will be drawn from magisterial and curial texts as well as from the corpus of Benedict XVI/Joseph Ratzinger; those principles will be illustrated in light of germane works on the subject by the emeritus pontiff. As before, the goal here is to provide a compelling alternative to Ehrman which at once respects the integrity of the Christian faith and the positive contributions of modern biblical scholarship.

Benedict XVI on St. Paul and the *Parousia*

Benedict treats the problem of the *parousia* in a number of places in his corpus. Each treatment contains particularities one would expect in texts deriving from a span of decades and composed for audiences ranging from biblical scholars to the lay faithful. I would like to begin by considering the treatment found in Benedict's general audiences for the year of St. Paul (2008–2009). Here the pontiff explicitly addresses 1 Thes 4:13–18 discussed above, bearing especially in mind the words, "We who are alive, who are left until the coming of the Lord, shall not precede those who have fallen asleep." The emeritus pontiff begins by observing that this text—the first of Paul's letters and what some have deemed the earliest New Testament document— was likely written around A.D. 52. Contextualizing the letter, he adds that its purpose was to aid the Thessalonian church being beset by doubts and problems.[22] This purpose will play an important role in our discussion below.

One who has persevered with me up to this point in the book will not be surprised at some of his ensuing observations which may af-

22. Benedict XVI, *St. Paul*, 72.

flict the comforted Catholic. He describes 1 Thessalonians as replete "with symbolic imagery, which, however, conveys a simple and profound message."[23] Benedict views 1 Thes 4 not as a literal depiction of the Second Coming but rather as concerned with theological truth through symbolic imagery. The "essential message," he says, is that "our future is to be with the Lord."[24] What we can take away from this is that, regardless of whether or not Paul expected an imminent *parousia*, he was not intending to make a claim or assertion on the subject of its timing. As the International Theological Commission wrote in its earlier work on eschatology, "The early Christians, whether they thought that the *parousia* was imminent or considered it to be quite remote, soon learned through experience that some of them would be taken away by death before the *parousia*."[25] Persecution and martyrdom were constant threats for early Christians, and Paul's letter served to guide the nascent community through these challenging times. Irrespective of the precise moment when Christ himself would return, many knew that they would be meeting him face to face in the near future one way or another.

Moreover, it can be argued that the sense of 1 Thes 4 remains the same even if it could be demonstrated that Paul literally expected the Second Coming to be ushered in with an angel blowing a trumpet. In the marvelous chapter of his book *Miracles* entitled "Horrid Red Things," C. S. Lewis offers an evocative treatment of this type of imagery. He says, "Even if it can be shown, then, that the early Christians accepted their imagery literally, this would not mean that we are justified in relegating their doctrines as a whole to the lumber-room."[26] The early Christian belief concerning the *parousia* and other doctrines like it "would survive substantially unchanged" even after "the falsity of the earlier images had been recognized."[27] Using terminology strikingly similar to the terminology employed by Benedict, Lewis argues that particular physical details about the end of time or the world to come "would not have been what [the sacred authors] cared about.... The

23. Ibid., 73.   24. Ibid.
25. International Theological Commission, *Some Current Questions in Eschatology*, 3.1
26. Lewis, *Miracles*, 119.   27. Ibid.

difficulty here is that they were not writing as philosophers to satisfy speculative curiosity about the nature of God and the universe."[28]

Like Benedict, Lewis affirms that images concerning how or when the *parousia* will take place do not constitute the purpose of the biblical texts in which they appear. According to the standards of *Dei Verbum* introduced in chapter 3, these images are not erroneous because they are not asserted or taught for their own sake in the first place. As Benedict and Lewis show time and again in their writings, Christians should not be afraid to admit the presence of symbolic imagery or even myth in the Bible. Read Lewis, Tolkien, or Chesterton, and it is quite clear that myth does not equal falsehood.[29] To be sure, in a certain sense this makes the theologian's task more difficult, as he has to search out the essential message of biblical texts and bring into relief their permanent dimension or core meaning as distinct from accidental features not part of the deposit of faith. This requires more patience and skill than simply saying every sentence of Scripture is true on its own terms apart from its context and without qualification.[30] On the other hand, following this approach of Benedict and Lewis is liberating because Christians can be confident that there is always a core message God wants to convey to us in the Bible and that this remains unchanged even if we grant the presence of certain difficulties in the text or have to emend our previous reading of it.

Interestingly, Ehrman himself seems to grasp the basic point about images as distinct from the message for which they are a vehicle:

---

28. Ibid., 119–20.

29. For just one of many possible illustrations from each author, see Tolkien, *Tree and Leaf*, 48; Lewis, *Miracles*, 146, 218; Chesterton, *The Everlasting Man*, 233–47.

30. "It follows straightaway that neither the criterion of inspiration nor that of infallibility can be applied mechanically. It is quite impossible to pick out one single sentence and say, right, you find this sentence in God's great book, so it must simply be true in itself." Ratzinger, *God and the World*, 153; cf. Benedict XVI, Address to Participants in the Plenary Meeting of the Pontifical Biblical Commission (May 2, 2011): "Lastly, I would only like to mention the fact that in a good hermeneutic it is not possible to apply mechanically the criterion of inspiration, or indeed of absolute truth by extrapolating a single sentence or expression. The plan in which it is possible to perceive Sacred Scripture as a Word of God is that of the unity of God, in a totality in which the individual elements are illuminated reciprocally and are opened to understanding."

The idea that "Jesus is coming back" is built on the idea that above us, in the sky, over the clouds, is a space where God lives, and that Jesus has gone up there to live with Him. He ascended bodily and he is coming, bodily, back down. No one any longer thinks that above the clouds is a place where God and Jesus live. Above the clouds is more of the atmosphere, and above that is space, and beyond that are billions of stars—and that's just our own galaxy. If the very notion that Jesus is coming back down assumes that there is an "up"—what does one do with that idea in a universe such as ours where there is, literally, no up and down, except in relation to where you happen to be standing at the moment? You obviously need to translate the idea into some kind of modern idiom for it to make sense.[31]

Of course, Ehrman ultimately disagrees with Benedict and Lewis on the implications that flow from distinguishing image and message. Unlike Ehrman, Christians continue to expect the second coming even as we envision *how* it is to happen differently than did our forebears.

Returning to Benedict's catechesis, he next turns his attention to 2 Thes 2:1–4, which reads:

Now concerning the coming of our Lord Jesus Christ and our assembling to meet him, we beg you, brethren, not to be quickly shaken in mind or excited, either by spirit or by word, or by letter purporting to be from us, to the effect that the day of the Lord has come. Let no one deceive you in any way; for that day will not come, unless the rebellion comes first, and the man of lawlessness is revealed, the son of perdition, who opposes and exalts himself against every so-called god or object of worship, so that he takes his seat in the temple of God, proclaiming himself to be God.

Paul here warns his church lest its members be deceived in thinking an imminent Second Coming can be determined based on human calculations. He reminds his audience that "the man of lawlessness" must come first, and that he plainly has not yet. Benedict for his part tells us that "the intention" of this text "is primarily practical."[32] How so? Paul wrote this because he needed to correct Thessalonians who were rationalizing their neglect of worldly duties with the claim that the end was approaching soon anyway: "For we hear that some of you are living in idleness, mere busybodies, not doing any work" (2 Thes 3:11).[33]

---

31. Ehrman, *Jesus, Interrupted*, 280.   32. Benedict XVI, *St. Paul*, 73.

33. It should be noted that Paul's exhortation regarding the end times in 1 Cor 10 might also be described as primarily practical. After saying that these things "were written down for our instruction, upon whom the end of the ages has come," he immediately

Teasing out Paul's thought, Benedict teaches that the expectation of Jesus' *parousia* does not dispense Christians of any epoch from working in the world but rather increases our responsibility to work *in* and *for* the world while not being *of* the world. This is but one of several examples in this catechesis of how Benedict characteristically follows his careful and critical exegesis with a spiritual exhortation for Christians to apply God's word to our lives. He concludes by teaching that, while Christians today might not pray for the end to come soon in the same way St. John did (cf. Rv 16:22), we can and should pray for the Lord to put the injustices of the world to an end. We can also work for the world to be "fundamentally changed" into a "civilization of love."[34]

That said, Benedict's catechesis does not completely resolve the problem of the early expectation of the *parousia*, but it does help us to see that teaching the precise moment of the Second Coming was not Paul's real point in the theologically thorny text of 1 Thessalonians.

Ratzinger's *Eschatology* and the *Parousia*

In contrast with his catechetical instructions on St. Paul discussed above, Ratzinger's *Eschatology: Death and Eternal Life* was written in his capacity as a private theologian, long before he became pope. This book is pivotal because its proper object is the *eschaton*. It is revealing—and perhaps startling—to read the very first sentence of the book's section entitled "The Expectation of an Imminent End." Ratzinger plainly states, "Beyond a shadow of a doubt, the New Testament does contain unmistakable traces of an expectation that the world will end soon. Where do these traces come from? Do they go back to Jesus?"[35] In characteristic fashion, Ratzinger soberly raises the possibility that the New Testament got it wrong with respect to the timing of Christ's second coming.

In the ensuing discussion, Ratzinger flexes his historical-critical muscles as he explores hypotheses that attempt to date the various

---

proceeds to add, "Therefore let any one who thinks that he stands take heed lest he fall" (1 Cor 10:11–12).

34. Benedict XVI, *St. Paul*, 77.
35. Ratzinger, *Eschatology*, 35.

New Testament texts dealing with the subject of the *parousia*. The standard maxim, he relates, is "the greater the stress on expectation of an imminent end, the older a text must be."[36] As evidence for this, he observes that Matthew and Luke, composed (according to the standard view of Ratzinger and most modern scholars) later than Mark, speak of a "delay of the arrival" of the Bridegroom, whereas Mark does not. Ratzinger tells us, "In such texts the waiting Church retrojects its own experience of the 'delay' of the *parousia* into the earlier sayings of Jesus."[37]

Next Ratzinger turns his attention to 2 Peter and observes, "In this epistle, one sees even more clearly how a later period reached a compromise between imminence and remoteness, and explained the *parousia*'s delay in theological fashion."[38] 2 Pet 3:4 confronts the argument of those who would scoff and ask, "Where is the promise of his return?" To this question Peter replies:

But do not ignore this one fact, beloved, that with the Lord one day is as a thousand years, and a thousand years as one day. The Lord is not slow about his promise as some count slowness, but is forbearing toward you, not wishing that any should perish, but that all should reach repentance. But the day of the Lord will come like a thief, and then the heavens will pass away with a loud noise, and the elements will be dissolved with fire, and the earth and the works that are upon it will be burned up. (2 Pet 3:8–10)

Emphasizing that we cannot know the precise day or hour, Peter enjoins Christians to "be zealous to be found by him without spot or blemish, and at peace" (2 Pet 3:14).

At this point, however, Ratzinger tweaks the standard scholarly chronology of New Testament texts dealing with the *parousia*:

In themselves the examples given are doubtless cogent evidence for the thesis [that the older the biblical text, the greater the stress on an imminent end to the world].... Nevertheless, it is open to question whether one can infer from this anything like a general chronological principle whereby Christian origins are marked by an eschatology of radical imminence which would then be gradually toned down until one finally arrives at John, where, for Bultmann

36. Ibid.
37. Ibid., 35–36. As evidence for this claim, Ratzinger cites Mt 24:48 and 25:5 as well as Lk 12:45.
38. Ibid., 36.

at least, temporal eschatology has been wholly eliminated in favor of its existential counterpart.[39]

As we have observed throughout this book, on the subject of historical-critical scholarship Ratzinger demonstrates great respect for the findings of modern scholarship while at the same time soberly acknowledging its limitations. In this case, while acknowledging the presence of development within the thought of the New Testament itself, he stresses modern scholarship's inability to furnish a strict chronology of biblical texts dealing with the *parousia*.[40] Not without a touch of irony does Ratzinger thus state, "Naturally, [the person who believes that later texts are more accurate with regard to the timing of the *parousia*] has to claim that John understood Jesus better than Jesus understood himself."[41]

Adducing evidence contrary to the presupposition that later means less imminent when it comes to the early Church's expectations of the *parousia*, Ratzinger writes that one commentator, Hans Conzelmann, "has shown that the gospel of Matthew, composed contemporaneously with Luke's (or perhaps even later) contains an undiminished imminent eschatology which may even be described as heightened in comparison with Mark."[42] How is this to be explained?

39. Ibid.
40. Particularly illuminating are his comments concerning developments in the later Gospel of John. "That deepening of the idea of the Parousia achieved in the Fourth Gospel is not, therefore, when compared with the Synoptic tradition, something different and strange. Rather does it clarify the relation of the Parousia to the worldly time, something only lightly sketched in the Synoptics." Ibid., 203. It is in this Gospel that the New Testament's conception of the *parousia* reaches full maturity: "It would take a careful analysis of the concepts of 'going' and 'coming' in the Farewell Discourse to display the idea of the Parousia in that mature form which was reached at the close of the New Testament development and passed on from there to the Church." Ibid., 203–4. For an important treatment of doctrinal development within the New Testament itself, see the International Theological Commission's 1990 document *The Interpretation of Dogma*: "There is evidence even in the New Testament that there were stages in the arrival at truth: these expressions of truth reinforce one another mutually, go from depth to depth, but never contradict one another. It is always the identical mystery of God's salvation in Jesus Christ which has found expression in many forms and from different aspects" (B.I.3).
41. Ratzinger, *Eschatology*, 36.
42. Ibid., 37.

In some circumstances, an extreme form of temporal expectation might well be the product of a re-Judaizing process. The Judaism of Jesus' day had an overwhelming expectation of the imminent end. Such an expectation cannot be regarded, then, as something peculiarly characteristic of Jesus. The schema of linear development simply does not correspond to the facts.[43]

As evidence for this claim, Ratzinger recalls that Matthew is the only one of the Synoptic Gospels to depict the coming of the Son of Man in sudden fashion: "For as the lightning comes from the east and shines as far as the west, so will be the coming of the Son of man" (Mt 24:27). In point of fact, he notes that Matthew is the only gospel to employ the precise term *parousia*.

What Ratzinger achieves here both helps our cause and simultaneously makes it more difficult. On the one hand, he makes it clear that the New Testament indeed contains an "imminent eschatology" at various points and does not merely appear to do so. On the other hand, he has not yet offered an explanation for how such an admission is consonant with the doctrine of biblical inerrancy. In other words, if we cannot respond to Ehrman's challenges concerning problematic texts by saying, "Dr. Ehrman, you're reading it wrong—the apostles didn't *really* think that the world was about to end," then how is one supposed to respond to this challenge? Furthermore, Ratzinger's thought introduces yet another problem: that not only the early Church, but possibly even Jesus himself, expected the consummation of the world to be at hand in his day.

To counter these challenges, Ratzinger next turns his attention to "the text which lies at the heart of the problem"—Jesus' eschatological discourse describing the fall of Jerusalem in Mark 13 along with its parallels in Matthew 24 and Luke 21.[44] In particular he focuses on Mt 24:29–31, Mk 13:24–27, and Lk 21:25—each of which contains a unique narrative connecting the fall of Jerusalem and the *parousia* temporally. Ratzinger remarks, "So far as our problem is concerned, it is

---

43. Ibid., 37–38. For a further critique of an attempt to perceive a strictly linear development within Scripture, see Benedict XVI, *Jesus of Nazareth: From the Baptism in the Jordan to the Transfiguration*, xix. On the possibilities and limits of tracing doctrinal development within Scripture, see my *Dark Passages of the Bible*, in particular chapter 6 on the afterlife.

44. Ratzinger, *Eschatology*, 38.

extremely important to note how these two aspects—the imminent destruction of Jerusalem and the Parousia—are temporally related."[45] After pointing out that what Luke portrays "is not the end of the world but the start of a new age in salvation history," he turns his attention to Mark, the most challenging of the texts concerning the problem under consideration in this chapter.[46] "By contrast," he relates, "Mark appears to present a direct temporal link between the fall of the city and the consummation of the world."[47] Noting that the issue is more complex than this, Ratzinger wraps up his discussion by acknowledging, "Nevertheless, the impression persists that the trials and tribulations entailed in the destruction of Jerusalem *are* connected in time with the events of the end of the world."[48] As further evidence of this connection, he adds later in the book, "Even in his own age, Paul believed that he had in fact offered the Gospel to the whole inhabited world. The demand that the Gospel would be preached to all the world seemed thus already fulfilled in the generation of the apostles, what the Markan Jesus calls 'this generation.'"[49]

As Ratzinger is always so good at doing, he moves to summarize and tell his readers what they are to take home from the foregoing discussion: "What ought we to think of these internal divergences within the Synoptic tradition and the issue which they concern?" He immediately answers: "In the first place, the single Gospel is heard only in

---

45. Ibid., 39.   46. Ibid.

47. Ibid.

48. Ibid., 40 (emphasis Ratzinger's). For example, recalling that Matthew converts Mark's schematic *in illo tempore* ("in those days") into his *euthys*, Ratzinger then argues that the latter should not be translated "immediately" but rather "suddenly," adding that "the entire assertion [should be] interpreted accordingly."

49. Ibid., 199. This is not the only place in Ratzinger's corpus in which he describes Paul's conviction in this manner. For example, he made the following remark in a speech to catechists: "Of course, at the end of his life Paul believed that he had proclaimed the Gospel to the very ends of the earth, but the Christians were small communities dispersed throughout the world, insignificant according to the secular criteria. In reality, they were the leaven that penetrates the meal from within and they carried within themselves the future of the world." Joseph Ratzinger, Address to Catechists and Religion Teachers for the Jubilee of Catechists (December 12, 2000). For an illuminating text concerning the assumption that the Gospel had been preached to all creatures, see Jean-Pierre Torrell, OP, "Saint Thomas et les non-chrétiens," *Revue thomiste* 106 (2006): 17–49.

the quartet of the four evangelists (for John belongs there too!). The word of Jesus persists only as something heard and received by the Church."[50] We find Ratzinger stating here what he has said in many other places, a teaching which is but an echo of *Dei Verbum*: the inerrancy of biblical texts is not to be found in looking at them in isolation, but rather within the unity of the entire Word of God contained in Scripture and tradition and lived by the Church.[51] Hence, if Mark's text seems to present problems, we need to look at what the other evangelists say on the topic and evaluate Mark's central purpose in light of that knowledge. We also must bear in mind the entirety of sacred tradition, cognizant that Christianity is not primarily a "religion of the book" but rather is a religion of the living Word, the person Jesus Christ. The ITC's recent work, echoing Ratzinger's language, thus teaches that the Scriptures are "witnesses of faith" and "testify" to the Gospel revelation which is something still greater within which the Bible finds its proper context.[52]

When it comes to the timing of the *parousia* and whether the early Church erred with an expectation that Christ would return in the apostolic era, Ratzinger argues:

> *The decisive point* is surely that the New Testament writings leave open the nature of the difference between literary schema and reality in this connection.... Schema and reality are differently related by different authors, but *none of them makes the bold claim* to an identity between the two.... Since *what interests them* is not the question of exact chronological succession or a possible causality of development but the inner unity of the whole, they are able to present their material in schematic *blocs*, united by schematic connections.... It can only be laid out in some way that *the governing affirmations* of their message suggest.[53]

50. Ratzinger, *Eschatology*, 40.

50. Ratzinger, *Eschatology*, 40.

51. On the importance of reading individual texts in light of the unity of Scripture, see *Dei Verbum*, 12, and *Theology Today*, 22.

52. This terminology appears a number of times within the document. For example, see *Theology Today*, 7, 26, and 30: "The gospel of God is fundamentally testified by the sacred Scripture of both Old and New Testaments.... Tradition is the faithful transmission of the Word of God, witnessed in the canon of Scripture by the prophets and the apostles and in the *leiturgia* (liturgy), *martyria* (testimony) and *diakonia* (service) of the Church." Ibid., 7. For a more thorough discussion of how the Scriptures witness or attest to revelation, see my *Dark Passages of the Bible*, especially 7n8 and 65–66.

53. Ratzinger, *Eschatology*, 41–42 (emphasis added).

By distinguishing "schema" from "reality," Ratzinger moves us away from a rigid literalism that would, in the name of reading the Bible "at face value," miss its primary message conveyed through the literary artistry of the various sacred authors. "What interests them," the emeritus pontiff observes, is not the issue of what precise moment the Second Coming will take place. Rather, "the governing affirmations of their message" suggest something different, something observable in the author's treatment of Paul above. For Ratzinger this is the critical point: *in dealing with the second coming, the biblical authors subordinate the question of timing to the question of how Christians ought to behave regardless of when Christ returns.* For all we know, some biblical authors may have expected Christ to return in their day, as many texts seem to indicate. But what Ratzinger demonstrates is that these expectations are not being asserted or taught, any more than the author of Genesis was trying to provide a timeline for the world's creation.[54] Jesus may return today, or he may return millennia upon millennia from now, but irrespective of this eventuality, the reality is that Christians of all ages have to be awake and prepared. For, even if Christ does not return to earth in our lifetime, this fact remains: we each will be meeting him face to face within a number of minutes to a number of decades, and the precise moment of this meeting will likely occur most unexpectedly.

---

54. For a formidable treatment of this point in relation to Genesis, see Ratzinger, *In the Beginning*. Concerning how to read the account of the world's creation in relation to the *parousia* at its end, it is also worth pondering Allison, *The Historical Christ and the Theological Jesus*, 98: "It matters not, once we understand Genesis aright, what year the book implicitly sets for the world's first dawn. Bishop Ussher's calculation of 4004 B.C. must be wrong because the series of events he ostensibly dated never took place.... In like fashion, locating the coming of the Son of Man in the distant future is no more sensible than locating the occasion in the near future: mythological events do not intersect the historical time line. The *parousia* is a parable, a projection of the mythopoeic imagination. Its date cannot be known because it has no date." While one may take issue with Allison's calling the *parousia* a parable, I believe his overall comparison remains helpful as it shows that the timing of the Second Coming is secondary and unknowable in much the same way as the events concerning our human origins remain shrouded in mystery, accessible only through the images the Church's faith has handed down to us.

Benedict XVI's *Jesus of Nazareth* and the *Parousia*

To see what excellent Catholic exegesis looks like, there is no better place to look than the three volumes of Benedict XVI's *Jesus of Nazareth*, which were examined in the previous chapter. In this section we will follow the lead of our emeritus pontiff in the chapter entitled "Jesus' Eschatological Discourse" from the second volume of the trilogy. The discourse Benedict has in his sights is roughly the same as that found in his work *Eschatology*, which we treated above. For insight into Benedict's mind on this matter, it is significant that he begins his discussion with these words: "This discourse, found in all three Synoptic Gospels with certain variations, could perhaps be described as the most difficult text in the whole of the Gospels."[55] This fear-inspiring claim should remain with us and keep us humble as we proceed in our work of exegeting Benedict's exegesis.

One of Benedict's first paragraphs on the subject reveals striking similarities with his treatment of the *parousia* explored above:

> While this vision of things to come is expressed largely through *images* drawn from tradition, *intended* to point us toward *realities* that defy description, the difficulty of the content is compounded by all the problems arising from the text's redaction history: the very fact that Jesus' words here are *intended* as continuations of tradition rather than literal descriptions of things to come meant that the redactors of the material could take these continuations a stage further, in the light of their particular situations and their audience's capacity to understand, while taking care to remain true to the *essential content* of Jesus' message.[56]

Here we find key terms and expressions which recur throughout Benedict's corpus and so reveal what he considers the key to solving our problem. In *Eschatology* we find "schema" or literary presentation distinguished from "reality," while in this text a similar distinction emerges between "images" and "realities." The images or literary presentation, he observes, are bound up with the Gospels' redaction history—referring to the process by which the biblical books were gradually compiled, edited, and adapted until reaching their canonical form.

---

55. Benedict XVI, *Jesus of Nazareth: Holy Week*, 26–27.
56. Ibid., 27 (emphasis added).

Like Ehrman and other historical-critical scholars, Benedict does not assume that the Gospels contain a word-for-word transcript of Jesus' discourses at every point. Rather, Jesus' words here represent "continuations of tradition"—tradition which preceded Jesus and was developed both by Jesus and by the early Church after his return to the Father. Thus Benedict relates that "the redactors of the material could take these continuations a stage further, in the light of their particular situations and their audience's capacity to understand."[57]

How, then, do we know what the truth of the matter is? Do we really know what Jesus said concerning his Second Coming? Could Jesus himself, whose teaching itself forms part of a continually developing tradition, have erred? What Benedict states—tersely but profoundly—is that the evangelists took care "to remain true to the essential content of Jesus' message."[58] Here again as elsewhere in his corpus, Benedict searches out the *intention* of a particular biblical passage in order to ascertain its *essential content*. He is clear that not every single word in Scripture is being asserted or taught for its own sake, and so difficult passages must be understood within the whole of each individual author's work and in light of the entirety of Scripture. For that matter, Benedict is even aware that Jesus himself employs images which are by their very nature imperfect. Jesus, he says, affirms the substance of said images without the intention of formally incorporating them in their entirety into his message.[59]

As for the question of whether a given statement can be verified as a direct quote from Jesus, Benedict is open to various answers, but he reminds his audience that this is actually a peripheral issue. To draw

57. Ibid.
58. Ibid.
59. For instance, in discussing the image of Hades in Luke 16, Benedict explains: "Jesus uses ideas that were current in the Judaism of his time. Hence we must not force our interpretation of this part of the text. Jesus adopts existing images, *without formally incorporating* them into his teaching about the next life. Nevertheless, *he does unequivocally affirm the substance of the images....* But, as we saw earlier, this is not the principal message that the Lord wants to convey in this parable. Rather, as Jeremias has convincingly shown, *the main point*—which comes in the second part of the parable—is the rich man's request for a sign." *Jesus of Nazareth: From the Baptism in the Jordan to the Transfiguration,* 215–16 (emphasis added).

a now-familiar distinction, we know the essence or substance of Jesus' message, but the extent to which we can verify its many features as issuing from Jesus' own human mouth is an accidental matter. Hence Benedict states, "The extent to which *particular details* of the eschatological discourse are attributable to Jesus himself we need not consider here. That he foretold the demise of the Temple—its theological demise, that is, from the standpoint of salvation history—is beyond doubt."[60] What is Benedict getting at with this talk of the Temple's "theological demise"? Why not just speak of the physical demise it underwent at the hands of the Romans in A.D. 70? It seems to me that Benedict speaks in this way so as to leave open the question of whether or not Jesus foretold the destructive events in question.[61] The pontiff thus argues:

[T]he *nucleus* of Jesus' prophecy is concerned not with the outward events of war and destruction, but with the demise of the Temple in salvation-historical terms, as it becomes a "deserted house." It ceases to be the locus of God's presence and the locus of atonement for Israel, indeed, for the world.[62]

60. Benedict XVI, *Jesus of Nazareth: Holy Week*, 34–35.

61. For a better understanding of this problem, it is important to recall the doubt of modern scholars concerning whether Jesus prophesied the end of the Temple. This approach assumes that the Gospel authors sought to convey Jesus' message by putting words into his mouth after the events had unfolded in history, and for this reason they would not consider the words in question here true prophecies. One of the criticisms that Benedict has leveled at certain scholars is precisely their presupposition that miracles and prophecy cannot occur. In particular, see the first volume of *Jesus of Nazareth*, especially where he identifies as the "fundamental dogma" of modernity the belief that "God cannot act in history." Ibid., 35. On this subject, see also Cardinal Ratzinger's famous lecture "Biblical Interpretation in Conflict: On the Foundations and the Itinerary of Exegesis Today," in *Opening Up the Scriptures*, 1–29. Just as incisive are his lesser-known remarks concerning modernity's assumption that only what is visible or empirically verifiable is true: "In today's context, the impossibility of passing beyond what is apparent, that is, of passing beyond phenomena, has indeed become a kind of dogma." This "so-called modern worldview," which Ratzinger associates with Bultmann in this text, entails a "dictatorship of appearances." Joseph Ratzinger, "Culture and Truth: Some Reflections on the Encyclical Letter *Fides et Ratio*," *The Patrician* (Winter 1999): 1–8. That said, Benedict does not throw the baby out with the bath water when it comes to modern exegesis. Not all those who practice historical-critical exegesis go about their business with a "ready-made philosophy" that is closed to the possibility of divine intervention in the world.

62. Benedict XVI, *Jesus of Nazareth: Holy Week*, 46.

In speaking of this "nucleus," Benedict wishes to signal carefully that whether Jesus prophesied the *physical* demise of the temple is accidental with respect to the gospel message. By no means does Benedict speak in this way out of indifference or lack of careful attention to the biblical text; rather, precisely out of respect for the text he draws a distinction to make sense out of what would otherwise be a contradiction. Here we witness the emeritus pontiff humbly welcoming the questions and observations of modern scholars which at first glance appear incompatible with the Christian tradition. His genius, however, does not lie in this charitable attitude alone. It consists in the fact that he engages the best of modern thought *while at the same time* remaining true to the constant tradition of the Church, endeavoring a synthesis between the two at points where most people (on both sides of the exegetical isle) say rapprochement is impossible.

Benedict does not stop here, however. Regarding the nucleus of Jesus' eschatological discourse, he adds that "the nucleus of Jesus' eschatological message includes the proclamation of an age of the nations."[63] This age is the time of the Church, which the Bible portrays as the intervening period following the time of Jesus' earthly pilgrimage and preceding his return in glory. For Benedict this point is highly relevant because it reveals there to be more than one voice in the New Testament concerning the question of when Jesus will return. For Benedict, the Bible is like a mosaic or stained-glass window with many different pieces that make sense only when looked at as a whole.[64] It is therefore not as if the entire Church were in a state of confusion in expecting an imminent *parousia*. Benedict writes, "It seems obvious to me that several of Jesus' parables ... speak of this time of the Church; from the perspective of a purely imminent eschatology, they would make no sense."[65] He likewise states, "From the content, it is clear that all three Synoptic Gospels recognize a time of the Gentiles: the end of the world can come only when the Gospel has been brought to all peoples."[66]

63. Ibid.
64. Ratzinger, *God and the World*, 101.
65. Benedict XVI, *Jesus of Nazareth: Holy Week*, 47.
66. Ibid., 42.

To be sure, the emeritus pontiff is not backing away from his earlier admission that certain passages explicitly state that "this generation will not pass away" before the end (Mt 24:34). At the same time, he is well aware that other texts suggest the *parousia* will not occur "until the times of the Gentiles are fulfilled" (Lk 21:24) and that "the Gospel must first be preached to all nations" (Mk 13:10; cf. Mt 24:14). To this he adds, "Paul, too, recognizes an age of the Gentiles, which is the present and which must be fulfilled if God's plan is to attain its goal."[67] In light of this evidence, one can see that drawing a one-to-one correspondence between Jesus' use of eschatological imagery and his thought concerning the chronological end of the world would constitute a "superficial reading" of the Gospels.[68] Granted that the Gospels witness to a time of the Gentiles expected to precede the *parousia*, we nevertheless remain faced with another stumbling block—the perception that certain early Christians thought the Gospel had in fact already reached all the nations.

How are we to square such an observation with our discussion up to this point? The reality is that certain biblical authors may have assumed that the Gospel had reached unto the ends of the earth and that Jesus was about to return in glory in their day. This cannot be proved beyond the shadow of a doubt, but neither can it be disproved simply by saying that they could not have thought this way, since saying that would be tantamount to admitting the presence of an error in Scripture. Benedict's approach is much more refined—and thus challenging—than this. Rather than coming down on one side or another on this question, he shows that the very issue is peripheral and could go either way:

The fact that the early Church was unable to assess the chronological duration of these *kairoi* ("times") of the Gentiles and that it was generally assumed they would be fairly short is ultimately *a secondary consideration. The essential point* is that these times were both asserted and foretold and that, above all else and prior to any calculation of their duration, they had to be understood and were understood by the disciples in terms of a mission.[69]

---

67. Ibid., 43.   68. Ibid., 41.
69. Ibid., 43 (emphasis added).

The bottom line in all of this is that the Bible does not formally assert the precise time of the Second Coming. Although we find indications of what individual apostles expected concerning the matter, Benedict understands that, for them also, this was "ultimately a secondary consideration." Whether they thought the world was going to end within a day or a decade or a millennium, he tells us that the "essential point" they were asserting concerned the need for spiritual preparation, for mission, and for endurance in the face of persecution. It turns out that these are realities that must govern Christians' lives regardless of the epoch in which they live and how much time remains in their earthly pilgrimage.[70] They are the core message, the true key, to understanding the Bible's *parousia* passages. This is exactly what one would expect Benedict to say in light of his synthetic exegetical approach, an approach adopted by the PBC in its latest document in the effort to take seriously the literal sense of Scripture while also asking how it can be applied in the lives of Christians in every age.[71]

70. Though located within a discussion of the Sermon on the Mount, the following insight from Servais Pincakers, OP, is equally applicable to the *parousia* texts in this chapter: "The expectation of the end time, the urging of the Spirit, and the threat of persecution certainly contributed a special vitality and forcefulness to the Gospel precepts. Yet nowhere in the Sermon itself do we find any textual reference to a time limit for the fulfillment of its injunctions." *The Sources of Christian Ethics* (Washington, D.C.: The Catholic University of America Press, 1993), 138. On the subject of the spiritual preparation and watchfulness that lies at the heart of the New Testament's imminent *parousia* passages, see Allison, *The Historical Christ and the Theological Jesus*, 98–99: "Proclaiming a near end confronts people with a decision that cannot wait. In addition, because such proclamation typically arises among the disenfranchised, it can rudely unmask the sins of the status quo." Citing B. H. Streeter, Allison rightly notes that for many the expectation of an imminent end had the effect that imminent death has upon individuals of any epoch: "So in ordinary life ultimate values and eternal issues are normally obscured by minor duties, petty cares, and small ambitions; at the bedside of a dying man the cloud is often lifted." Streeter, *Foundations: A Statement of Christian Belief in Terms of Modern Thought: By Seven Oxford Men* (Longdon, Macmillan, 1913), 119–20.

71. See *Theology Today*, 22: "It is in this context that exegesis searches for the literal sense and opens itself to the spiritual or fuller sense (*sensus plenior*) of scripture." The PBC here cross-references the commission's earlier work *The Interpretation of the Bible in the Church* as well as the *Catechism of the Catholic Church*, 115–18. In the following sentence the commission explicitly cites Benedict XVI to further its case: "Only where both methodological levels, the historico-critical and the theological, are respected, can one speak of a theological exegesis, an exegesis worthy of this book." *VD*, 34. For an in-depth treatment of how Benedict weds a critical reading of the literal sense with a theological

The *Adventus Medius* in Benedict's Theology

The epilogue to Benedict's second volume of the *Jesus* trilogy offers a final fascinating angle from which to make sense of thorny *parousia* texts within the New Testament. Reflecting on the subject of Christ's Ascension and return in glory, he begins by dispelling a common yet mistaken assumption concerning the risen Jesus' message that he will come to judge all men and establish God's kingdom in the world:

> There has been a substantial trend in recent theology to view this proclamation as the principal content, if not the very heart of the message. Thus it is claimed that Jesus himself was already thinking in exclusively eschatological categories. The "imminent expectation" of the kingdom was said to be the specific content of his message, while the original apostolic proclamation supposedly consisted of nothing else. Had this been the case, one might ask how the Christian faith could have survived when that imminent expectation was not fulfilled. In fact, this theory goes against the texts as well as the reality of nascent Christianity, which experienced the faith as a force in the present and at the same time as hope. The disciples undoubtedly spoke of Jesus' return, but first and foremost they bore witness to the fact that he is alive now.[72]

Benedict responds here to those who would claim that the "specific content" or core of Jesus' post-resurrection teaching concerned the prediction of his imminent return in glory. As we already have seen above, he does not deny that the early Church may have expected an imminent *parousia*, but to make the further claim that the message "consisted of nothing else" would be utterly mistaken. To be sure, the disciples spoke of Jesus' return, but their primary concern was with the present. Again, as Benedict demonstrated above, the essential content of the apostolic message concerning the *parousia* was not its timing but rather the spiritual preparation and mission to be cultivated with urgency regardless of when Christ's return was to take place.[73]

---

reading of the spiritual sense and its relation to *lectio divina*, see my *Dark Passages of the Bible*, especially chapters 2, 5, and 6.

72. Benedict XVI, *Jesus of Nazareth: Holy Week*, 279.

73. Not only is this the essential content of the Gospel message concerning the *parousia*, but in an illuminating linguistic move Benedict also says that this spiritual dimension is the content of the Christian life: "The content of the Christian life, we said, is not predicting the future, but it is, on the one hand, the gift of the Holy Spirit and, on the other hand, the disciples' worldwide testimony to Jesus, the crucified and risen Lord." Ibid., 286–87.

In subsequent pages Benedict turns from this issue of Christ's final return to ponder the possibility that there might be another "coming" of Christ between his coming in the flesh and his coming in glory at the end of time:

Is it not the case that he will come to us only on some unknown last day? *Can he come today as well?* These questions have left their mark on John's Gospel, and Saint Paul's letters also attempt to answer them. Yet *the essential content* of this answer can be gleaned from the accounts of the "Ascension" at the end of Luke's Gospel and the beginning of the Acts of the Apostles.[74]

How does Christ come to Christians today? The Gospel of John reveals that by going away Christ is able to come again with a new closeness and presence through the Holy Spirit.[75] In the following passages Benedict spells this out at greater length and illustrates with a few examples:

Specific reference is made [in the Gospel of John] to a "coming" of the Father and the Son: it is an eschatology of the present that John has developed. It does not abandon the expectation of a definitive coming that will change the world, but it shows that the interim time is not empty: it is marked by the *adventus medius*, the middle coming, of which Bernard speaks. This anticipatory presence is an *essential element* in Christian eschatology, in Christian life.... The "middle coming" takes place in a great variety of ways. The Lord comes through his word; he comes in the sacraments, especially in the most Holy Eucharist; he comes into my life through words or events.[76]

The idea of an *adventus medius* developed by St. Bernard is identified here as an "essential element" in eschatology and the concept of the *parousia.* Christ enters our lives every day, especially in the Eucharist.

We can see how this connection is developed at greater length by returning to Ratzinger's *Eschatology* for a moment:

The cosmic imagery of the New Testament cannot be used as a source for the description of a future chain of cosmic events. All attempts of this kind are misplaced. Instead, these texts form part of a description of the mystery of the Parousia in the language of liturgical tradition.... The Parousia is the highest intensification and fulfillment of the Liturgy. And the Liturgy is Parousia, an event taking place in our midst.[77]

74. Ibid., 280 (emphasis added).

75. Ibid., 283–84. Benedict refers here to the speech of Jesus narrated in Jn 14:25–31.

76. Ibid., 291 (emphasis added).

77. Ratzinger, *Eschatology*, 202–3. See also Joseph Ratzinger, *A New Song for the Lord: Faith in Christ and Liturgy Today* (New York: Crossroad, 1996), 129.

Once again, Ratzinger denies that the New Testament has its sights set on a literal description of how future events will unfold. Instead, he picks up on a point that many fail to consider in the whole *parousia* debate, namely that the Scriptures depict the Lord's coming in the language of *liturgy*, not cosmology. "Every Eucharist is Parousia," Ratzinger emphatically reasserts.[78] Thus the words "Come, Lord Jesus!" (Rv 22:20) can and should be prayed by everyone who is blessed to partake in the marriage supper of the Lamb (cf. Rv 19:7–9). To put it in Benedict's own words from one of his last catecheses as Roman pontiff, "Jesus repeats several times: 'Behold, I am coming soon' (Rv 22:7, 12). This affirmation does not only indicate the future prospect at the end of time but also that of the present: Jesus comes, he makes his dwelling place in those who believe in him and receive him."[79] To be sure, this explanation does not suffice on its own to account for all the Bible's problematic *parousia* passages, but it does provide another important angle from which to glimpse the concerns of early Christians and thereby to provide an alternative to approach that respects both the integrity of the faith and the enterprise of scholarly exegesis.

Conclusion: Toward a Reconciliation of Past and Present Magisterial Teaching on the *Parousia*

Having advanced Ratzinger's approach toward reconciling problematic biblical texts concerning the *parousia*, I would like to conclude

---

78. Ratzinger, *Eschatology*, 203. My aim here is not to develop Ratzinger's argument in favor of this connection. For an accessible treatment of this, see Scott Hahn's chapter "Come Again? The Real Presence as Parousia," in *Catholic for a Reason III: Scripture and the Mystery of the Mass* (Steubenville, Ohio: Emmaus Road, 2004), 31–48. In connection with the *parousia* and the Book of Revelation, see his *The Lamb's Supper: The Mass as Heaven on Earth* (New York: Doubleday, 1999). Also highly valuable is the excellent history of doctrine upon which Hahn draws: Jaroslav Pelikan, *The Emergence of the Catholic Tradition (100–600)*, Vol. 1: *The Christian Tradition* (Chicago: University of Chicago Press, 1971), especially 126–27 where he states: "The Eucharistic liturgy was not a compensation for the postponement of the parousia, but a way of celebrating the presence of one who had promised to return." For another accessible treatment of the issue, see Michael Barber, *Coming Soon: Unlocking the Book of Revelation and Applying Its Lessons Today* (Steubenville, Ohio: Emmaus Road, 2005).

79. Benedict XVI, *A School of Prayer: The Saints Teach Us How to Pray* (San Francisco: Ignatius Press, 2012), 270.

with a few considerations regarding the PBC decrees on the same subject. It is clear that in many ways the corpus of Joseph Ratzinger differs both in principle and in practice from the magisterial texts surveyed above. To be sure, the PBC decisions are not themselves dogmas, but they are concerned with upholding the dogma of the Second Coming in its full integrity and were issued with magisterial authority. How are they to be reconciled with the biblical text in light of modern exegesis and the teaching of today's Magisterium?

While the constraints of the present chapter do not make it possible to provide the more lengthy treatment this question could easy receive, for present purposes I would like simply to summarize a few key elements in such a solution to the problems posed by the PBC decree described above—a solution which follows along the same lines advanced in the case of similar problems posed above by the text of Scripture. Both in Ratzinger's works and in the recent magisterial tradition one finds an emphasis on the need to situate dogmas within the Church's living and developing tradition. From the awareness that dogmas have a historical dimension follows the need to ascertain the precise context, meaning, intent, and content of dogmatic formulas. Ratzinger/Benedict and the International Theological Commission refer to the latter variously as the core, principles, or permanently valid content of dogmas.[80] The key to discernment here lies in grasping the precise question under consideration in a given magisterial statement.[81] Ascertaining the relevant question and answer within

80. "Without doubt a distinction must be made between the permanently valid content of dogmas and the form in which this is expressed." International Theological Commission, *The Interpretation of Dogma*, C.III.3. The document at this point summarizes Newman's seven criteria for discerning true from false developments of doctrine. Concerning how said dogmas are to be rendered accessible to believers today, the commission teaches that "the dogma must be stripped down to the original kernel to make it intelligible in a new culture. It is a problem involving all evangelization today, and especially where new factors affect the process of evangelization." Ibid., A.II.1. Benedict employs similar language, underscoring the need to distinguish "permanent" principles from "contingent" practical forms of magisterial teaching, which are subject to change. See Benedict XVI, Christmas Address to the Roman Curia (December 22, 2005). For an informative discussion of the historical condition that affects magisterial decisions, see the Congregation for the Doctrine of the Faith's 1973 declaration *Mysterium Ecclesiae*, 5.

81. International Theological Commission, *Theology Today*, 29: "Dogmas belong to

their context thus enables one to distinguish truths of sacred tradition which constitute the deposit of faith from human traditions which may be ancient yet stand in need of critique and are thus amenable to change over time.[82]

What is needed therefore is a "critique" that distinguishes the specific pastoral decisions of the commission at the time from the essence of the message they wished to affirm. We have already seen that Ratzinger explicitly locates the core of Scripture's *parousia* passages within their message concerning spiritual preparation, mission, and endurance in times of persecution. What, then, is the core or kernel of those troublesome PBC decrees on the subject of the Second Coming? Asking this question necessarily entails another question: What was the primary interest of the PBC in drafting such documents, and

---

the living and ongoing Apostolic Tradition. Theologians are aware of the difficulties that attend their interpretation. For example, it is necessary to understand the precise question under consideration in light of its historical context, and to discern how a dogma's meaning and content are related to its formulation. Nevertheless, dogmas are sure points of reference for the Church's faith and are used as such in theological reflection and argumentation." The commission here cites its earlier document *The Interpretation of Dogma*, B.III.3, as well as John XXIII's opening speech at Vatican II and the latter's constitution *Gaudium et Spes*, 62. See also the ITC's earlier document cited in *The Interpretation of Dogma*, B.II.2, which describes the Second Vatican Council as having "presented the Church's traditional doctrine on a much greater canvas" and, in so doing "accepted that dogma has an historical dimension." The document adds that "a dogmatic definition is not only the end of a development but equally a new start." Ibid., C.III.1.

82. International Theological Commission, *Theology Today*, 31: "Vatican II distinguished between Tradition and those traditions that belong to particular periods of the Church's history, or to particular regions and communities, such as religious orders or specific local churches.... While criticism is not appropriate with reference to Apostolic Tradition itself, traditions must always be open to critique, so that the 'continual reformation' of which the Church has need can take place, and so that the Church can renew herself permanently on her one foundation, namely Jesus Christ. Such a critique seeks to verify whether a specific tradition does indeed express the faith of the Church in a particular place and time, and it seeks correspondingly to strengthen or correct it through contact with the living faith of all places and all times." The ITC here cites the following texts from the Second Vatican Council: *Dei Verbum*, 8; *Lumen Gentium*, 13–14; *Unitatis Redintegratio* 6, 15, 17; *Ad Gentes* 22. See also *The Interpretation of Dogma*, C.II.2: "The discernment of spirits (1 Cor 12:10; 1 Thes 5:21; 1 Jn 4:1) is therefore an element in the entrance through the agency of the Holy Spirit into 'the fullness of truth.' The problem is to make a distinction between Tradition as received from the Lord (1 Cor 11:23) and the traditions of men (Mk 7:8; Col 2:8)."

of what lasting relevance are their findings that stand in such stark contrast with magisterial writings today?[83] While we cannot speak for the members of the 1915 PBC, a clear indication of their underlying intent is offered by none other than Ratzinger himself in a work written while he was head of the PBC. He provides a vivid comparison to illustrate:

> The process of intellectual struggle over these issues that had become a necessary task can in a certain sense be compared with the similar process triggered by the Galileo affair. Until Galileo, it had seemed that the geocentric world picture was inextricably bound up with the revealed message of the Bible, and that champions of the heliocentric world picture were destroying the core of Revelation. It became necessary fully to reconceive the relationship between the outward form of presentation and the real message of the whole, and it required a gradual process before the criteria could be elaborated.... Something analogous can be said with respect to history. *At first it seemed as if the ascription of the Pentateuch to Moses or of the Gospels to the four individuals whom tradition names as their authors were indispensable conditions of the trustworthiness of Scripture and, therefore, of the faith founded upon it.* Here, too, it was necessary for the territories to be re-surveyed, as it were; the basic relationship between faith and history needed to be re-thought. This sort of clarification could not be achieved overnight.[84]

In this passage Ratzinger sheds light on the reason certain features of early PBC decrees stand "in need of correction." Those who crafted the statements had assumed that the trustworthiness of Scripture—and thereby the faith itself—would be undermined if the Church entertained findings of modern scholarship that contradicted ancient

---

83. In a section of its work *Unity of the Faith and Theological Pluralism* entitled "Permanent Nature of Doctrinal Formulations," the ITC states: "Dogmatic formulations must be considered as responses to precise questions, and it is in this sense that they remain always true. *Their permanent interest* depends on the lasting relevance of the questions with which they are concerned; at the same time it must not be forgotten that the successive questions that Christians ask themselves about the understanding of the divine word as well as already discovered solutions grow out of one another, so that today's answers always presuppose in some way those of yesterday, although they cannot be reduced to them." Ibid., §10 (emphasis added). This document is cited twice in the ITC's most recent work, *Theology Today*.

84. Ratzinger, "Exegesis and Magisterium of the Church," 134 (emphasis added). Benedict XVI also reflected on this dimension of the Galileo affair in a poignant speech about Vatican II near the end of his pontificate. Benedict XVI, Address to the Parish Priests and Clergy of Rome (February 14, 2013).

traditions concerning such matters as the authorship and dating of biblical books. Applying Ratzinger's principles to the case of the *parousia*, with the rising tide of modernism in the early twentieth century the commission had a reasonable fear of an exegetical slippery slope. In other words, they could see no way to reconcile the inspiration and inerrancy of Scripture with an admission that at least some New Testament authors expected the Second Coming within their generation.

Having come to terms with the problems entailed in maintaining both of these seemingly incongruous positions (the inspiration of Scripture and the expectation of an imminent *parousia*), Ratzinger explains that some magisterial decisions are not intended to be definitive but rather "provisional" determinations of pastoral prudence. In keeping with the terminology employed in magisterial works discussed above, he indicates that such statements have a kernel that remains valid throughout history as well as certain "particulars" or changeable accidental features.[85] Regarding what he calls "the anti-Modernist decisions of the then Biblical Commission," Ratzinger makes two observations. On the one hand, "with respect to particular aspects of their content, they were superseded after having fulfilled their pastoral function in the situation of the time."[86] On the other hand, he observes that "as warning calls against rash and superficial accommodations, they remain perfectly legitimate," for "the anti-Modernist decisions of the Church performed the great service of saving her from foundering in the bourgeois-liberal world."[87]

---

85. These citations come from a document then-Cardinal Ratzinger presented to the press upon the publication of the instruction *Donum Veritatis* on the ecclesial vocation of the theologian: "The text also presents the various forms of binding authority which correspond to the grades of the Magisterium. It states—perhaps for the first time with such candor—that there are magisterial decisions which cannot be the final word on a given matter as such but, despite the permanent value of their principles, are chiefly also a signal for pastoral prudence, a sort of provisional policy. Their kernel remains valid, but the particulars determined by circumstances can stand in need of correction." Joseph Ratzinger, "On the 'Instruction Concerning the Ecclesial Vocation of the Theologian,'" in *The Nature and Mission of Theology*, 106. For the background to this statement see especially Congregation for the Doctrine of the Faith, *Donum Veritatis*, 24.

86. Ratzinger, "On the 'Instruction Concerning the Ecclesial Vocation of the Theologian,'" 106.

87. Ibid.

Thus from our privileged vantage point a century later, we can see with Benedict that the core of the PBC decrees did not consist in their assertions concerning particular matters which prominent faithful exegetes today dispute. Rather, the substance of what the Magisterium intended to convey at the time, and that remains true today, is the desire to safeguard the truth of Scripture. In the case of our topic in this chapter, this entails upholding the dogma of the *parousia* while letting our precise understanding of it be illumined by modern exegesis. This has been the central thrust of our book: to provide a compelling approach to contemporary problems that does not dismiss but rather thinks *through* them with the conviction that doing so will only serve to strengthen our faith in Christ and his Church.

7

❧

"TO WHOM SHALL WE GO?" TOWARD AN *APOLOGIA* FOR THE CHRISTIAN APPROACH TO JESUS

In the preceding chapters I endeavored to show that Benedict XVI's exegetical vision offers a compelling, faith-affirming alternative to the prevalent secular approach to the life of Christ epitomized in the writings of Bart Ehrman. While at times I have indicated that Benedict's particular conclusions are more warranted than those of Ehrman, on the whole I only claim to have offered Benedict's approach as a viable alternative rather than arguing specifically why one should be inclined to choose it. In this concluding chapter I would like to offer some of my own reflections on this question that I hope will be of value to others pursuing it.

Benedict XVI: Pure Objectivity Does Not Exist

"The debate about modern exegesis is not at its core a dispute among historians, but among philosophers."[1] This all-important quote I mentioned in the introduction to this volume has remained with us throughout our quest and demands a final word here by way of conclusion. As we have seen in the pages above, Ratzinger's call for a "criti-

---

1. Ratzinger, "Biblical Interpretation in Conflict," 19.

cism of the criticism," made a generation ago, remains as relevant as ever for those who wish to engage modern biblical criticism seriously from a perspective of faith.

Whether we are aware of it or not, every reader—agnostic and Christian alike—when sitting down to read the Bible brings philosophical presuppositions to the table. These first principles are "spectacles" we wear which color our entire view of reality, including what we think is going on within Scripture. Ratzinger for his part argues that Heisenberg's uncertainty principle has an analogy here: "Pure objectivity is an absurd abstraction," he says, for "the observer's perspective is an essential determinant of the outcome of an experiment."[2] What this means in the context of this book is that the answers to particular questions we ask of Scripture are in large part determined before we ever open up the text in the first place. What are we to make of Jesus' miracles and of his resurrection in particular? If one is an agnostic like Ehrman, then a natural explanation will be adduced for these phenomena. Such an explanation could take many forms: for example, a putative healing miracle could be explicable in light of modern medicine, or more likely it was invented by the gospel authors decades after Jesus' life in order to convince others of his divinity.

On the other hand, a person who approaches the Bible assuming theism to be true will be open to taking the healing story at face value and will attribute it to Jesus' divine mastery over the natural order. Or perhaps the believer will take a position similar to that of the agnostic but with the understanding that God in his providence shows us the face of Jesus by working through natural causes, whether medicine or human authors with their own agendas. My point here is not to adjudicate which if any of these explanations best explains a given miracle story in the gospels. Rather, I simply wish to underscore the reality that our conclusions about a given text are in large part governed by principles and commitments we had before opening up the Bible.

Throughout his career, Joseph Ratzinger has shown himself to be at once a great admirer and practitioner of modern exegesis as well as one of its most incisive critics. While the above chapters should have

2. Ibid., 9.

made it clear that Ratzinger by no means rejects the modern approach to Scripture, he nevertheless admits that it "has brought forth great errors" caused in no small part by an unquestioning allegiance to certain "academic dogmas."[3] Perhaps the principal mainstream assumption the emeritus pontiff finds problematic is the belief (and I use that word here deliberately, meaning something one cannot prove) that God cannot enter in and work in human history. However improbable divine intervention in our world might appear, Ratzinger argues that this cannot be excluded *a priori* unless one has definitive proof that God does not exist. The miraculous is by its very nature something unexpected and highly improbable. The jump from calling it improbable to impossible is what Ratzinger finds problematic, and he thinks that many people today read the Bible in this way without reflecting upon whether their assumption of such a conclusion is warranted or not.

Ehrman: Everyone Has Presuppositions

Approaching the question from a very different angle, the agnostic Ehrman does both sides of the debate a great service in debunking the notion that we hold our respective convictions about Scripture on the basis of certain proofs. For example, in *Jesus, Interrupted* he writes that we can neither prove nor disprove the Resurrection:

I am decidedly not saying that Jesus was not raised from the dead. I'm not saying the tomb was not empty. I'm not saying that he did not appear to his disciples and ascend into heaven. Believers believe that all these things are true. But they do not believe them because of historical evidence. They take the Christian claims on faith, not on the basis of proof. There can be no proof.[4]

These words may alarm some Christians who think that we can "prove" the Resurrection. To be sure, we Christians can and must adduce reasons for our belief and be prepared to defend our faith against objections. But Ehrman is perfectly right to push us on the reality that these reasons do not amount to a definitive proof. This indeed is why we call it faith, not science.

---

3. Ibid., 27.
4. Ehrman, *Jesus, Interrupted*, 180.

Now the Catholic position is by no means saying that faith is "un-scientific" or at odds with history. Rather, the point here is that the Christian and the agnostic may look at the same evidence and draw different conclusions because of our prior commitments, specifically our adherence to the Christian faith, which itself is a gift from God meditated by the Church. Aquinas puts this well in his discussion of the cause of faith:

As regards ... man's assent to the things which are of faith, we may observe a twofold cause, one of external inducement, such as seeing a miracle, or being persuaded by someone to embrace the faith: neither of which is a sufficient cause, since of those who see the same miracle, or who hear the same sermon, some believe, and some do not. Hence we must assert another internal cause, which moves man inwardly to assent to matters of faith ...

[S]ince man, by assenting to matters of faith, is raised above his nature, this must needs accrue to him from some supernatural principle moving him inwardly; and this is God. Therefore faith, as regards the assent which is the chief act of faith, is from God moving man inwardly by grace.[5]

Ultimately, various factors influence one's approach to the Christian mystery, and it is difficult to articulate how two intelligent, well-meaning people can look at the same evidence and draw radically different conclusions. Politically incorrect and unsatisfying as it may sound, the Christian response of Aquinas is that it has everything to do with the mystery of grace. Not even witnessing a miracle is sufficient to produce faith. Good arguments may dispose one to belief, but faith itself is a gift given by God.

Granted that believing above all depends upon God's grace, this is by no means to say that we simply need to "leave it in God's hands" and do nothing to help people come to Christ. On the contrary, I think

5. Aquinas, *Summa theologiae*, II-II, q. 6, a. 1. Ehrman is right to criticize the common simplistic responses offered by Christians when they are faced with the findings of modern biblical scholarship: "The reason historians cannot prove or disprove whether God has performed a miracle in the past—such as raising Jesus from the dead—is not that historians are required to be secular humanists with an anti-supernaturalist bias. I want to stress this point because conservative Christian apologists, in order to score debating points, often claim that this is the case. In their view, if historians did not have anti-supernaturalist biases or assumptions, they would be able to affirm the historical 'evidence' that Jesus was raised from the dead." Ehrman is right that the historical method alone cannot yield a decision as to whether Jesus rose from the dead.

that one of the most helpful things we can do is to help people think
about their assumptions or first principles. In his book *How Jesus Became God*, Ehrman himself has a helpful overview of the fundamen-
tals for doing history properly at the level of first principles. As I mentioned in the introduction, he says something here which I could have
mistaken as coming from the pen of Benedict XVI had I not known
otherwise:

> The first thing to stress is that everyone has presuppositions, and it is impos-
> sible to live life, think deep thoughts , have religious experiences, or engage in
> historical inquiry without having presuppositions. The life of the mind can-
> not proceed without presuppositions. The question, though, is always this:
> What are the appropriate presuppositions for the task at hand?[6]

This issue lies at the heart of Benedict's conviction that the debate
in exegesis is at bottom a philosophical one. We can never completely
suspend our biases, but we can at least do our best to remain conscious
of their presence and engage in a self-critique that helps to purify our
thought and attune it with the breadth of knowledge we can gain from
the sources available to us. In view of this critique, the pivotal question is: *whose philosophical presuppositions best position us for an accurate
understanding of the Bible and of the nature of things in general?* While I
ultimately disagree with the assumptions he chooses to operate upon,
John Dominic Crossan puts the matter quite well:

> I repeat, once again, that you must decide your presuppositions about gospel
> traditions before reconstructing either the historical Jesus or earliest Chris-
> tianity. Everyone must. Everyone does.... [N]obody can avoid presupposi-
> tions, although you can avoid these in favor of those. You can refuse mine and

---

6. Ehrman, *How Jesus Became God*, 144. These remarks are refreshing coming as
they do from a scholar who approaches the gospels with a hermeneutic of suspicion. In
particular, they contrast with those of Julius Wellhausen, who alleged that philosophy
does not precede, but rather follows biblical criticism. Note that I do not construe this
observation to be a back-door attack on the Documentary Hypothesis but simply an observation of how much more realistic I find Ehrman's philosophical sense. I concur with
Hahn and Wiker, who observe on this score, "A critical approach and a deeper knowledge of history do not produce these presuppositions.... Rather, the presuppositions determine the way that exegetes are critical and the way that they use history." *Politicizing
the Bible*, 12. Hahn and Wiker's evaluation of Wellhausen can be found on p. 561 of the
same work.

choose your own. In historical Jesus research, nobody can avoid presuppositions about the gospels—about their number, their nature, and their relationships. And nobody can dismiss another's presuppositions using the grounds that they are just that. Presuppositions can be rejected only by judgments of inadequacy, illegitimacy, or invalidity.[7]

This leads us right to the heart of the matter: whose presuppositions are more adequate—the Christian's or the agnostic's?

Whose Philosophical Presuppositions Are Better? Ehrman's Case

As I mentioned above, the conclusions we draw about the Bible are largely determined by the presuppositions that governed our worldview before we ever opened up the sacred page in the first place. What this means for our book is that our position on Christ's divinity, Resurrection, and return ultimately hinges on how we answer a prior question: whether or not the natural world we know is the only reality that exists—in other words, whether or not the supernatural or divine exists. While a positive answer to this question does not guarantee the truth of Jesus Christ (one can be a theist without being a Christian), a negative answer necessarily entails the conclusion that purported miracles such as Christ's resurrection cannot be true. Ehrman's position is

7. Crossan, *The Birth of Christianity*, 95. It should be recalled from chapter 4 that significant arguments against Ehrman's exegetical criteria (especially the criterion of dissimilarity) have been adduced by contemporary scholars. According to Luke Timothy Johnson, "It should be obvious that these are not 'criteria' at all, but assumptions that are attached to a predetermined vision of the Jesus who is supposedly sought." Johnson, *The Real Jesus: The Misguided Quest for the Historical Jesus and the Truth of the Traditional Gospels* (San Francisco: HarperSanFrancisco, 1996), 25. Regarding these criteria, Dale Allison soberly acknowledges, "Because our criteria are not strong enough to resist our wills, we almost inevitably make them do what we want them to do: we, with all our expectations and presuppositions, bend them more than they bend us.... Once a paradigm about Jesus is in place, cognitive bias will also be in place.... Honesty moves me to indict myself here.... My Jesus is the same yesterday, today, and probably forever." Allison, *The Historical Christ and the Theological Jesus*, 58–59. In a sobering remark that all academics would do well to ponder, he writes (p. 60): "A historian's Jesus is never just the consequences of reading sources through a screen of criteria. Rather, we conduct our intellectual rituals, that is, invent and/or apply our criteria, only after we have adopted some firm ideas about Jesus. Our criteria are less routes to our destination than ways of persuading others to end up where we have."

not strictly negative in the sense of claiming to have disproven God's existence, but he rejects miracles nonetheless.[8]

Ehrman is quite open about how he came to his current persuasion. It was the problem of evil—not a devastating encounter with historical biblical criticism—that drove him to agnosticism:

For many people who inhabit this planet, life is a cesspool of misery and suffering. I came to a point where I simply could not believe that there is a good and kindly disposed Ruler who is in charge of it.... I can't believe in that God anymore, because from what I now see around the world, he doesn't intervene.[9]

Ehrman recently dedicated his entire book entitled *God's Problem* to the problem of evil as addressed in different, and even what appear to be contradictory, ways throughout the Bible. In the course of his text, the author examines the entire gamut of biblical theodicies and finds all of them wanting. Moreover, he finds both unbiblical and unconvincing the standard Christian appeal to man's free will as the explanation of evil in our world. And within the free will theodicy, most appalling to Ehrman is the suggestion that a divine being would torture humans eternally for only a very brief misuse of their free will while on earth. As he puts it in *Jesus, Interrupted*, "There is not literally a place of eternal torment where God, or the demons doing his will, will torture poor souls for 30 trillion years (as just the beginning) for sins they committed for thirty years. What kind of never-dying eternal divine Nazi would a God like that be?"[10] In light of this qualm and others like it, Ehrman concludes, "I don't 'know' if there is a God; but I think that if there is one, he certainly isn't the one proclaimed by the Judeo-

---

8. I for one appreciate Ehrman's general attitude toward the question of God's existence insofar as it differs in tone and quality from that of many strident atheists. In the author's own words: "I should stress that it is not the goal of this book to convince you, my reader, to share my point of view about suffering, God, or religion. I am not interested in destroying anyone's faith or deconverting people from their religion. I am not about to urge anyone to become an agnostic. Unlike other recent agnostic or atheist authors, I do not think that every reasonable and reasonably intelligent person will in the end come to see things my way when it comes to the important issues of life." Ehrman, *God's Problem*, 17.

9. Ibid., 3.

10. Ehrman, *Jesus, Interrupted*, 276.

Christian tradition, the one who is actively and powerfully involved in this world."[11]

One of the most interesting and telling dimensions of Ehrman's thought regarding evil comes at the end of his book-length treatment of it: "I have to admit that at the end of the day, I do have a biblical view of suffering. As it turns out, it is the view put forth in the book of Ecclesiastes.... In my opinion, this life is all there is."[12] He then proceeds to elaborate upon what he takes to be the moral implications of this naturalistic view:

In any event, the idea that this life is all there is should not be an occasion for despair and despondency, but just the contrary. It should be a source of joy and dreams—joy of living for the moment and dreams of trying to make the world a better place, both for ourselves and for others in it. This means working to alleviate suffering and bringing hope to a world devoid of hope.... By all means, and most emphatically, I think we should work hard to make the world—the one we live in—the most pleasing place it can be for ourselves. We should love and be loved. We should cultivate our friendships, enjoy our intimate relationships, cherish our family lives. We should make money and spend money. The more the better. We should enjoy good food and drink. We should eat out and order unhealthy desserts, and we should cook steaks on the grill and drink Bordeaux. We should walk around the block, work in the garden, watch basketball, and drink beer. We should travel and read books and go to museums and look at art and listen to music. We should drive nice cars and have nice homes. We should make love, have babies, and raise families. We should do what we can to love life—it's a gift and it will not be with us for long.

But we should also work hard to make our world the most pleasing place it can be for others—whether this means visiting a friend in the hospital, giving more to a local charity or an international relief effort, volunteering at the local soup kitchen, voting for politicians more concerned with the suffering in the world than with their own political futures, or expressing our opposition to the violent oppression of innocent people. What we have in the here and now is all that there is. We need to live life to its fullest and help others as well to enjoy the fruits of the land. In the end, we may not have ultimate solutions to life's problems. We may not know the why's and wherefore's. But just because we don't have an answer to suffering does not mean that we cannot have a response to it. Our response should be to work to alleviate suffering wherever possible and to live life as well as we can.[13]

11. Ehrman, God's Problem, 4.   12. Ibid., 276.
13. Ibid., 278.

As a Catholic, I find myself agreeing with most of Ehrman's moral imperatives mentioned above, and I think he lays them out eloquently. Indeed, from the perspective of natural law as taught in the Catholic Church, a person does not need explicit faith in God to know that the above things are good.

In any event, the problem of evil is not the only point in Ehrman's favor when it comes to assessing the strength of his presuppositions. As we saw above, Ehrman's case that the early Church mythologized the man Jesus is by no means something to be dismissed out of hand. While I have endeavored to show that Benedict XVI's alternate hermeneutic of the evidence is just as plausible as Ehrman's, this is a far cry from demonstrating Ehrman's agnostic assumptions to be wrong. In other words, it is possible that the clearer insight into Jesus' divinity we find in later strands of tradition was the work of providence and genuine divine revelation, but it is also possible that the early Church invented Jesus' divinity. Likewise, it is possible that the New Testament authors found genuine foreshadowing in the Old Testament after they had encountered Jesus in his real historical Resurrection, but it is also possible that these same authors artfully crafted events in Jesus' life to make him "fulfill" Old Testament texts that fit their agenda. Bearing in mind that the Resurrection is a miracle and by definition highly improbable, I think it is unreasonable to dismiss Ehrman's agnostic approach to the gospels as illegitimate based on internal evidence alone.

Whose Philosophical Presuppositions Are Better?
The Case for Benedict

Regarding the Problem of Evil

Ehrman is by no means the first person driven to agnosticism by the problem of evil, nor will he be the last. It would be pretentious to claim that I can diffuse this timeless conundrum in a few short words, but since the issue bears so directly on our exegetical presuppositions, I would at least like to point the reader in the direction of a compelling Christian response.

First, there is the classical Christian answer to the problem of evil, represented in the thought of such figures as Augustine and Aquinas.

In short, God would not allow evil in the first place unless his om-
nipotence and goodness were such as to bring greater good out of the
evil he allows.[14] For this wisdom these patristic and medieval authors
themselves were indebted to an even more authoritative and ancient
source: Scripture itself. Whether it is Paul teaching that where sin
abounds, grace abounds all the more (Rom 5:20) or Joseph the patriarch telling his brothers that what they meant for evil, God meant
for good (Gn 50:20), the Bible affirms that God allows certain evils
precisely in order to bring about an even greater good. Ehrman does
not accept this argument, but many Christians including myself find it
invaluable even while recognizing that it does not constitute a comprehensive solution to the problem of evil.

Second, I would like to highlight a dimension of the problem
that many authors fail to address. The question here is: what kind of
world ought we to expect from God? As Brian Davies writes, many
anti-theistic writers embrace the notion that relief from suffering is
an intrinsically good thing, but many theists reject this assumption.
A Christian who thinks like Aquinas and Augustine will argue that
sacrifice and pain can lead to desirable results in accordance with the
belief (also rooted in experience, even if it is not always verifiable) that
God brings even greater good out of evil. Another way Davies takes
up this issue is to challenge the temptation to suppose that "Maximize
happiness" is an imperative that any decent-minded God would act
upon. Davies suggests that such an imperative is unintelligible, since
God could always make a person happier.[15]

Davies refers to various Christian thinkers who have urged that
reason alone cannot say very much vis-à-vis the question of what kind
of world God should be expected to make. In particular he calls upon
the Angelic Doctor to show that, insofar as anything can be deemed a
"characteristic effect" of God, it is being (esse)—the fact that there is
any world at all. He continues:

14. Aquinas, *Summa theologiae*, I, q. 2, a. 3, ad 1; Augustine, *Enchiridion*, xi.

15. Brian Davies, *The Reality of God and the Problem of Evil* (London: Continuum,
2006), 23. My thanks to James Madden for putting me onto this and a couple other philosophical works to which I appeal in this conclusion.

For Aquinas, we have to start by noting what God has, in fact, made to be. Reflections on the topic of God and evil must, so he thinks, start from that, and not from assumptions we might have dreamed up (on what basis?) concerning what God is or is not likely to create.[16]

If this is the case, then are there any grounds other than intuition on which we might base our convictions regarding God in relation to evil, so that we would avoid endorsing a voluntaristic view of God? Referencing Herbert McCabe, Davies writes:

Like Aquinas, McCabe is suggesting that, since God accounts for there being something rather than nothing, we have no basis *as philosophers* (i.e. apart from recourse to divine revelation) for expectations concerning the kind of world which God (if he chooses to create) will make.[17]

There does, however, exist another channel by which to understand the relationship between God and evil. According to Christianity, this mode of knowledge consists in divine revelation, something not available to all on the basis of human reason alone. If Davies is right, then ironically many who reject the existence of God on the basis of the problem of evil are drawing on capital left over from Christianity. Cognizant of it or not, it is the worldview furnished by a Christian culture that leads one to demand that God be good in the way most today presume him to be good. But this was not an assumption shared by most religions or philosophies prior to Christianity. In fact, Ehrman puts this rather well in his discussion of the Book of Job:

Do we think that everything would be made right if the six million Jews killed in the Holocaust were "replaced" by six million additional Jews born in the next generation? As satisfying as the book of Job has been to people over the ages, I have to say I find it supremely dissatisfying. If God tortures, maims, and murders people just to see how they will react—to see if they will not blame him, when in fact he is to blame—then this does not seem to me to be a God worthy of worship. Worthy of fear, yes. Of praise, no.[18]

Ehrman can only claim that God as presented in Job is unworthy of man's devotion, but he cannot go so far as to conclude that the divine does not exist. Indeed, from the standpoint of natural reason as reflected in the history of religion, it would seem right to believe that

16. Ibid., 24.   17. Ibid., 25 (emphasis added).
18. Ehrman, *God's Problem*, 172.

God (or gods) exists and that he (or they) is indeed worthy of fear. Who is to say that the divinity ought to be loved or that God loves? Argues Davies:

Christian teaching warrants those who accept it in thinking that God is loving in something like the sense of "loving" that we have in mind when we are concerned with love between equals.... [T]he *doctrine of the Trinity* licenses those who accept it in believing that, as the New Testament says, "God is love."[19]

Although there may be philosophical grounds for thinking of God as good and loving, for Davies it is ultimately only the additional pool of evidence furnished by Christian revelation that warrants our belief in God being good in the way that we who (consciously or unconsciously) have inherited a Christian worldview commonly presume him to be good.

Morality and the Notion of Evil Itself Are Vacuous without God

In addition to missing the mark on the problem of evil, I would argue that agnostics like Ehrman also find themselves in a contradictory position when it comes to the moral norms they profess. This line of criticism is expressed well by C. S. Lewis, who appeals to the absolute nature of the value judgments we all make as an indication that there exists some transcendent ground to them:

There is no escape along these lines. If we are to continue to make moral judgments ... then we must believe that the conscience of man is not a product of Nature. It can be valid only if it is an offshoot of some absolute moral wisdom, a moral wisdom which exists "on its own" and is not a product of non-moral, non-rational Nature.[20]

In other words, if the natural world is all that exists and human rationality is entirely explicable as an evolution from the subrational, then why should we trust our own moral judgments? How can we be convicted that an action such as rape or murder is evil if the notions of "good" and "evil," "justice" and "injustice," are merely the conceptual

---

19. Davies, *The Reality of God*, 240–41 (emphasis added).
20. Lewis, *Miracles*, 60.

byproducts of blind evolution?[21] If naturalism is true, argues Lewis, then all moral judgments are merely statements about their speakers' feelings.[22] As Benedict XVI writes on the alluring supposition of a world without God, "On closer examination, though, it seems suspicious. Who is to say what justice is?"[23] Paul Williams, in his fascinating book detailing his conversion from Buddhism to Catholicism, writes in a similar vein: "We can truly say God is good. But for us his goodness is bound up with his being the source of all good things (Aquinas). Apart from that we cannot know what we mean, as it were 'from God's side' by saying God is good."[24] Like Benedict and Davies, Williams finds it nonsensical for the agnostic to claim that God has moral obligations toward humans and that he should have made a better world. Rather, it is only in light of the revelation that God is love that evil becomes a problem in relation to God: "The issue of evil in the world becomes an issue of a particular type of mystery *for the believer*, rather than an argument against the existence of God."[25] In sum, I think that Dostoevsky's character Ivan Karamazov has it right when he insinuates that if there is no God, everything is permitted.

One of Lewis's more crucial observations on this score concerns agnostics who subscribe to moral relativism: "A moment after they have admitted that good and evil are illusions, you will find them exhorting us to work for posterity, to educate, revolutionize, liquidate, live, and die for the good of the human race."[26] While the above state-

---

21. Note that the Catholic need not deny evolution here—the point is whether the process is guided by divine reason or not.

22. Lewis, *Miracles*, 56. Scott Hahn writes similarly in one of his popular works, "People who allow evil to drive them to atheism suddenly have no standard by which to judge something evil. Instead of solving the problem, they've institutionalized it—written it into the very fabric of the cosmos. If there is no God, then there is no transcendent, ultimate goodness, no perfect measurement of righteousness; and so there can be no true evil, either. Without God, everything becomes a matter of moral indifference or mere human preference." *Reasons to Believe: How to Understand, Explain, and Defend the Catholic Faith* (New York: Doubleday, 2007), 49.

23. Benedict XVI, *Jesus of Nazareth: From the Baptism in the Jordan to the Transfiguration*, 54.

24. Paul Williams, *The Unexpected Way: On Converting from Buddhism to Catholicism* (London: T and T Clark, 2002), 45.

25. Ibid.

26. Lewis, *Miracles*, 57.

ments from Ehrman demonstrate that he does not consider himself a moral relativist, I think that Lewis's argument holds for all those who in one way or another fall short of affirming the existence of a supernatural ground to the universe. As we saw above, Ehrman wraps up his book *God's Problem* with a beautiful exhortation to drink fine wine and enjoy making love, but when putting the book down I cannot help but think, "Amen to that—but *why* should we all agree that these things ought to be done?" Brian Davies expresses my point here better than I could hope to put it in my own words:

> We cannot, I think, make good progress when trying to think about God and evil if we do not (and apart from the issue of evil) ask if there are positive grounds for believing in God to start with. If there are such grounds, the next obvious question to ask is "What should we suppose God to be?" God is often (though certainly not always) said to be omnipotent, omniscient, and good. But how, when it comes to God, should we construe "omnipotent," "omniscient," and "good"? You might reply, "It is obvious, is it not?" My view, however, is that it is not obvious.[27]

In other words, the problem of evil is meaningless in the absence of a prior discussion of whether or not we have good reasons to believe that God exists in the first place.

Our Rationality Itself Depends on God

In addition to arguing that an agnostic worldview is incompatible with belief in absolute moral norms, Lewis contends that our rationality itself is unreliable if God does not exist. According to Lewis, "[I]t is not dependence simply but dependence on the non-rational which undermines the credentials of thought.... It is only when you are asked to believe in Reason coming from non-reason that you must cry Halt, for, if you don't, all thought is discredited."[28] As in the case of morality above, there is no reason to believe that my reasoning is valid if it is merely the product of sub-rational causes.

More recently and in a more developed scholarly fashion, Alvin Plantinga has argued that there is deep conflict between naturalism and the scientific theory of evolution which most naturalists accept.

27. Davies, *The Reality of God*, 26–27.
28. Lewis, *Miracles*, 41–42; cf. ibid., 46.

Far from rejecting evolution as such, Plantinga finds untenable a common naturalistic gloss or add-on to this scientific theory: the claim that evolution is unorchestrated by God or anyone else. Like Lewis, Plantinga maintains that human rationality itself is undermined in an agnostic universe:

> I argue that it is improbable, given naturalism and evolution, that our cognitive faculties are reliable. It is improbable that they provide us with a suitable preponderance of true belief over false. But then a naturalist who accepts current evolutionary theory has a defeater for the proposition that our faculties are reliable. Furthermore, if she has a defeater for the proposition that her cognitive faculties are reliable, she has a defeater for any belief she takes to be produced by her faculties. But of course all of her beliefs have been produced by her faculties—including, naturally enough, her belief in naturalism and evolution. That belief, therefore—the conjunction of naturalism and evolution—is one that she can't rationally accept. Hence naturalism and evolution are in serious conflict: one can't rationally accept them both. And hence, as I said above, there is a science/ religion conflict (maybe a science/quasi-religion conflict) to be sure, but it is between science and naturalism, not science and theistic belief.[29]

Put in another way, the non-theist who argues that reason has led him to the conclusion of atheism or agnosticism has no rational grounds for believing that this conclusion itself is any more true than its opposite.

Addressing more specifically the mechanism of natural selection, Plantinga appeals to naturalistic philosophers who acknowledge a tension between their own premises and conclusions. Thus Thomas Nagel: "If we came to believe that our capacity for objective theory [e.g., true beliefs] were the product of natural selection, that would warrant serious skepticism about its results."[30] Barry Stroud likewise admits, "There is an embarrassing absurdity in [naturalism] that is revealed as soon as the naturalist reflects and acknowledges that he believes his naturalistic theory of the world.... I mean he cannot say it and consistently regard it as true."[31] Concerning Patricia Churchland's affirma-

29. Alvin Plantinga, *Where the Conflict Really Lies: Science, Religion, and Naturalism* (New York: Oxford University Press, 2011), xiv.

30. Thomas Nagel, *The View from Nowhere* (Oxford University Press, 1989), 79.

31. Barry Stroud, "The Charm of Naturalism" in *Naturalism in Question*, ed. Mario De Caro and David Macarthur (Cambridge, Mass.: Harvard University Press, 2004), 28.

tion that the "chore" of our cognitive faculties is to promote survival, Plantinga summarizes:

> Churchland's point, clearly, is that (from a naturalistic perspective) what evolution guarantees is (at most) that we behave in certain ways—in such ways as to promote survival, or more exactly reproductive success. The principal function or purpose, then, (the "chore" says Churchland) of our cognitive faculties is not that of producing true or verisimilitudinous (nearly true) beliefs, but instead that of contributing to survival by getting the body parts in the right place.... Our beliefs *might* be mostly true ... but there is no particular reason to think they *would* be: natural selection is interested, not in truth, but in appropriate behavior.[32]

On our cognitive faculties being aimed not necessarily at truth but at some other property such as survival, Plantinga contrasts the critiques of Christian belief made by Marx and Freud: "Marx's claim is that religious belief arises from cognitive dysfunction; as a result of living in a dysfunctional society the believer's cognitive faculties are not working properly."[33] Freud, on the other hand, contests that the problem has to do with the reality that our cognitive faculties are not aimed at truth in the first place:

32. Plantinga, *Where the Conflict Really Lies*, 315; cf. Patricia Churchland, *Journal of Philosophy* 84 (October 1987): 548. Plantinga demonstrates that these philosophical reservations are by no means new. Friederich Nietzsche, for example, writes: "It is unfair to Descartes to call his appeal to God's credibility frivolous. Indeed, only if we assume a God who is morally our like can 'truth' and the search for truth be at all something meaningful and promising of success. This God left aside, the question is permitted whether being deceived is not one of the conditions of life." Nietzsche, *Nietzsche: Writings from the Late Notebooks* (Cambridge Texts in the History of Philosophy), ed. Rüdiger Bittner (Cambridge: Cambridge University Press, 2003), Notebook 36, June–July 1885, 26. For Descartes, even our knowledge of mathematics hinges upon the existence of a God who is not an evil deceiver: "Thus I concluded that it is at least as certain as any geometrical proof that God, who is this perfect being, is or exists." *Discourse on Method* (Cambridge: Cambridge University Press, 1999), 129. Plantinga notes that even Darwin himself expresses serious doubts along these lines: "With me the horrid doubt always arises whether the convictions of man's mind, which has been developed from the mind of the lower animals, are of any value or at all trustworthy. Would any one trust in the convictions of a monkey's mind, if there are any convictions in such a mind?" Darwin, Letter to William Graham, Down, July 3rd, 1881, in *The Life and Letters of Charles Darwin Including an Autobiographical Chapter*, ed. Francis Darwin (London: John Murray, Albermarle Street, 1887), vol. 1, 315–16.

33. Alvin Plantinga, *Knowledge and Christian Belief* (Grand Rapids, Mich.: Eerdmans, 2015), 22.

Belief in God is an illusion ... but illusion has its uses, in particular in enabling us to live in this cold, bleak, miserable world in which we find ourselves. Someone with properly functioning cognitive faculties might very well form religious belief. Still, there is a problem with such belief: it isn't produced by cognitive faculties whose purpose is to furnish us with true beliefs about our world.[34]

In making this analysis, by no means is Plantinga insinuating along with Freud that our cognitive faculties are unreliable. Rather, Plantinga's *reductio* argues that the naturalist who accepts evolution is rationally obliged to give up the assumption that his thinking itself is reliable.[35]

On the other hand, the alternative, theistic approach does not entail this deep conflict between itself and science or between itself and absolute moral norms as discussed above. Indeed, according to Plantinga,

[The believer] will see the shoe as on the other foot. According to St. Paul, it is *unbelief* that is a result of dysfunction, or brokenness, failure to function properly, or impedance of rational faculties. Unbelief, he says, is a result of sin; it originates in an effort, as Romans 1 puts it, to "suppress the truth in unrighteousness." Indeed, unbelief can also be seen as resulting from wish-fulfillment—a result of the desire to live in a world without God, a world in which there is no one to whom I owe worship and obedience.[36]

34. Ibid., 25.

35. Plantinga, *Where the Conflict Really Lies*, 326. Concerning his own epistemological assumptions, the author continues, "So the belief that my cognitive faculties are reliable is one for which I don't need evidence or argument—that is, I don't need evidence or argument in order to be rational in believing it. I can be fully and entirely rational in believing this even though I have no evidence or argument for it at all. This is a belief such that it is rational to hold it in the basic way, that is, not on the basis of argument or evidence from other things I believe." Ibid., 341.

36. Plantinga, *Knowledge and Christian Belief*, 43. Continues Plantinga: "And God himself, the source of my very being, can also be a threat. In my prideful desire for autonomy and self-sufficiency I can come to resent the presence of someone upon whom I depend for my every breath and by comparison with whom I am small potatoes indeed. I can therefore come to hate him too. I want to be autonomous, beholden to no one. Perhaps this is the deepest root of the condition of sin, and a motivation for atheism as wish-fulfillment." Ibid., 50. On the cause of atheism, also worthy of our meditation are Dale Allison's reflections on the correlation between secularization and our growing separation from the natural world that has led to the loss of our ability to wonder. See Allison, *The Luminous Dusk* (Grand Rapids, Mich.: Eerdmans, 2006), especially 1–23

Ultimately, then, Plantinga disagrees with Freud: our belief-forming faculties really are aimed at truth. With Marx, however, he will admit that these faculties sometimes fail to achieve their proper end—only it turns out that the people whose faculties malfunction are not believers but rather *non*believers.

Are Divine Interventions Plausible?

For C. S. Lewis the upshot of the above arguments against naturalism is clear: "If we decide that Nature is not the only thing that is, then we cannot say in advance whether she is safe from miracles or not."[37] In other words, if there exists a Being who is not limited by the confines of the natural world but is rather the very ground of this world, then we can never conclusively deny that this Being sometimes acts in a way other than that which we tend to expect based on our observations of nature. But how is the Christian to explain positively the phenomena of miracles or divine interventions?

While Christians often speak of miracles as divine "interventions," unfortunately this turn of phrase appears to presuppose that God is somehow "absent" from his creation and then "intrudes" upon it to perform a miracle. As Brian Davies puts it, "For something can only intervene by entering into a situation from which it is first of all absent, while God [as the Catholic conceives of him] cannot be thought to be absent from anything he creates.... God is creatively present to everything at all times."[38] According to Davies, it is best to follow Aquinas on this subject. Aquinas holds that miracles are not explicable in natural terms, and yet this is not due to God's "intervention." Rather, for Aquinas what specifies a miracle is that it is an event which has nothing but God as its cause.[39]

Similarly for Lewis, the miracles we take to be "interruptions" of nature's history are in reality "expressions of the truest and deepest

---

and 177–78. Natural theology without nature, argues Allison, loses its potency. Ibid., 17–18. According to Allison, other factors that, in today's world, make believing more difficult include urbanization, industrialization, increasing distance from nature's terrors, and the ubiquity of artificial noise. Ibid., 32.

37. Lewis, *Miracles*, 14.

38. Davies, *The Reality of God*, 75.

39. Ibid., 76; cf. Aquinas, *Summa theologiae*, I, q. 8, a. 1.

unity in [God's] total work."[40] He in turn proposes that within the universe "there are rules behind the rules, and a unity which is deeper than uniformity."[41] This articulation aligns well with Plantinga's discussion of miracles in light of Newtonian and quantum physics. As for the former, Plantinga points out that Newton himself believed that God providentially guides the world and periodically adjusts the orbits of the planets. This classical view is summarized well here:

> [I]t is no part of Newtonian mechanics or classical science generally to declare that the material universe is a closed system.... Classical science, therefore, doesn't assert or include causal closure. The laws, furthermore, describe how things go when the universe is causally closed, subject to no outside causal influence. They don't purport to tell us how things always go; they tell us, instead, how things go when no agency outside the universe acts in it.[42]

So thought of, the natural laws offer no threat to special divine action. Miracles are often thought to be problematic, in that God, if he were to perform a miracle, would be involved in "breaking," going contrary to, abrogating, suspending, a natural law. But given this conception of law, if God were to perform a miracle, it wouldn't at all involve contravening a natural law. That is because, obviously, any occasion on which God performs a miracle is an occasion when the universe is not causally closed; and the laws say nothing about what happens when the universe is not causally closed.[43]

So much for miracles in relation to classical physics, but what happens if we turn to contemporary quantum mechanics (QM)? Like Plantinga, in matters of science I am reduced to arguing from authority here, but based on this authority Plantinga concludes that the following is what we can say:

> QM doesn't determine a specific outcome for a given set of initial conditions, but instead merely assigns probabilities to the possible outcomes. This means that, even apart from that proviso, QM doesn't constrain special divine action in anything like the way classical deterministic mechanics does.[44]

Miracles may be highly improbable, but there is nothing inherently contradictory in the supposition that God sometimes deviates from the usual way we observe him governing his creation. To this point Plantinga adds something that resonates with Davies's point above:

40. Lewis, *Miracles*, 154.   41. Ibid., 153.
42. Plantinga, *Where the Conflict Really Lies*, 78–79.
43. Ibid., 82.   44. Ibid., 94.

given contemporary quantum physics, it might not even make sense to speak of intervention in the first place, let alone find something in science with which it is incompatible.[45]

Even if one accepts this defense of the miraculous offered by Plantinga, there still remains the question of whether the miracles presented in Scripture are credible or not. In other words, granted that God *can* act independently of created causes within our universe, do we have any reason to suppose that he has done so in any given instance? Ironically, in the name of science biblical scholars and theologians commonly answer "no" to this question. In so doing, they are (whether consciously or unconsciously) assuming the Laplacean picture of a causally closed physical universe which itself is a metaphysical worldview unsupported by classical science. Plantinga observes:

> [T]here is an interesting irony in these theologians urging the deterministic, Laplacean picture, when that picture is no part of the classical science to which they solemnly pledge fealty. There is a further irony: the classical science they so eagerly meant to accommodate was well out of date at the time they were eagerly accommodating it.[46]

As a theologian, I myself am keenly aware of how tempting it is to think that God did not perform the various miracles attributed to him in Scripture. Whether we like it or not, even traditionally minded thinkers like myself are children of our age, an age indelibly marked by the widespread conviction that history is a closed continuum that cannot be rent by the interference of supernatural, transcendent powers.[47] It pains me to admit it, but I will probably never be able to completely shake off Rudolph Bultmann's famous assertion that I learned in college: "It is impossible to use electric light and the wireless and to avail ourselves of modern medical and surgical discoveries, and at the same time to believe in the New Testament world of spirits and miracles."[48] Like many other theologians and biblical scholars, I do not object to the truth that God creates and sustains the world. What I myself

45. Ibid., 97.
46. Ibid., 91.
47. Ibid., 70 ; cf. Rudolf Bultmann, *Existence and Faith*, ed. Schubert Ogden (New York: Meridian Books, 1960), 291–92.
48. Bultmann, *New Testament and Mythology and Other Basic Writings*, selected, edited and translated by Schubert Ogden (Philadelphia: Fortress Press, 1984), 4.

have difficulty with—and which Plantinga rightly challenges people like myself on—is the claim that God does or has done anything *in addition to* creating the world and sustaining it in existence. In other words, from this point of view it is what Plantinga calls *special divine action* that is the problem.[49]

When I am tempted to write off the possibility of special divine action, I ask myself the question Plantinga poses to exegetes: is there any reason to think that my assumption is true? I think that Plantinga hits the nail on the head in exposing this assumption for what it is: "Here the objection, obviously, is theological. It has nothing to do with science. The idea is that God simply wouldn't do such a thing; this sort of action is inconsistent with his unfathomable augustness and unsurpassable greatness."[50] Special divine action, so the claim goes, would make God fall into inconsistency, arbitrariness, or caprice by dealing in two different manners within the universe.[51] In a vein that is similar to Lewis's argument above, Plantinga responds with a pointed question:

But is this really true? There would be arbitrariness and inconsistency only if God had no special reason for acting contrary to the usual regularities; but of course he might very well have such reasons. This is obvious for the case of raising Jesus from the dead: God intends to mark the special status accruing to Jesus by this mighty act of raising him from the dead. In other cases too, however, he might have reasons for "dealing in two different manners" with his cosmos; how could we be even reasonably sure that he doesn't?[52]

As Lewis said above, the Christian believes that within the universe there lies a unity which is deeper than uniformity. Within this grand providential plan, God's special action (through miracles, grace, etc.) is no more out of place than the most mundane and uncontroversial actions few find objectionable. The trouble is, of course, that we mortals cannot glimpse this plan fully. For us, in this vale of tears,

49. Plantinga, *Where the Conflict Really Lies*, 72. For another thorough treatment of these topics, see Plantinga's *Warranted Christian Belief* (New York: Oxford University Press, 2000).

50. Plantinga, *Where the Conflict Really Lies*, 74, 105.

51. Ibid., 106.

52. Ibid., 107.

God's reply to Job must suffice. But it is also worth considering Paul Williams's response to the problem of miracles' improbability. Like Lewis, he argues that the miraculous is far from out of place for one who accepts the existence of God and his providence:

Perhaps those who deny [miracles such as] the virgin birth do so on the basis that a virgin birth is just not very likely. But why should our understanding of God's actions, or the incarnation of Christ, be based on what is more likely? One might expect the exact opposite. It is indeed not very likely that what God would do is what is most likely, what would be most expected. The Christian message is indeed one of God behaving in the most unexpected way. Denial of the virgin birth on these grounds would suggest doubt as regards the whole message of Christianity.[53]

For Williams, miracles and mysteries are precisely what we should expect if the Christian message that God became man is true, and they only make the Christian that more compelling.

Dale Allison says something similar about what makes Christianity compelling. Writing of his own work *The Historical Christ and the Theological Jesus*, Allison states:

The upshot of the foregoing pages is that the historical Jesus remains, in Schweitzer's familiar words, a stranger and an enigma. As a Christian, however, I do not find this so dreadful. What good is Jesus if he does not trouble our theological dreams? Certainly the character in the gospels combats complacency and self-satisfaction, and what but complacency and self-satisfaction can come from a historical Jesus who confirms us in our theological ways, whether those ways be liberal or conservative? A domesticated Jesus who sounds like us, makes us comfortable, and commends our opinions is no Jesus at all.[54]

Like Williams, in the case of the radical improbability of miracles Allison finds that the troubling endeavor of historical Jesus research does not undermine his faith, but rather enhances it. Allison's account of his own experience resonates with my own:

The inexplicable divine mystery still speaks through the old pages and through my hermeneutical confusion.... Despite my modernity and my cynical nature, despite my dissection of it and my quarrels with it, the Bible re-

53. Williams, *The Unexpected Way*, 63–64.
54. Allison, *The Historical Christ and the Theological Jesus*, 89–90.

mains profitable for teaching, for correction, and for training in righteousness. It comforts. It inspires. It commands. When I push its pages apart, I lay my finger on God's heart.[55]

Christian Belief and the Evidence of Religious Experience

To this criticism of the criticism regarding miracles, I would add that there also exist compelling positive reasons for accepting the miraculous even if we personally are not conscious of having experienced it. In particular, Lewis reminds us not to discount the fact that our world is full of testimonies of people who claim to have experienced miracles. To be sure, miracles are by definition improbable, and it is *prima facie* more likely that the witnesses to an alleged miracle are lying or deluded than that the miracle actually occurred. And yet, even as we know fraudulent cases exist, these by no means discredit all such claims regarding the miraculous. Indeed, upon closer inspection, it may actually end up being more probable that a putative miracle occurred than that it did not. How so? David Hume held that a miracle is always improbable, but he also admitted that this probability increases dramatically in the presence of a credible witness we know and trust. Says Hume: "If the falsehood of his testimony would be more miraculous, than the event which he relates; then, and not till then, can he pretend to command my belief or opinion."[56] I wonder whether Hume's criterion might be met when we come face to face with the testimony of a living saint whom we can scarcely imagine being delusional or dishonest. Thus Ratzinger's oft-repeated conviction that "the true apology of Christian faith, the most convincing demonstration of its truth ... are the saints and the beauty that the faith has generated."[57]

In this connection I find it helpful to employ a concept developed by Sandra Lee Menssen and Thomas Sullivan. The authors propose a

55. Ibid., 111.

56. Hume, *An Enquiry Concerning Human Understanding* (Indianapolis: Hackett Pub. Co, 1977), Part I, 77.

57. Ratzinger, "The Feeling of Things, the Contemplation of Beauty" (August 24, 2002). Other formulations of Ratzinger's leading apologetics principle are found in *Feast of Faith*, 124; *The Ratzinger Report*, 129–30; *Principles of Catholic Theology*, 373; *Truth and Tolerance*, 226; Meeting with the Clergy of the Diocese of Bolzano-Bressanone (August 6, 2008).

potentially fruitful way of evaluating revelatory claims by appealing
to what they call *conditional upon explanation facts* (CUE-facts). These
are putative facts "one does not accept as true but *would* accept, provided they are appropriately linked to a plausible explanation."[58] Ex-
tending this framework beyond the authors' own application of it, I
would suggest that a given miracle receives precisely this sort of plausible explanation when we—though skeptical of the purported miracle
examining it in isolation—know that the one testifying to it is a living
saint who would not be delusional or dishonest. When it comes to the
CUE-fact of Jesus' Resurrection, I would suggest this sort of plausible
explanation may come from a variety of places: through our personal
experience of beauty and holiness in the same Church that claims that
Jesus rose from the dead; through the freedom and happiness that
come through obedience to the Church's moral teachings; through the
Church's indefectibility over the centuries; through the peaceful forti-
tude of martyrs across the ages (in particular Jesus' first disciples) who
have given their lives for Christ, etc. Another author, Paul Williams,
even goes so far as to claim that, after considering all arguments for
and against the resurrection of Jesus, one may "reach the stage where
the onus of proof is on the other side to construct a more convincing
and plausible case of what did happen instead of the resurrection."[59]

Concerning miracles, I myself tend to be very skeptical when
people talk to me of miraculous healings on the one hand or demonic
possessions on the other. But then every once in a while I hear an account of some such phenomenon directly experienced by someone I
trust and know not to be delusional. These are the moments that make
me reconsider the possibility that such things happen after all even if
I (thankfully, in the case of possessions) have never consciously experienced them. On this very point, George Mavrodes does well to call out
David Hume on his mistaken assumption that one's personal lack of

---

58. Sandra Lee Menssen and Thomas D. Sullivan, *The Agnostic Inquirer: Revelation from a Philosophical Standpoint* (Grand Rapids, Mich: William B. Eerdmans Pub,
2007), 211.

59. Williams, *The Unexpected Way*, 121; see pp. 121–35 of the same work for Williams's full argument wherein he counters suggestions that Jesus' risen body was only
"spiritual," that his disciples had suffered from hallucinations, etc.

experiencing the miraculous is at all relevant to probability judgments about miracles as such. This is in harmony with Lewis, who observes that we could go on and on our whole lives and never obtain a sample size large enough to support a probability judgment regarding the possibility of miracles. Hume categorically claims that a resurrection has never been observed in any age or country, but this is merely an ungrounded assertion. Mavrodes thus writes:

The clearest fact in this whole area would seem to be that *the testimony about resurrections, and other apparently miraculous happenings, is not uniform.* . . . In the case of miracles, the fact that there are these other troubling minority testimonies, the testimonies of those who claim to have experienced miracles themselves, becomes part of the data with which we must deal.[60]

On a related note, skeptics sometimes point to the prevalence of clearly false miracle stories throughout the world as an indication that the miracles of Christ were also mythical in character. Dale Allison turns this analogy on its head:

The argument from analogy has usually been employed to argue that the miracles stories in the Gospels are not memories but inventions. Being like so many obviously fictional tales, they likewise must be unhistorical. I have swapped this argument for another, urging instead that the numerous accounts of purported wonders from sincere eyewitnesses should moderate our skepticism and keep us open-minded.[61]

Perhaps more common than grandiose miraculous events are experiences of another sort that point directly to God: experiences of grace. Though one may not think of them as miraculous, the grace of the Holy Spirit active in one's life and miraculous healings are events that have God alone as their cause. I would venture that all living members of Christ's body at some moment have had an experience that was too perfect to be a coincidence, something that God alone could have orchestrated—or at least something so improbable that it would be more incredible *not* to attribute it to God's direct orchestration.[62]

---

60. George Mavrodes, "David Hume and the Probability of Miracles," *International Journal for Philosophy of Religion* 43 (1998): 176, 180.

61. Allison, *The Historical Christ and the Theological Jesus*, 77–78.

62. In speaking of "probability" here, by no means am I insinuating that the certitude of faith is only probable. Thus John Henry Newman: "[T]he very idea of Christianity in

One particularly powerful way God's grace moves the believer is through his encounter with beauty and holiness in our world. As Benedict (quoted above) said, in his view the greatest apology for the Christian faith lies in the saints and the beauty that the Church's faith has generated. Throughout his career, the emeritus pontiff has time and again emphasized that the *via pulchritudinis*, the way of beauty, is a privileged path toward God, especially in a de-Christianized society that is often hostile to the Church's truth claims and moral norms. In a couple of places he even gives us an autobiographical glimpse into how the beauty of music bolstered his faith. One time, after attending a Bach concert with a Lutheran bishop, the two spontaneously looked at each other and said, "Anyone who has heard this, knows that the faith is true." Benedict later reflected on the experience, saying, "The music had such an extraordinary force of reality that we realized, no longer by deduction, but by the impact on our hearts, that it could not have originated from nothingness, but could only have come to be through the power of the Truth that became real in the composer's inspiration."[63] In experiencing beauty like this, the believer intuitively sees it as incredible that such power could be at work in a universe without God.

---

its profession and history, is ... to be positively acknowledged, embraced, and maintained as true, on the ground of its being divine, not as true on intrinsic grounds, not as probably true, or partially true, but as absolutely certain knowledge, certain in a sense in which nothing else can be certain, because it comes from Him who neither can deceive nor be deceived." Elsewhere we find him writing, "No man can worship, love, or trust in a probable God." And yet Newman himself argues that certitude can be found through an "accumulation of probabilities," none of which may be certain on its own but which taken together can lead to a real assent of faith. All this goes to show that the certitude of the faith ultimately derives from the authority of the God revealing himself to man rather than from man's effort to grasp him. John Henry Newman, *An Essay in Aid of a Grammar of Assent* (Garden City, N.Y.: Image, 1955), 302, 320; Letter to David Brown, Jan. 14, 1875, in *Letters and Diaries of John Henry Newman*, vol. XXVII, ed. C. S. Dessain and E. E. Kelly (Oxford: Clarendon, 1961), 188. On the certitude of faith see also Aquinas, *Summa theologiae*, I, q. 1, a. 5, ad 1; II-II, q. 4, a. 8. For a helpful popular treatment of the question, see Thomas Dubay, SM, *Faith and Certitude: Can We Be Sure of the Things That Matter the Most to Us?* (San Francisco: Ignatius, 1985).

63. Joseph Ratzinger, "The Feeling of Things, the Contemplation of Beauty" (August 24, 2002). See also his account of this experience in his catechesis "Art and Prayer" (August 31, 2011).

In saying this, one should not get the false impression that only art connoisseurs can come to God through the experience of beauty. There have been many times in my life when I have looked out on the world and said something similar to what Benedict is reporting here: the beauty of an encounter with a friend in deep conversation, the beauty of a film that brought tears, the beauty of my newborn child— these are just a few experiences wherein I, like Benedict, have had occasion to say: "This could not have originated from nothingness." I recently experienced this reality in the most profound way when my father unexpectedly suffered a heart attack and passed away within hours. Although his death was probably the most earth-shattering event of my life thus far, the week I spent at my childhood home after Dad's passing was one in which God rained down countless reminders of his love and providential care for my family. My dad had died a holy death, and everyone surrounding him at his passing and burial knew it. I was not the only one who could not stop thinking, amidst so much suffering, just how *beautiful* the whole affair was. In our pain God did not just whisper that he was still there—he shouted it, especially in the Church's liturgy throughout the week.

To give just one example of how the beauty of the Church's funeral rites moved me to faith, I would like to recall what happens in a Catholic funeral right before the Mass begins. Immediately after my father's casket was closed for the final time, I was handed the funeral pall and helped my siblings lay it over the casket. The pall is the reminder of the faithful departed's baptism into Christ—an indelible mark that he now carries into eternity. As we laid the pall over my father's casket, I could not help but draw the connection to the Catholic baptismal liturgy. After baptizing the child, the priest clothes him with a little white garment and says, "You have become a new creation, and have clothed yourself in Christ. See in this white garment the outward sign of your Christian dignity. With your family and friends to help you by word and example, bring that dignity unstained into the everlasting life of heaven." It hit me more strongly than ever before that this is what the funeral pall recalls.

My liturgical experience of Dad's death spoke volumes about the truth of Christianity in general and the Catholic Church in particular. I think Benedict captures the reason this is so: "Why, in brief, does the faith still have a chance? I would say the following: because it is in harmony with what man is. Man is something more than what Kant and the various post-Kantian philosophers [and, I might add, exegetes] wanted to see and concede."[64] The Catholic Church's doctrine and practice is in harmony with who man is: the Church forces us to confront death in all its awfulness, but then she also gives us all the grace we need to face it well.

Closely related to the liturgy and to our own experience of death, the epitome of beauty is glimpsed by the Christian in the experience of God's love in his bearing of the cross for us. Christ's total gift of self on the cross is the most beautiful of human actions ever to have been performed, and it challenges the superficial notion of beauty dominant in our culture today. According to Benedict, the beauty of the crucified Jesus is not simply an aesthetic harmony of proportion and form. While Christ is surely "the fairest of the sons of men" (Ps 45:2), he is also the one "who had no form or comeliness that we should look at him, and no beauty that we should desire him" (Is 53:2). From the suffering Christ we learn one of life's most important lessons: that true beauty also embraces the ugliness of pain and even the dark mystery of death. Jesus on the cross reminds us that true beauty, true freedom, and ultimately true happiness are ultimately found when we embrace suffering as part of God's plan for our sanctification.[65] In short, it is the crucible of suffering with Christ on the cross that draws us away from the transitory, detaches us from what is opposed to God, and unites us intimately to him. Dostoyevsky's character Prince Myskin famously remarked that beauty will save the world. But here Benedict reminds us of something people usually forget: salvific beauty is not any beauty whatsoever but specifically the redeeming beauty of Christ crucified who invites us to share in his cross.

Reading the lesser-known writings of Benedict XVI one frequently discovers unexpectedly delightful gems, and it is with one of these

64. Joseph Ratzinger, "Relativism: The Central Problem for Faith Today," https://www.ewtn.com/library/CURIA/RATZRELA.HTM

65. Joseph Ratzinger, "The Feeling of Things, the Contemplation of Beauty" (August 24, 2002); cf. Benedict XVI, Sacramentum Caritatis, 35.

that I would like to draw these brief remarks on religious experience and beauty to a close. When he celebrated Mass in St. Patrick's Cathedral in New York, Benedict gave a fascinating homily in which he reflected upon the great building as an allegory of faith and the search for truth. Like any Gothic cathedral, from the outside its windows appear dark and heavy, even dreary. But once one enters the Church, these same windows suddenly come alive with resplendent light passing through their stained glass. The allegory is clear: "It is only from the inside, from the experience of faith and ecclesial life, that we see the Church as she truly is: flooded with grace, resplendent in beauty, adorned by the manifold gifts of the Spirit."[66] Here Benedict teaches in poetic fashion a truth he has reiterated in many different places and ways throughout his career. The truth of the Catholic Church ultimately can be seen only *from the inside* when we fast from our own preconceptions and desires with a willingness to embark upon "the experiment of faith."[67] I agree with Benedict's contention that is only from the inside—from a posture of obedience to the truth—that the power of Christianity is clearly seen. Paradoxically, it is when we lose our life for Christ's sake that we truly find it. It is when we relinquish our freedom to do as we please that we discover the truth that authentic freedom lies in pleasing God. It is when we learn to die with Christ that we truly live.[68]

66. Benedict XVI, Homily for Votive Mass for the Universal Church (April 19, 2008). Related to this image, I appreciate Dale Allison's remark: "The Sermon on the Mount does not look the same from the outside as it does from the inside." Allison, *The Historical Christ and the Theological Jesus*, 48. See also Allison, *The Luminous Dusk*, 62–63. Recalling the wisdom of Albert Schweitzer, who long ago emphasized that Christ reveals himself to us fully only when we hearken to him, Allison exhorts us to "the first-hand experience of heeding and following Jesus, of personally striving, as best we can, to enter into his moral vision. Without such effort, our knowledge of him will be less. As the Jesus of Mt 11:29 says, 'Take my yoke upon you, and learn of me.'" Ibid., 48; see also Schweitzer, *The Quest of the Historical Jesus* (Minneapolis: Fortress Press, 2000), 487.

67. Joseph Ratzinger, "Why I Am Still in the Church," in *Fundamental Speeches from Five Decades* (San Francisco: Ignatius Press, 2012), 132–53. For a fuller treatment of Ratzinger/Benedict's theology of beauty in relation to the truth of Christianity, see Matthew Ramage, "Benedict XVI's Theology of Beauty and the New Evangelization," *Homiletic and Pastoral Review* (January 29, 2015; online).

68. For a fuller treatment of Christian freedom in contrast with the prevailing contemporary notion of freedom in our culture, see Matthew Ramage, "Benedict XVI and

To be sure, none of what has been said above changes the fact that the believer can and must always be prepared with reasonable arguments to defend faith in Christ in our world today. Indeed, that is what this book has been all about. Yet Benedict wishes to remind us that we are rarely if ever going to argue someone into believing. One thing a Christian can certainly do every day—even on those days when the subject of faith never comes up explicitly in our conversations—is to live beautifully a life of grace and Christian freedom. A life lived in the quest for holiness has great power to draw others to Christ. This Christian witness epitomizes what Benedict has in mind in calling the Church's saints and her beauty the greatest apology of Christian faith.

Conclusion

My argument has been that the testimony of religious experience (direct and indirect) ought to form an integral part of our evidence base when it comes to discussing the miraculous. In concluding, I would like to make a now-familiar observation, namely, that rejecting this pool of evidence out of hand is not a scientific conclusion but an-

---

Freedom in Obedience to the Truth: A Key for the New Evangelization," *Homiletic and Pastoral Review* (May 12, 2014; online). The "experiment of faith" of which Ratzinger speaks necessarily involves a communitarian dimension. Indeed, according to Alasdair MacIntyre, membership within a community is a precondition for rational enquiry: "Reason can only move towards being genuinely universal and impersonal insofar as it is neither neutral nor disinterested, that membership in a particular type of moral community, one from which fundamental dissent has to be excluded, is a condition for genuinely rational enquiry, and more especially for moral and theological enquiry." MacIntyre, *Three Rival Versions of Moral Enquiry: Encyclopaedia, Genealogy, and Tradition* (Notre Dame, Ind.: University of Notre Dame Press, 1990), 60–61. Also helpful in this regard is MacIntyre's description of a "practice." See his *After Virtue: A Study in Moral Theory* (Notre Dame, Ind.: University of Notre Dame Press, 2003), especially p. 242. Finally, see also his *Whose Justice? Which Rationality?* (Notre Dame, Ind: University of Notre Dame Press, 1988), 367 and 388, where he says, "It follows that the only rational way for adherents of any tradition to approach intellectually, culturally, and linguisitic alien rivals is one that allows for the possibility that in one or more areas the other may be rationally superior to it in respect precisely of that in the alien tradition which it cannot as yet comprehend.... Only those whose tradition allows for the possibility of its hegemony being put into question can have rational warrant for asserting such hegemony. And only those traditions which recognize the possibility of untranslatability into their own language-in-use are able to reckon adequately with that possibility."

other unwarranted philosophical presupposition like others discussed further above. As one who daily engages in the craft of historical-critical exegesis, I find Benedict XVI's comments on this subject refreshing and liberating. In contrast with what he calls a naturalist "ready-made philosophy" that precludes the possibility of such experience, Benedict urges us to approach the Bible with an "open philosophy" that refuses to exclude the possibility that God himself "can work in history and enter into it without ceasing to be himself, however improbable this might appear."[69] This posture, deeply rooted in the Catholic tradition with its conviction that the boundary of time and eternity is permeable, allows for the Bible to be what the Church has always claimed it to be: the word of God in human words.

As we have seen in the chapters above, this is by no means to deny that there exist certain tensions between the Catholic faith and the findings of historical-critical biblical scholarship. If there did not, then this book would have been superfluous. While admitting that difficulties do and likely always will remain, I think Plantinga does well to conclude that these alleged conflicts do not provide defeaters for Christian belief:

> The reason … is that the scientific evidence base, constrained as it is by methodological naturalism, is only a part of the Christian evidence base. Perhaps certain Christian beliefs are improbable from that partial evidence base; it doesn't follow that they are improbable from a Christian's complete evidence base.[70]

The key to the Christian evidence base, a key absent in the non-theist's arsenal, is of course God himself, and thus the real question undergirding our exegetical debates is the prior issue of whether or not God exists and governs our world. It is the question of whether we have independent reasons to believe that there exists a supernatural Being beyond the natural order, a Being to whom nature owes its existence

69. Ratzinger, "Biblical Interpretation in Conflict," 22.
70. Plantinga, *Where the Conflict Really Lies*, xii. See also Plantinga, *Knowledge and Christian Belief*, 106: "The traditional Christian thinks he knows by faith that Jesus was divine and that he rose from the dead. Hence, he will be unmoved by the fact that these truths are not especially probable on the evidence to which Duhemian HBC [historical biblical criticism] limits itself—that is, evidence which explicitly excludes what one knows by faith."

and who may act within that order in ways we do not typically observe. In the arguments from Lewis and Plantinga surveyed above, I think we find well-argued reasons to believe that the answer to this question is "yes."

I would like to conclude by returning to my point of departure for this volume and reiterating a theme that has run throughout it. If the debate in modern exegesis is at bottom philosophical in nature, then we desperately need to carry out a criticism of the criticism, identifying and evaluating the philosophical presuppositions that believers and nonbelievers alike bring to their reading of the biblical text. A key contention I have made in this regard is that the impossibility of miracles like Christ's Incarnation and Resurrection is not something that can be proved; it can only be assumed. Indeed, I would say with Lewis that this agnostic premise is held by faith rather than reason. Furthermore, in light of the arguments outlined above I am convinced that holding to God's nonexistence while making claims to truth or morality requires more "faith" than accepting the Christian hypothesis. But if we are to entertain this hypothesis—even if we only come to the conclusion that theism is true—then we cannot consider ourselves "safe" from miracles and from the Christian narrative so deeply interwoven with them.

BIBLIOGRAPHY

Note: All of the addresses, homilies, etc. of Pope Benedict XVI and all the works of the International Theological Commission listed here are available on the Vatican website, w2.vatican.va.

Allison, Dale. *Constructing Jesus: Memory, Imagination, and History*. Grand Rapids, Mich.: Baker Academic, 2010.

———. "The Historians' Jesus and the Church." In *Seeking the Identity of Jesus: A Pilgrimage*, edited by Richard B. Hays and Beverly R. Gaventa, 84–85. Grand Rapids, Mich.: Eerdmans, 2008.

———. *The Historical Christ and the Theological Jesus*. Grand Rapids, Mich.: Eerdmans, 2009.

———. *The Luminous Dusk: Finding God in the Deep, Still Places*. Grand Rapids, Mich.: Eerdmans, 2006.

Arias Reyero, Maximino. *Thomas von Aquin als Exeget: Die Prinzipien seiner Schriftdeutung und seine Lehre von den Schriftsinnen*. Einsiedeln: Johannes Verlag, 1971.

Balthasar, Hans Urs von. *The Office of Peter and the Structure of the Church*. San Francisco: Ignatius Press, 1986.

Barber, Michael. *Coming Soon: Unlocking the Book of Revelation and Applying Its Lessons Today*. Steubenville, Ohio: Emmaus Road Publishing, 2005.

Bauckham, Richard. *Jesus and the Eyewitnesses: The Gospels as Eyewitness Testimony*. Grand Rapids, Mich.: Eerdmans, 2006.

Béchard, Dean. *The Scripture Documents*. Collegeville, Minn.: The Liturgical Press, 2002.

Benedict XVI. Address to the Parish Priests and Clergy of Rome. February 14, 2013.

———. Address to Participants in the Plenary Meeting of the Pontifical Biblical Commission. May 2, 2011.

———. *Angelus*. October 26, 2008.

———. "Art and Prayer." August 31, 2011.

———. Christmas Address to the Roman Curia. December 22, 2005.

———. "Faith, Reason, and the University: Memories and Reflections," Address at the University of Regensburg. September 12, 2006.

———. General Audience. March 20, 2010.

———. Homily for Votive Mass for the Universal Church. April 19, 2008.

———. *Jesus, the Apostles, and the Early Church*. San Francisco: Ignatius Press, 2007.

———. *Jesus of Nazareth: From the Baptism in the Jordan to the Transfiguration*. New York: Doubleday, 2007.

———. *Jesus of Nazareth: Holy Week: From the Entrance into Jerusalem to the Resurrection*. San Francisco: Ignatius Press, 2011.

———. *Jesus of Nazareth: The Infancy Narratives*. New York Image, 2012.

———. *Light of the World: The Pope, the Church, and the Signs of the Times*. San Francisco: Ignatius Press, 2010.

———. Meeting with the Clergy of the Diocese of Bolzano-Bressanone. August 6, 2008.

———. *Sacramentum Caritatis*. 2007.

———. *A School of Prayer: The Saints Teach Us How to Pray*. San Francisco: Ignatius Press, 2012.

———. *St. Paul*. San Francisco: Ignatius Press, 2009.

———. *Verbum Domini*. 2010.

Bird, Michael, Craig Evans, Simon Gathercole, Charles Hill, and Chris Tilling. *How God Became Jesus: The Real Origins of Belief in Jesus' Divine Nature—A Response to Bart Ehrman*. Grand Rapids, Mich.: Zondervan 2014.

Borg, Marcus. *The God We Never Knew: Beyond Dogmatic Religion to a More Authentic Contemporary Faith*. San Francisco: HarperSanFrancisco, 1997.

———. *Meeting Jesus Again for the First Time: The Historical Jesus and the Heart of Contemporary Faith*. San Francisco: HarperSanFrancisco, 1995.

———. *Reading the Bible Again for the First Time: Taking the Bible Seriously but Not Literally*. San Francisco: HarperSanFrancisco, 2001.

Brown, Raymond E. *The Birth of the Messiah: A Commentary on the Infancy Narratives in Matthew and Luke*. Garden City, N.Y.: Doubleday, 1977.

———. *The Gospel According to John*. Garden City, N.Y.: Doubleday, 1966.

Bultmann, Rudolf. *Existence and Faith*. Edited and translated by Schubert Ogden. New York: Meridian Books, 1960.

———. *The Gospel of John: A Commentary*. Edited by G. R. Beasley-Murray Philadelphia, Penn.: Westminster Press, 1971.

———. *Jesus and the Word*. Translated by Louise Pettibone Smith and Erminie Huntress Lantero. New York: Scribner's, 1958.

———. "The Primitive Christian Kerygma and the Historical Jesus." In *The*

Historical Jesus and the Kerygmatic Christ: Essays on the New Quest of the Historical Jesus, edited by Carl E. Braaten and Roy A. Harrisville, 15–42. New York: Abingdon Press, 1964.

Bultmann, Rudolf, Hans Werner Bartsch, and Reginald H. Fuller. *Kerygma and Myth: A Theological Debate*. Translated by Reginald H. Fuller. New York: Harper and Row, 1961.

Burridge, Richard. *What Are the Gospels? A Comparison with Graeco-Roman Biography*. Cambridge: Cambridge University Press, 1992.

Burtchaell, James Tunstead. *Catholic Theories of Biblical Inspiration since 1810: A Review and Critique*. London: Cambridge University Press, 1969.

Catechism of the Catholic Church. Translated by United States Catholic Conference. Washington, D.C.: Libreria Editrice Vaticana, 1994.

Chesterton, G. K. *The Everlasting Man*. In *The Collected Works of G. K. Chesterton*. San Francisco: Ignatius Press, 1986.

Congregation for the Doctrine of the Faith. "Doctrinal Commentary on the Concluding Formula of the *Professio Fidei*." 1998.

———. *Donum Veritatis*. 1990.

———. *Mysterium Ecclesiae*. 1973.

Crossan, John Dominic. *The Birth of Christianity: Discovering What Happened in the Years Immediately after the Execution of Jesus*. San Francisco: Harper-SanFrancisco, 1998.

———. *The Historical Jesus: The Life of a Mediterranean Jewish Peasant*. San Francisco: HarperSanFrancisco, 1991.

———. *How to Read the Bible and Still Be a Christian: Struggling with Violence from Genesis through Revelation*. New York: HarperOne, 2015.

———. *Jesus: A Revolutionary Biography*. San Francisco: HarperSanFrancisco, 1994.

———. *The Power of Parable: How Fiction by Jesus Became Fiction about Jesus*. New York: HarperOne, 2013.

Daniélou, Jean. *The Infancy Narratives*. Translated by Rosemary Sheed. New York: Herder and Herder, 1968.

Darwin, Charles, and Francis Darwin. *The Life and Letters of Charles Darwin: Including an Autobiographical Chapter*. New York: D. Appleton and Co., 1887.

Davies, Brian. *The Reality of God and the Problem of Evil*. London: Continuum, 2006.

Descartes, René. *Discourse on Method*. Cambridge: Cambridge University Press, 1999.

Dostoyevsky, Fyodor. *The Brothers Karamazov: The Constance Garnett Translation Revised by Ralph E. Matlaw: Backgrounds and Sources, Essays in Criticism*. New York: Norton, 1976.

Dostoyevsky, Fyodor. *The Idiot*. Translated by Richard Pevear and Larissa Volokhonsky. New York: Everyman's Library, 2002.

Dubay, Thomas, S.M. *Faith and Certitude: Can We Be Sure of the Things That Matter the Most to Us?* San Francisco: Ignatius, 1985.

Dulles, Avery, S.J., "Benedict XVI: Interpreter of Vatican II." In *Church and Society: The Laurence J. McGinley Lectures, 1988–2007*, 468–84. New York: Fordham University Press, 2008.

Ehrman, Bart. *God's Problem: How the Bible Fails to Answer Our Most Important Question—Why We Suffer.* New York: HarperOne, 2008.

———. *Forged: Writing in the Name of God: Why the Bible's Authors Are Not Who We Think They Are.* New York: HarperOne, 2011.

———. *How Jesus Became God: The Exaltation of a Jewish Preacher from Galilee.* New York: HarperOne, 2014.

———. *Jesus: Apocalyptic Prophet of the New Millennium.* Oxford: Oxford University Press, 1999.

———. *Jesus, Interrupted: Revealing the Hidden Contradictions in the Bible (And Why We Don't Know about Them).* New York: HarperOne, 2009.

———. *Misquoting Jesus: The Story Behind Who Changed the Bible and Why.* New York: HarperOne, 2007.

———. *The New Testament: A Historical Introduction to the Early Christian Writings.* New York: Oxford University Press, 2012.

Enns, Peter. *The Bible Tells Me So: Why Defending Scripture Has Made Us Unable to Read It.* San Francisco : HarperOne, 2014.

———. "Fuller Meaning, Single Goal: A Christotelic Approach to the New Testament Use of the Old in Its First-Century Interpretive Environment." In *Three Views on the New Testament Use of the Old Testament*, 167–217. Grand Rapids: Zondervan, 2008.

———. *Inspiration and Incarnation.* Grand Rapids, Mich.: Baker Academic, 2005.

Evans, Craig. "Getting the Burial Traditions and Evidences Right." In *How God Became Jesus: The Real Origins of Belief in Jesus' Divine Nature—A Response to Bart Ehrman*, edited by Michael Bird, 94–116. Grand Rapids, Mich.: Zondervan 2014.

———. *Mark 8:27–16:20.* Nashville, Tenn.: Thomas Nelson Publishers, 2001.

Farkasfalvy, Denis. *Inspiration and Interpretation: A Theological Introduction to Sacred Scripture.* Washington, D.C.: The Catholic University of America Press, 2010.

Francis, Pope, and Antonio Spadaro, SJ. "A Big Heart Open to God." *America.* September 30, 2013. http://americamagazine.org/pope-interview.

Funk, Robert W. *The Acts of Jesus: The Search for the Authentic Deeds of Jesus.* San Francisco: HarperSanFrancisco, 1998.

Funk, Robert W., and Roy W. Hoover. *The Five Gospels: The Search for the Authentic Words of Jesus: New Translation and Commentary.* New York: Macmillan, 1993.

Gathercole, Simon. "What Did the First Christians Think about Jesus?" In *How God Became Jesus: The Real Origins of Belief in Jesus' Divine Nature—A Response to Bart Ehrman*, edited by Michael Bird, 94–116. Grand Rapids, Mich.: Zondervan 2014.

Glare, P. G. W. *Oxford Latin Dictionary*. Oxford: Clarendon Press, 1982.

Gnilka, Joachim. *Das Matthäusevangelium*. Freiburg: Herder, 1986.

———. *Jesus of Nazareth: Message and History*. Peabody, Mass.: Hendrickson Publishers, 1997.

Goodacre, Mark. *The Case Against Q*. Harrisburg, Pa.: Trinity Press International, 2002.

———. *The Synoptic Problem: A Way through the Maze*. London: Sheffield Academic Press, 2001.

———. *Thomas and the Gospels: The Case for Thomas's Familiarity with the Synoptics*. Grand Rapids, Mich.: Eerdmans, 2012.

Grillmeier, Alois. *Christ in Christian Tradition: From the Apostolic Age to Chalcedon (451)*. Mowbray, 1965.

Grisez, Germain. "The Inspiration and Inerrancy of Scripture." In *For the Sake of Our Salvation: The Truth and Humility of God's Word*, St. Paul Center for Biblical Theology, 181–90. Steubenville, Ohio: Emmaus Road Publishing, 2010.

Hahn, Scott. "Come Again? The Real Presence as Parousia." In *Catholic for a Reason III: Scripture and the Mystery of the Mass*, 31–48. Steubenville, Ohio: Emmaus Road Publishing, 2004.

———. *The Lamb's Supper: The Mass as Heaven on Earth*. New York: Doubleday, 1999.

———. *Reasons to Believe: How to Understand, Explain, and Defend the Catholic Faith*. New York: Doubleday, 2007.

Hahn, Scott, and Benjamin Wiker. *Politicizing the Bible: The Roots of Historical Criticism and the Secularization of Scripture, 1300–1700*. New York : Crossroad Publishing Company, 2013.

Harnack, Adolf von. *What Is Christianity?* Translated by Thomas Bailey Saunders. Philadelphia: Fortress Press, 1986.

Harrison, Brian. "Does Vatican Council II Allow for Errors in Sacred Scripture?" *Divinitas*, LII, 3 (2009): 279–30.

———. "Restricted Inerrancy and the 'Hermeneutic of Discontinuity.'" In St. Paul Center for Biblical Theology, *For the Sake of Our Salvation: The Truth and Humility of God's Word*, 225–46. Steubenville, Ohio: Emmaus Road Publishing, 2010.

Hays, Richard. "Benedict and the Biblical Jesus." *First Things* (August, 2007). http://www.firstthings.com/article/2007/08/001-benedict-and-the-biblical-jesus

———. *Reading Backwards: Figural Christology and the Fourfold Gospel Witness*. Waco, Tex.: Baylor University Press, 2014.

Hengel, Martin. *The Four Gospels and the One Gospel of Jesus Christ.* Translated by John Bowden. Harrisburg, Penn: Trinity Press, 2000.

———. *The Son of God: The Origin of Christology and the History of Jewish-Hellenistic Religion.* Translated by John Bowden. London: SCM, 1975.

Heschel, Susannah. *The Aryan Jesus: Christian Theologians and the Bible in Nazi Germany.* Princeton, N.J.: Princeton University Press, 2008

Hume, David. *An Enquiry Concerning Human Understanding.* Indianapolis, Ind.: Hackett Publishing Co., 1977.

Hurtado, Larry. *Lord Jesus Christ: Devotion to Jesus in Earliest Christianity.* Grand Rapids, Mich.: Eerdmans, 2003.

International Theological Commission. *God the Trinity and the Unity of Humanity. Christian Monotheism and Its Opposition to Violence.* 2014.

———. *The Interpretation of Dogma.* 1990.

———. *Some Current Questions in Eschatology.* 1992.

———. *Theology Today: Perspectives, Principles and Criteria.* 2012.

———. *Unity of the Faith and Theological Pluralism.* 1972.

James, William. *The Varieties of Religious Experience.* Cambridge, Mass.: Harvard University Press, 1985.

Jaubert, Annie. *The Date of the Last Supper.* Staten Island, N.Y.: Alba House, 1965.

Jeremias, Joachim. *The Parables of Jesus.* Translated by S. H. Hooke. London: SCM Press, 1963.

Johnson, Luke Timothy. *The Real Jesus: The Misguided Quest for the Historical Jesus and the Truth of the Traditional Gospels.* San Francisco: HarperSanFrancisco, 1996.

Journet, Charles. *What Is Dogma?* Translated by Mark Pontifex, OSB. New York: Hawthorn Books, 1964.

Keener, Craig. *The Historical Jesus of the Gospels.* Grand Rapids, Mich.: Eerdmans, 2009.

Kleinhaus, Arduin. "De nova Enchiridii Biblici editione." *Antonianum* 30 (1955): 63–65.

Kreeft, Peter, and Ronald Tacelli, *Handbook of Christian Apologetics: Hundreds of Answers to Crucial Questions.* Downers Grove, Ill.: InterVarsity Press, 1994.

Lagrange, Marie-Joseph. *Historical Criticism and the Old Testament.* Translated by Edward Myers. London: Catholic Truth Society, 1905.

Laurentin, René. *The Truth of Christmas beyond the Myths: The Gospels of the Infancy of Christ.* Translated by Michael J. Wrenn. Petersham, Mass.: St. Bede's Publications, 1986.

Leiva-Merikakis, Erasmo. *Fire of Mercy, Heart of the Word: Meditations on the Gospel According to Saint Matthew.* Volume 2. San Francisco: Ignatius Press, 2004.

Lienhard, Joseph, S.J. "Pope Benedict XVI: Theologian of the Bible." *Homiletic and Pastoral Review* 110, 10 (2010): 66–78.

Leo XIII. *Providentissimus Deus* (November 18, 1893).

Levenson, Jon. *The Death and Resurrection of the Beloved Son: The Transformation of Child Sacrifice in Judaism and Christianity.* New Haven, Conn.: Yale University Press, 1993.

———. *Resurrection and the Restoration of Israel: The Ultimate Victory of the God of Life.* New Haven, Conn.: Yale University Press, 2006.

Levine, Amy-Jill. *The Misunderstood Jew: The Church and the Scandal of the Jewish Jesus.* New York: HarperOne, 2006.

Lewis, C. S. *Miracles: A Preliminary Study.* New York: Macmillan, 1978.

———. *Reflections on the Psalms.* London: Harvest Books, 1964.

———. *The Weight of Glory, and Other Addresses.* New York: Macmillan, 1980.

Loisy, Alfred. *L'Évangile et l'Église.* Paris: Picard, 1902.

MacIntyre, Alasdair C. *After Virtue: A Study in Moral Theory.* Notre Dame, Ind.: University of Notre Dame Press, 2003.

———. *Three Rival Versions of Moral Enquiry: Encyclopaedia, Genealogy, and Tradition.* Notre Dame, Ind.: University of Notre Dame Press, 1990.

———. *Whose Justice? Which Rationality?* Notre Dame, Ind.: University of Notre Dame Press, 2003.

Martin, Francis. "Joseph Ratzinger, Benedict XVI, on Biblical Interpretation: Two Leading Principles." *Nova et Vetera* 5 (2007): 285–314.

Mavrodes, George I. "David Hume and the Probability of Miracles." *International Journal for Philosophy of Religion* 43 (1998): 167–82.

Meier, John P. *A Marginal Jew: Rethinking the Historical Jesus.* 4 vols. Anchor Yale Bible Reference Library; New Haven, Conn.: Yale University Press, 1991, 1994, 2001, 2009.

Menssen, Sandra Lee, and Thomas D. Sullivan. *The Agnostic Inquirer: Revelation from a Philosophical Standpoint.* Grand Rapids, Mich: William B. Eerdmans, 2007.

Metzger, Bruce, and Bart Ehrman. *The Text of the New Testament: Its Transmission, Corruption, and Restoration.* New York: Oxford University Press, 2005.

Miller, Athanasius. "Das neue biblische Handbuch." *Benediktinische Monatschrift* 31 (1955).

Nagel, Thomas. *The View from Nowhere.* New York: Oxford University Press, 1989.

Neusner, Jacob. *A Rabbi Talks with Jesus.* Montreal: McGill-Queen's University Press, 2000.

Newman, John Henry. *An Essay in Aid of a Grammar of Assent.* Garden City, N.Y.: Image, 1955.

―――. *An Essay on the Development of Christian Doctrine.* Notre Dame, Ind.: University of Notre Dame Press, 1989.

―――. Letter to David Brown. January 14, 1875. In *Letters and Diaries of John Henry Newman.* Volume 27. Edited by C. S. Dessain and E. E. Kelly. Oxford: Clarendon Press, 1961.

―――. "The Theory of Developments in Religious Doctrine." In *Fifteen Sermons Preached before the University of Oxford,* 312–51. Notre Dame, Ind.: University of Notre Dame Press, 1998.

Nietzsche, Friedrich Wilhelm, Rüdiger Bittner, and Kate Sturge. *Writings from the Late Notebooks.* Translated by Kate Sturge. Cambridge: Cambridge University Press, 2003.

O'Collins, Gerald, SJ. "Does Vatican II Represent Continuity or Discontinuity?" *Theological Studies* 73 (2012).

Origen. *Commentary on the Gospel of John.* Translated by Allan Menzies. In vol. 9 of *The Ante-Nicene Fathers: Translations of the Writings of the Fathers down to A.D. 325,* edited by Rev. Alexander Roberts and James Donaldson. Grand Rapids, Mich.: W. B. Eerdmans: 1989.

―――. *Contra Celsum.* In vol. 4 of *The Ante-Nicene Fathers: Translations of the Writings of the Fathers down to A.D. 325,* edited by Rev. Alexander Roberts and James Donaldson. Grand Rapids, Mich.: W. B. Eerdmans: 1989.

―――. *On First Principles.* Translated by Frederick Crombie. In vol. 4 of *The Ante-Nicene Fathers: Translations of the Writings of the Fathers down to A.D. 325,* edited by Rev. Alexander Roberts and James Donaldson. Grand Rapids, Mich.: W. B. Eerdmans: 1989.

Paul VI, *Mysterium Fidei.* 1965.

―――. *Sedula Cura.* 1971.

Pelikan, Jaroslav. *The Emergence of the Catholic Tradition (100–600),* Volume 1: *The Christian Tradition.* Chicago: University of Chicago Press, 1971.

Pesch, Rudolf. *Das Markusevangelium.* Freiburg: Herder, 1976.

Pidel, Aaron, SJ. "Joseph Ratzinger and Biblical Inerrancy." *Nova et Vetera* 12.1 (2014).

Pinckaers, Servais, OP. *The Sources of Christian Ethics.* Washington: The Catholic University of America Press, 1993.

Pitre, Brant. *Jesus, the Tribulation, and the End of the Exile: Restoration Eschatology and the Origin of the Atonement.* Tübingen: Mohr Siebeck, 2005.

Pius IX. *Syllabus of Errors.* 1864.

Pius X. *Lamentabili Sane.* 1907.

―――. *The Oath Against Modernism.* 1910.

―――. *Pascendi Dominici Gregis.* 1907.

―――. *Praestantia Sacrae Scripturae.* 1907.

Pius XI. *Mit brennender sorge.* 1937.

Pius XII. *Humani Generis.* 1950.

———. *Divino Afflante Spiritu*. 1943.

Plantinga, Alvin. *Knowledge and Christian Belief*. Grand Rapids, Mich.: Eerdmans, 2015.

———. *Warranted Christian Belief*. New York: Oxford University Press, 2000.

———. *Where the Conflict Really Lies: Science, Religion, and Naturalism*. New York: Oxford University Press, 2011.

Pontifical Biblical Commission. *On the Authorship, Date of Composition, and Historicity of the Gospel of Matthew*. 1911.

———. *On the Authorship and Historicity of the Fourth Gospel*. 1907.

———. *On the Authorship, Time of Composition, and Historicity of the Gospels of Mark and Luke*. 1912.

———. *On the Character and Authorship of the Book of Isaiah*. 1908.

———. *On the False Interpretation of Two Texts*. 1933.

———. *The Historicity of the Gospels*. 1964.

———. *The Inspiration and Truth of Sacred Scripture*. Collegeville, Minn.: The Liturgical Press, 2014.

———. *The Interpretation of the Bible in the Church*. 1994.

———. *On the Mosaic Authorship of the Pentateuch*. 1906.

———. *On the Parousia or Second Coming of Our Lord in the Letters of St. Paul the Apostle*. 1915.

———. *On the Synoptic Question or the Mutual Relations among the First Three Gospels*. 1912.

Pontifical Council for Interreligious Dialogue. *Dialogue and Proclamation*. 1991.

Ramage, Matthew. "Benedict XVI and Freedom in Obedience to the Truth: A Key for the New Evangelization." *Homiletic and Pastoral Review*. May 12, 2014.

———. "Benedict XVI's Theology of Beauty and the New Evangelization." *Homiletic and Pastoral Review*. January 29, 2015.

———. *Dark Passages of the Bible: Engaging Scripture with Benedict XVI and Thomas Aquinas*. Washington, D.C.: The Catholic University of America Press, 2013.

———. "Farewell to the Devil?" *Gregorian Institute*. October 25, 2013. http://www.thegregorian.org/blog/farewell-to-the-devil

Rahner, Karl, and Joseph Ratzinger. *Revelation and Tradition*. Translated by W. J. O'Hara. New York: Herder, 1966.

Ratzinger, Joseph. *In the Beginning: A Catholic Understanding of the Story of Creation and the Fall*. Translated by Boniface Ramsey. Grand Rapids, Mich.: Eerdmans, 1995.

———. "Biblical Interpretation in Conflict: On the Foundations and the Itinerary of Exegesis Today." In *Opening Up the Scriptures: Joseph Ratzinger and the Foundations of Biblical Interpretation*, 1–29. Edited by José Granados, Carlos Granados, and Luis Sánchez-Navarro. Grand Rapids, Mich.: Eerdmans, 2008.

———. "Biblical Interpretation in Crisis: On the Question of the Foundations and Approaches of Exegesis Today." In *Biblical Interpretation in Crisis: The Ratzinger Conference on Bible and Church,* edited by Richard John Neuhaus, 1–23. Grand Rapids, Mich.: Eerdmans, 1989.

———. *Called to Communion: Understanding the Church Today.* San Francisco: Ignatius Press, 1996.

———. "Christ, Faith, and the Challenge of Cultures." Speech given in Hong Kong to the presidents of the Asian bishops' conferences and the chairmen of their doctrinal commissions during a March 2–5, 1993, meeting.

———. "Culture and Truth: Some Reflections on the Encyclical Letter *Fides et Ratio.*" *The Patrician* (Winter, 1999): 1–8.

———. *Daughter Zion: Meditations on the Church's Marian Belief.* San Francisco: Ignatius Press, 1983.

———. *Eschatology: Death and Eternal Life.* Translated by Michael Waldstein. Washington, D.C.: The Catholic University of America Press, 1988.

———. "Exegesis and the Magisterium of the Church." In *Opening Up the Scriptures: Joseph Ratzinger and the Foundations of Biblical Interpretation,* 126–36. Edited by José Granados, Carlos Granados, and Luis Sánchez-Navarro. Grand Rapids, Mich..: Eerdmans, 2008.

———. "Farewell to the Devil?" In *Dogma and Preaching: Applying Christian Doctrine to Daily Life,* translated by Michael J. Miller and Matthew J. O'Connell. 197–206. San Francisco: Ignatius Press, 2011.

———. *Feast of Faith: Approaches to a Theology of the Liturgy.* Translated by Graham Harrison. San Francisco: Ignatius Press, 1986.

———. "The Feeling of Things, the Contemplation of Beauty." Message of His Eminence Card. Joseph Ratzinger to the Communion and Liberation (CL) Meeting at Rimini (24-30 August 2002).

———. *God and the World: A Conversation with Peter Seewald.* Translated by Henry Taylor. San Francisco: Ignatius Press, 2002.

———. "On the 'Instruction Concerning the Ecclesial Vocation of the Theologian.'" In *The Nature and Mission of Theology: Approaches to Understanding Its Role in Light of the Present Controversy,* 101–20. Translated by Adrian Walker. San Francisco: Ignatius Press, 1995.

———. *Introduction to Christianity.* Translated by Michael J. Miller. San Francisco: Ignatius Press, 2004.

———. *Milestones: Memoirs 1927 1977.* Translated by Erasmo Leiva-Merikakis. San Francisco: Ignatius Press, 1998.

———. *A New Song for the Lord: Faith in Christ and Liturgy Today.* Translated by Martha M. Matesich. New York: Crossroad, 1996.

————. Presentation on the Occasion of the First Centenary of the Death of Cardinal John Henry Newman. April 28, 1990. Vatican website.

————. "Zum Problem der Entmythologisierung Des Neuen Testamentes." *Religionsunterricht an höheren Schulen* 3 (1960): 2–11.

————. *Principles of Catholic Theology: Building Stones for a Fundamental Theology.* Translated by Sr. Mary Frances McCarthy, SND. San Francisco: Ignatius Press, 1987.

————. "Relativism: The Central Problem for Faith Today." https://www.ewtn.com/library/CURIA/RATZRELA.HTM

————. *Salt of the Earth: The Church at the End of the Millennium—An Interview with Peter Seewald.* Translated by Adrian Walker. San Francisco: Ignatius Press, 1997.

————. "Sources and Transmission of the Faith." *Communio* 10, no. 1 (1983): 17–34.

————. *Theological Highlights of Vatican II.* New York: Paulist Press, 1966.

————. *Theology of History in St. Bonaventure.* Translated by Zachary Hayes. Chicago: Franciscan Herald Press, 1971.

————. *Truth and Tolerance: Christian Belief and World Religions.* Translated by Henry Taylor. San Francisco: Ignatius Press, 2004.

————. "Why I Am Still in the Church." In *Fundamental Speeches from Five Decades,* translated by Michael J. Miller, J. R. Foster, and Adrian Walker, 132–53. San Francisco: Ignatius Press, 2012.

Ratzinger, Joseph, and Vittorio Messori, *The Ratzinger Report: An Exclusive Interview on the State of the Church.* Translated by Salvator Attanasio and Graham Harrison. San Francisco: Ignatius Press, 1985.

Reiser, Marius. *Bibelkritik und Auslegung der Heiligen Schrift: Beiträge zur Geschichte der biblischen Exegese und Hermeneutik.* Tübingen: Mohr Siebeck, 2007.

Rhonheimer, Martin. "Benedict XVI's 'Hermeneutic of Reform' and Religious Freedom.'" *Nova et Vetera* 9, no. 4 (2011): 1029–54.

Sanders, E. P. *Jesus and Judaism.* Philadelphia: Fortress Press, 1985.

Schnackenburg, Rudolf. *Freundschaft mit Jesus.* Freiburg im Breisgau: Herder, 1996.

————. *The Gospel According to St. John.* Translated by Cecily Hastings. New York: Seabury Press, 1980.

————. *Jesus in the Gospels: A Biblical Christology.* Translated by O. C. Dean Jr. Louisville, Ky.: Westminster John Knox Press, 1995.

Schürmann, Heinz, and Klaus Scholtissek. *Jesus, Gestalt und Geheimnis: gesammelte Beiträge.* Paderborn: Bonifatius, 1994.

Schweitzer, Albert. *The Quest of the Historical Jesus.* Translated by W. Montgomery, J. R. Coates, Susan Cupitt, and John Bowden. Minneapolis, Minn.: Fortress Press, 2000.

Solovyov, Vladimir Sergeyevich. *The Antichrist*. Edinburgh: Floris Books, 1982.

Sparks, Kenton. *God's Word in Human Words*. Grand Rapids, Mich.: Baker Academic, 2008.

Stallsworth, Paul T. "The Story of an Encounter." In *Biblical Interpretation in Crisis: The Ratzinger Conference on Bible and Church*, edited by Richard John Neuhaus, 102–90. Grand Rapids, Mich.: Eerdmans, 1989.

Streeter, Burnett Hillman. *Foundations: A Statement of Christian Belief in Terms of Modern Thought: By Seven Oxford Men*. London: Macmillan, 1913.

Stroud, Barry. "The Charm of Naturalism." In *Naturalism in Question*. Edited by Mario De Caro and David Macarthur, 21–35. Cambridge, Mass.: Harvard University Press, 2004.

Synave, Paul, and Pierre Benoit. *Prophecy and Inspiration: A Commentary on the Summa Theologica II-II, Questions 171–178*. New York: Desclée Co., 1961.

Theissen, Gerd. *The Gospels in Context: Social and Political History in the Synoptic Tradition*. Minneapolis: Fortress Press, 1991.

Thomas Aquinas. *Commentary on Saint Paul's Epistle to the Ephesians*. Translated by Matthew Lamb. Albany, N.Y.: Magi Books, 1966.

———. *S. Thomae Aquinatis Opera Omnia: ut sunt in Indice Thomistico, additis 61 scriptis ex aliis medii aevi auctoribus*. Edited by Robert Busa. 6 vols. Stuttgart-Bad Cannstatt: Frommann-Holzboog, 1980.

———. *Summa Theologica [Summa theologiae]*. Translated by the Fathers of the English Dominican Province. Westminster, Md.: Christian Classics, 1981.

Tolkien, J. R. R. *Tree and Leaf: Including the Poem Mythopoeia*. Boston: Houghton Mifflin, 1965.

Torrell, Jean-Pierre, OP. "Saint Thomas et les non-chrétiens." *Revue Thomiste* 106 (2006): 17–49.

Vall, Gregory. "Psalm 22: Vox Christi or Israelite Temple Liturgy?" *The Thomist* 66 (2002): 175–200.

Vatican Council I. *Dei Filius*. 1870.

Vatican Council II. *Ad Gentes*. 1965.

———. *Dei Verbum*. 1965.

———. *Gaudium et Spes*. 1965.

———. *Lumen Gentium*. 1964.

———. *Unitatis Redintegratio*. 1964.

Vorgrimler, Herbert. *Commentary on the Documents of Vatican II*. New York: Herder and Herder, 1967.

Watson, Francis. *Gospel Writing: A Canonical Perspective*. Grand Rapids, Mich.: Eerdmans, 2013.

Wicks, Jared. "Six Texts by Prof. Joseph Ratzinger as Peritus before and during Vatican Council II." *Gregorianum* 89 (2008): 233–311.

Williams, Paul. *The Unexpected Way: On Converting from Buddhism to Catholicism*. London: T&T Clark, 2002.

Wright, N. T. *The Challenge of Jesus: Rediscovering Who Jesus Was and Is*. Downers Grove, Ill.: InterVarsityPress Books, 2015.

———. *Jesus and the Victory of God*. Minneapolis: Fortress Press,1996.

———. *The New Testament and the People of God*. Minneapolis: Fortress Press,1992.

———. *The Resurrection of the Son of God*. Minneapolis: Fortress Press, 2003.

Wurthwein, Ernst. *The Text of the Old Testament: An Introduction to the Biblia Hebraica*. Translated by Erroll F. Rhodes. Grand Rapids, Mich.: Eerdmans, 2014.

SCRIPTURE INDEX

Jesus, Interpreted: Benedict XVI, Bart Ehrman, and the Historical Truth of the Gospels was designed in Adobe Jensen and composed by Kachergis Book Design of Pittsboro, North Carolina. It was printed on 60-pound Natural Recycled Tradebook and bound by Thomson Reuters of Eagan, Minnesota.